From Apartheid to Democracy

From Apartheid to Democracy

A BLUEPRINT FOR PEACE IN ISRAEL-PALESTINE

Michael Schaeffer Omer-Man
and Sarah Leah Whitson

UNIVERSITY OF CALIFORNIA PRESS

University of California Press
Oakland, California

Cataloging-in-Publication data is on file at the Library of Congress.

ISBN 978-0-520-40199-0 (cloth : alk. paper)
ISBN 978-0-520-40200-3 (pbk. : alk. paper)
ISBN 978-0-520-40201-0 (ebook)

Manufactured in the United States of America

GPSR Authorized Representative: Easy Access System Europe, Mustamäe
tee 50, 10621 Tallinn, Estonia, gpsr.requests@easproject.com

34   33   32   31   30   29   28   27   26   25
10   9   8   7   6   5   4   3   2   1

Contents

Preface

Sarah Leah Whitson

The fields of human rights and journalism, where my co-author and I have spent the majority of our careers, tend to be driven by similar intellectual and analytical tools that can be boiled down to criticism: analyzing and examining the policies and behaviors of states and government officials, investigating the results of those policies and behaviors and their impact on human beings, and evaluating their compliance with various laws. Human rights work most typically concludes with a finding that a government and its officials have violated the law, followed by recommendations urging them to end the offensive policies and practices, and urging third parties to pressure them to end the violations and maybe to hold them accountable. Rarely do we venture into positive prescriptions about how to fix problems beyond stopping abuses. That work is typically relegated to policymakers, academics, and conflict resolution experts.

Human rights investigations documenting gross abuses and violations of laws in Israel-Palestine over many decades are no exception to this critical approach. The international human rights movement has expanded its critical lens, however belatedly, beyond merely documenting individual incidents of human rights and humanitarian law abuses in the region to evaluating the broader, systemic problems of permanent military occupation and apartheid rule. But this approach has tended to preclude proposing, much less envisioning, the structural changes and process needed not only to end the abuses but to transform the status quo into rights-respecting governance. To be sure, human rights practitioners, academics, and journalists have done critical work building analyses that have led to a growing, global understanding that there indeed exists an undemocratic and oppressive one-state reality in Israel-Palestine, but those analyses do not provide a framework for fixing it.

The idea for the Blueprint first emerged from an accidental encounter with a stranger seated next to me on a four-hour train from New York to Washington, DC. After engaging in polite small talk, I noticed that open on the stranger's computer was a document titled "Talking Points," on the letterhead of the American Israel Public Affairs Committee (AIPAC). A lively discussion ensued over the following hours, culminating in the stranger asking, "OK, so what if I concede it's apartheid rule? What if I concede the occupation is illegal? I agree that the Oslo Accords are dead and the situation is not sustainable! What do you want us to do? Jump in the sea? Give up our country? We have to accept the situation as is because there's no alternative. What's your solution?"

Mr. AIPAC's question put an end to that particular discussion, but it also managed to burrow into the depths of my intellectual curiosity, manifesting as a challenge, which ultimately resulted in this book. I simply had no answer to his question that day, and acknowledged as much.

A short while later, when I met my eventual co-author, Michael Schaeffer Omer-Man, I found a partner who was just as perplexed and vexed by the lack of an answer. A journalist and analyst who had been working and living in Israel-Palestine for fifteen years, Michael had written extensively on the vacuum—the lack of political vision to transform apartheid and occupation into something better—left behind by the Oslo Accords and nearly three decades of failed peace processes.

We set out in search of an alternative plan. We started by interviewing dozens of political experts and activists, only to discover that while many had very serious ideas about what they wished could emerge as a new reality for Israel-Palestine—a single democratic state, a binational state, a confederation, or even the resurrection of the two-state solution—there was a dearth of plans for how to turn those ideas into reality. It was clear to us that this void had allowed the status quo of permanent occupation, intermittent wars of horrendous destruction, and criminal apartheid to prevail without any serious political challenge.

We set out to fill this vacuum by developing a new plan, presented here as the Blueprint. As experts at information-gathering and analysis but novices at state-building, we first conducted two years of research and investigation, focusing on input from approximately a hundred specialists with vast knowledge and experience in questions about Israel, Palestine, political transition, history, and conflict resolution, the vast majority of them stakeholders in the conflict. We were determined not to repeat the failures of the processes and approaches of the past, which we believed resulted from two critical errors: attempting to resolve political questions of governance and land borders before remedying Israel's ongoing crimes in the territory between the Jordan River and the Mediterranean Sea (which, for the sake of clarity we call "the Territory"), and seeking to resolve these political questions without the legitimate consent of the governed. Our Blueprint is radical in its commitment to the primacy of democratic decision-making. This democratic deference is the principal reason why the Blueprint does not prescribe a singular solution to the question of how the people in the Territory should be governed but does prescribe how to create a level playing field—based on principles of democracy and equality—from which they can, and should, decide their future democratically.

While we are confident about our own knowledge and expertise on the situation of Israel-Palestine, with nearly five decades of combined experience working on the subject as researchers and writers, we are cognizant that our personal identities may be deemed inadequate or unsuitable for prescribing a solution for Israelis and Palestinians. One of us is an American journalist and researcher who spent nearly half his life living and working in Israel-Palestine and who holds Israeli citizenship, and the other is an American-Armenian human rights lawyer whose family lived as refugees in Jerusalem for three decades. Because of and despite our backgrounds, we believe that—like the international community writ large—we share responsibility for the problem of Israel-Palestine. It is one of great concern to all humanity, testing not only our capacity to accept the permanent subjugation of a people but also risking the obliteration of international human rights and humanitarian laws as meaningful rules for states and their governments. It is a problem created by the institutions of the international community, namely the United Nations, which undertook the partition of the territory, created the State of Israel, and continues to tolerate the ongoing military occupation and oppression of Palestinians. Our own country, the United States, in which we were both raised and live today, has an even greater role, more accurately described at this stage of history as an accomplice to Israel's crimes, providing long-standing military and political support for successive Israeli governments. Accordingly, as Americans, we believe that we have a particularly great responsibility to contribute to finding a solution.

Until the shocking, unlawful Hamas attacks of October 7, 2023, most global observers had settled on the comfortable notion that Israeli oppression of Palestinians could continue in perpetuity. There was no urgency. There was no visible path out of that entrenched reality. As of this writing, Israel's genocidal war in Gaza continues. The atrocities Israel has perpetrated during this war have reawakened the world to the suffering of Palestinians in Gaza and resulted in the unprecedented indictment of Israel's top leaders by the International Criminal Court and, albeit short-lived, US government sanctions on abusive Israeli settlers and settlements in the West Bank. But it has also reignited a sense of urgency, from college campuses in the United States to the halls of power around the world, of the need for a fair and just plan that doesn't lead right back to occupation and apartheid on the day after. We hope this book provides such a plan, or inspiration for an even better plan, and we offer it in all humility as an effort to make a positive contribution to the pursuit of peace, equality, and freedom for all of the people in the Territory.

Introduction and FAQs

A single state from the river to the sea might appear
unrealistic or fantastical or a recipe for further bloodshed.
But it is the only state that exists in the real world—not in
the fantasies of policymakers. The question, then, is: How
can it be transformed into one that is just?

Tareq Baconi, "The Two-State Solution Is an Unjust,
Impossible Fantasy," April 1, 2024

Long before the war in Gaza that started in October 2023 (the "Gaza War"), there was a growing consensus among global policymakers, political activists, and the broader foreign policy community that Israel-Palestine was stuck in a political and diplomatic vortex. It was becoming clear that the Oslo process—and the very idea of a two-state solution negotiated under the skewed and coercive power dynamics of permanent military occupation—was no longer a relevant framework for resolving the situation in Israel-Palestine, and that a growing chorus of experts no longer believed it to be viable.[1] As of 2025, it is undeniable that even the broadest interpretation of the Oslo process offers no viable path forward that can be translated into policy.

Instead of pushing for progress to remedy the conflict, prior to the Gaza War, the international community appeared relatively resigned to the quasi stability of a brutish, perpetual, but manageable Israeli military occupation, relentlessly expanding settlements in the West Bank; unlawful annexations on top of those in East Jerusalem and the Golan Heights; intermittent wars and episodes of armed conflict marked by indiscriminate and deliberate attacks on civilians; and a near-total siege of Gaza. Within the international legal and human rights communities, a growing

1

consensus had also emerged that Israel was committing the crimes of apartheid and persecution against the Palestinians it ruled over, and that the occupation, because of its permanent nature marked by violations of occupation laws and deliberate denial of Palestinian rights to self-determination, was itself illegal. The International Court of Justice affirmed that consensus in its July 19, 2024, advisory opinion, determining that Israel's occupation is illegal and must end.[2]

Yet the United States and Israel seemed to believe this state of affairs was stable and acceptable enough to keep pushing forward efforts to normalize Israel's relationship with Arab dictatorships. It was only Hamas's unprecedented attack on Israel on October 7, 2023, kidnapping over 250 Israelis and killing some 800 civilians and over 300 members of the Israeli security forces, and the doubly unprecedented genocidal war and destruction Israel unleashed in Gaza in response, that shook the sleep-walking international community into the understanding that there could be no stability or security without a real resolution to the conflict.[3]

Alternatives to the two-state solution envisioned by the Oslo Accords exist as theoretical visions for the future. Different groups and thinkers have put forth and advocated for one democratic state, a confederation, a federal system, a binational state, and even different proposals for regional integration. Others have sidestepped the question of self-determination for Palestinians, offering only a plan for economic development.[4] None of them, however, offer practical road maps or a plan for how to achieve those visions or translate them into policy. Various states and international actors have encouraged and even helped fund groups advocating some of those visions for peace, but none have developed into articulated plans for implementation.

Frustratingly, in the absence of a policy plan to break the stalemate, successive US administrations and other international actors have remained rhetorically committed to the Oslo Accords or, more vaguely, a resumption of the Oslo process, the 2002 Arab Peace Initiative, and what they describe as efforts to "preserve conditions for a two-state solution."[5] Under the Biden administration, this rhetoric reemerged, with the phrase "pathway to a two-state solution" appearing in government statements, including a grand vision to redesign the regional order, but without any pathway attached. The Trump administration was expected to pursue a regional framework of some sort but as of early 2025 offered no detailed process or even end-goal beyond proposing a "takeover" of Gaza by the United States, the complete displacement of Gaza Palestinians, and the building of luxury resorts there. In practice, the absence of a comprehensive alternative to the Oslo process has translated into a fortification of the status quo: permanent Israeli occupation and apartheid and, in the case of Gaza, as of April 2025, an ongoing genocide and siege, thereby sentencing generations of Palestinians and Israelis to living under an undemocratic, rights-abusing, apartheid regime, whether as victims or beneficiaries. The march toward permanent occupation and apartheid has not been a subtle development or even particularly difficult to identify. As far back as 1979, then–Israeli Prime Minister Menachem Begin openly declared that Israel did not intend to withdraw to the 1949 Armistice Lines, stating that "the green line no longer exists—it has vanished forever."[6]

For more than a decade, academics, analysts, and even former Israeli government officials have described that situation as a "one-state reality," largely based on the understanding that the occupation is, at this point, no longer temporary—if it ever was.[7] "Israel's [current] government did not create this reality but rather made it impossible to deny. The temporary status of 'occupation' of the Palestinian territories is now a permanent condition in which one state ruled by one group of people rules over another group of people."[8]

With no prospect of ending the occupation, and an Israeli leadership that has explicitly ruled out Palestinian statehood in any recognizable sense of the word, these analysts argue that it is far more helpful to view reality as it is: one regime that controls the entire area between the Jordan River and the Mediterranean Sea. To be clear, those making the case that we are living in a one-state reality are not necessarily advocating for a one-state solution; they are merely offering a realistic assessment of the current status quo. And while there are mountains of reports documenting the dismal situation in Israel-Palestine and the devastating harms caused by Israeli abuses and demanding an end to abuses and the imposition of sanctions and accountability, there is a dearth of ideas for a positive vision of how to move forward.

The Blueprint accepts the premise of a one-state reality and picks up where the punitive steps offered by a legal and human rights framework naturally end. It provides a positive policy vision for how to move forward—practical steps to transform an undemocratic, de facto one-state reality into a democratic, rights-respecting regime with equality for all peoples under its control and to afford both Jewish Israelis and Palestinians the opportunity to exercise self-determination in one, two, or more states if they choose. It seeks to inject energy and creativity into what we believe can be a renewed, vibrant debate about what should happen in Israel-Palestine to ensure a democratic, rights-respecting outcome. All of this is rooted in two basic understandings: that Israel's occupation and apartheid regimes must be ended as quickly as possible, and that there exists no current or seemingly viable process that could end them peacefully, fairly, or justly.

A WINDOW OF OPPORTUNITY?

Much has changed since October 7, 2023. The international community initially rallied around Israel in the wake of what was a devastating and horrifying attack, largely against civilians. Simultaneously, the United States under the Biden administration and much of the international community recognized that if Israel succeeded in its declared aims of its war—to remove the Hamas government in Gaza and eliminate its ability to threaten Israel—that could create an opportunity to revive the idea of a two-state solution. Israel had for decades argued that the Gaza Strip-based Hamas and the schism between it and the West Bank–based, Fatah-controlled Palestinian Authority stood in the way of any political progress. The urgency and dramatic shift in international rhetoric and diplomacy also clearly came from a genuine desire to give Israelis—and Palestinians—a chance at achieving real security, freedom, and prosperity. The response from Israel was an unequivocal "no," coupled with bewilderment at why anybody would dare speak of "a path to Palestinian statehood" at a moment that they felt the world should have seen as proof that Palestinians can never be trusted with power of any kind.

Despite their horrors, the events of October 7 and the war that followed have created a window of opportunity to advance new ideas and seek new solutions. Whereas before October 7, the global community was relatively comfortable resigning itself to what appeared to be a stable status quo of occupation and apartheid with no serious resistance, the situation is different today. Where there was certainty, there is now uncertainty in the face of tremendous volatility and confusion about how to end this war or restore relative stability and security. This volatility corresponds with a tremendously dangerous moment for Palestinians in particular, who are facing possible extermination and complete expulsion from Gaza and parts of the West Bank.

But it is also a potentially hopeful moment because there is space for changed conceptions and approaches. Faced with Israeli rejectionism and a war that many scholars, international legal practitioners, and casual observers now recognize as a genocide, much of the international community is pivoting back to punitive steps against Israel, demanding an end to the occupation and war, while some governments are again vaguely referring to a "pathway" to Palestinian statehood. The 2024 International Court of Justice opinion concluding that member states must end any assistance to Israel for its occupation and apartheid rule has added additional legal impetus to challenging the status quo and encouraged a growing international movement of states and civil society to sanction Israel.[9]

What's still missing, however, is a plan that would actually result in an end to the occupation and apartheid; an end to the conflict, and self-determination for Palestinians. We are in many ways back where we started: the world is outraged by Israel's policies but has little to offer beyond outrage and condemnation. Even if Israel faces international prosecutions, isolation, and crippling sanctions, the international community is still unable to articulate any positive policy demands or a vision for a just peace and rights-respecting governance. Alongside historical guilt over the Holocaust that makes it difficult for some governments to criticize Israel, as well as the outright sanction and ostracization of those who do criticize Israel in many countries today, this sad state of affairs is also a result of simply running out of ideas—or at least ones Israelis are willing to entertain.

A SUMMARY OF THE BLUEPRINT: DESIGN AND LIMITATIONS

The Blueprint is not a peace plan. It does not aim to address all of the social, economic, environmental, and political needs of the people living in the Territory. It does not guarantee a just and equal society, nor does it provide comprehensive remedies for historical crimes and injustices that would realistically satisfy their myriad victims. It does not favor any particular political solution, arrangement of states, or system of governance beyond an insistence on basic democratic and human rights norms.

The international community's approach to Israel-Palestine has, for the most part, prioritized resolving national-political aspects of the conflict over steps to ensure an end to Israeli crimes—namely the illegal occupation and apartheid rule—and protecting basic individual civil, political, and human rights. Instead, and particularly in the absence of any political or diplomatic horizon, the Blueprint urges the international community to reevaluate its priorities and insist first and foremost on ending Israel's ongoing crimes. Instead of seeking a negotiated solution between Israelis and Palestinians as two separate but monolithic blocs, we believe there should be no negotiation over ending some of the worst crimes under international law or the non-derogable human rights of Palestinians. Furthermore, because Palestinians currently have no legitimate, elected, or accountable leadership and because no leader has the authority to negotiate away individual rights, the Blueprint argues that the best way to resolve differing views on the future governance of Israel-Palestine should be through a democratic process in which every person in the Territory can participate.

Thus, the Blueprint places the onus on the State of Israel—as the state exercising effective control over all peoples in Israel, East Jerusalem, the West Bank, and Gaza—to meet its international legal obligations by ending its crimes and respecting the rights of all people under its rule. Only once Palestinians have political, civic, and human rights equal to Israeli Jews living in the Territory will Palestinians and Israelis be able to democratically determine what political structures and outcomes best serve their collective, national, political, ethnic, and religious interests. The Blueprint is not a plan for *achieving* national self-determination; it is a plan to create the conditions under which achieving self-determination and deciding political issues of governance are possible.

To that end, each section of the Blueprint describes practical policy steps that, taken together, would end apartheid and occupation and effectively transform an undemocratic one-state reality into a democratic one.

The sections detail the legislative, institutional, and policy changes necessary to achieve that transformation and the timetable for achieving them.
The nine sections of the Blueprint include:

1. Establishing a Caretaker Government to implement the Blueprint,
   incorporating the authorities of the State of Israel and the Palestinian
   Authority, bound by a set of Guiding Principles that enshrine
   democracy and equality.
2. Ending military rule and revoking all emergency regulations.
3. Restoring full freedom of movement, temporarily leaving internal
   checkpoints in place but codifying the right of everyone to pass
   through them, subject to physical security screening.
4. Replacing Israel's High Court of Justice with a High Court for the
   Transition, with Palestinian, Israeli, and international judges to
   shepherd the democratic transition.
5. Implementing a comprehensive process for revoking racist and
   discriminatory laws, including "Basic Laws," and replacing or
   reforming them in accordance with the Guiding Principles.
6. Extending citizenship and rights to all people living between the
   Jordan River and the Mediterranean Sea.
7. Integrating Israeli and Palestinian civilian police, forbidding military
   forces from domestic operations, and instituting a comprehensive
   plan for disarming and demobilizing remaining militant groups and
   security services.
8. Releasing all administrative detainees and political prisoners,
   recognizing the rights of Palestinian refugees, and planning policy
   options for a transitional justice program that a post-transition
   government can adopt.
9. At the end of three years, holding democratic elections that will result
   in a representative government, as well as preparing for a possible
   referendum in which all citizens can decide whether to remain as one
   state or seek an alternative formulation, be it two states,
   confederation, or something else.

Together, these steps lay the foundations for a political order built
on principles of equality and democracy and provide the support and
supervision to bolster its chances of success. They include systems for
ensuring proportional political representation alongside safeguards

against majoritarianism. The plan strives to do all of this without discounting the legitimate fears and needs of Israeli Jews and Palestinians alike, including security.

The political reality that the Blueprint creates would indeed look and act very much like a single state, and some readers may argue that it is a thinly veiled plan for a "one-state solution." The Blueprint is not, however, designed to create an immutable structure or structures. Because the starting point is a one-state reality marked by vicious and harmful criminal rule over Palestinians with no visible or viable path to a resolution, prioritizing ending these crimes and other systemic injustices while laying the groundwork for equitably determining an ultimate configuration is both a legal obligation and a practical and ethical necessity. Ideally, following a successful transition to a democratic reality, the people of the Territory can decide by referendum what type of state or states they want more permanently and what relationship they might have with each other. Those choices are not available to Israelis and Palestinians today. The Blueprint is designed to make them possible.

.   .   .   .   .

The Blueprint cannot be forced upon Israelis or Palestinians; it requires a level of earnest political will where there is almost none today. That type of change does not typically come about spontaneously, particularly on the part of privileged groups with the most to lose by giving up their privilege; the most privileged group in Israel-Palestine, Jewish Israelis, will not give up that privilege under the current power dynamics in the Territory, the region, and the world. The Blueprint is therefore predicated on the assumption that it will only become relevant for adoption and implementation as a result of dramatic shifts in Israelis'—and relatedly, Palestinians'—strategic outlooks. An event, series of events, or major shifts in the international system must first create the conditions in which the Israeli government and Jewish Israelis are forced to reevaluate their core values and interests. That can only occur if Israelis believe that their country's security, prosperity, or political survival is no longer tenable or that the current situation poses an existential threat to their lives and livelihood.

Such a turning point can come about in several ways. Prior to the Gaza War, we found that the easiest scenario for most people to imagine was one in which growing outrage over Israel's illegal occupation and apartheid rule led to sanctions, diplomatic isolation, and economic pressure similar to those used against Apartheid South Africa. These would be the ideal means for the international community to pursue a coercive but nonviolent, diplomatic, and multilateral effort to resolve Israeli intransigence. A second path that could lead to such a reckoning was more difficult to articulate before the Gaza War: unimaginably painful, intractable violence from which neither side can see a path to lasting victory—an unacceptably painful stalemate. More people are able to imagine the latter scenario today, although it does appear that Israel will be successful in militarily defeating its adversaries on the battlefield. What's more, at least at the time of writing, it appeared that the criminal devastation Israel has wrought on Gaza, which the International Court of Justice has found is plausibly genocide, combined with now-institutionalized Israeli rejection of the idea of a two-state outcome, may have a correlative relationship with and even amplify momentum toward sanctions and international isolation. Some of this is already taking place.

Even with massive pressure, however, the Blueprint cannot be forced upon Palestinians and Israelis, cannot be willed into existence, and is not designed to be an aspirational peace plan to capture the hearts of the people living there. Rather, it is a practical policy vision that the United States and other global powers can adopt and use to guide their approaches and strategic thinking vis-à-vis Israel-Palestine, replacing their unhelpful policies and helping them see past the long-expired idea of a negotiated two-state solution in the Oslo framework. The Gaza War has demonstrated quite clearly that there are hard limits to the United States' ability to coerce Israel into policies and diplomatic initiatives it opposes, even by nominally leveraging the military assistance Israeli military analysts describe as critical for survival. Yet, while the United States and international community cannot force Israel to end the occupation and apartheid rule, they can and must provide a practical, positive vision for how to do so and design their diplomatic, economic, and military policies vis-à-vis Israel so that those policies advance the viability of this new vision.

Finally, despite our belief that the Blueprint is implementation- or adoption-ready more or less as written, we do not believe it articulates the only possible path forward. Presenting the Blueprint to policymakers, think tanks, and other experts in the foreign policy community, and working to start conversations about its value, the details of its steps, its political practicality, and the best timing and methods for seeking its implementation, will, we hope, spur the creation of competing and complementary plans, policies, and outlooks. That outcome alone would be a positive development compared to the current situation of stasis, wherein various foreign policy communities clearly recognize that the status quo is not tenable but have no actionable plans to move things in a different direction.

Lastly, scholars advocating for a settler-colonial analysis of Israel-Palestine have rightfully warned against any approach that over-relies on the provision of individual human rights and democracy alone. "Such statements imagine that formal rights can be provided as a remedy to apartheid, even within an overarchingly unequal constitutional structure."[10] We accept that argument and believe we have heeded their warnings by putting forth a plan not just to dismantle the illegal occupation or the crime and system of apartheid, but also to fundamentally transform the institutions, systems, and structures they were implemented to serve. However, additional work to address the impact of historic injustices throughout society will have to come after a successful democratic transition, particularly as the scholarship is clear that these processes must be locally led to succeed.

METHODOLOGY

We designed and drafted the Blueprint based on input from nearly a hundred stakeholders and experts who have been engaged on the Blueprint's various focal points and themes. To the greatest extent possible, they are representative of the various stakeholder populations of Israelis and Palestinians (Jewish and Palestinian citizens of Israel, those living under Israeli occupation and siege, Palestinian refugees, and members of both diasporas). We consulted, interviewed, and otherwise engaged on a one-to-one basis with roughly half of those stakeholders and experts prior to drafting the Blueprint's first outline. They constitute civil society leaders, intellectuals, academics, policy experts, international legal and human rights experts, human rights defenders, and former politicians and diplomats in Israel and Palestine as well as the United States and elsewhere.

With the help of our dedicated research intern, Joseph Frankel, we conducted in-depth comparative research of other postconflict, postcolonial, and democratic transitions that encountered challenges with parallels in Israel-Palestine. This was done to gain a broad view of what has worked and what hasn't in similar situations, with an understanding that no two political transformations are the same and the needs and constraints of historical, societal, geopolitical, and religious factors in every case will be unique. In later stages, we looked at specific transitional steps that have been taken in other contexts and attempted to draw appropriate lessons for ours. That, of course, comes on top of a historical analysis of previous peace processes, with a particular focus on the Oslo process and the unintended negative consequences it produced.

This book is the result of that research, analysis, thinking, discussing, and debating not only what future has the best chance of achieving peace and justice for Palestinians and Israelis alike, but with a stubborn insistence on what is possible, if not yesterday, then tomorrow. It is an attempt to shake world leaders out of their complicity in more than half a century of occupation and arguably a much longer legacy of apartheid. It must be said that popular movements across the world are beginning to demand much of the same from their leaders in the wake of the Gaza War, a development we find encouraging and hope will help ripen the moment when those very leaders might start to consider bold policy shifts like the one that we propose here.

We offer our plan with the utmost humility and deference to those on the ground in Israel-Palestine who have sacrificed and lost more than can be imagined in their struggle for self-determination and liberation from occupation and apartheid. As authors, while our own personal histories have entailed family losses, suffering, and trauma in Israel-Palestine over the past century and in decades of our own work and activism there, we are cognizant that today we are Americans living in the United States; our perspective on what will best serve the interests of the people living between the River and the Sea will inevitably include blind spots and reflect the emotional and spiritual gap created by our difference and distance from Israelis and Palestinians in Israel-Palestine. We offer our Blueprint in the spirit of our belief that we have a collective, shared obligation to address the collective, shared problems of Israeli occupation, apartheid, and now, genocide. We feel we have a particular responsibility to play an active role in ending these problems as Americans, whose government buttresses and reinforces these problems. Ultimately, our vision is to create the conditions that prize, protect, and equalize the individual voices of every Palestinian and Israeli in the Territory and beyond.

.   .   .   .   .

While we did our best to answer anticipated questions and criticisms in each relevant section of the book, the following is a short list of the most common questions we have faced while building this plan.

IS THE BLUEPRINT A PLAN FOR A ONE-STATE SOLUTION?

The Blueprint is a transitional plan to create a single, temporary, transitional government with a mandate to end occupation and apartheid rule and establish inclusive, democratic governance mechanisms for all of the people living under Israeli sovereignty, including Israelis and Palestinians. The Blueprint creates the conditions and infrastructure that will allow citizens to decide democratically how they wish to be governed after the Transition is complete, whether in one state, two states, or other configurations. We argue that it is not possible to arrive at any just resolution or make final decisions about any future governance structure (or structures) under the current *undemocratic* one-state reality of apartheid and occupation rule, but that it is possible to do so in an interim *democratic* state. At the end of the Transition, if the citizens fail to change, or choose not to change, the interim government's temporary single-state configuration, the default would be a single democratic state. We believe this would be a preferable outcome to endless apartheid and occupation under an undemocratic, one-state reality.

WHY DON'T YOU PRESCRIBE A NEW PLAN FOR A TWO-STATE SOLUTION?

For over three decades, the only plan for a "two-state solution" has been the one set forward in the Oslo Accords, requiring representatives of Israelis and Palestinians to negotiate the final boundaries of their states, the status of annexed territories like Jerusalem, and the return of Palestinian refugees as a precondition to ending apartheid and occupation and establishing two states. This approach has failed, resulting in a de facto one-state apartheid reality. The authority of the declared leadership of the Palestinian Authority, who were last elected nearly twenty years ago, is also dubious. In addition, many now believe it is not possible to separate or deconstruct the Israeli land confiscations of Occupied Palestinian Territory (OPT) and that the existing configuration of a proposed Palestinian state is not viable, particularly as it includes noncontiguous territory. As well, growing numbers of Israelis and Palestinians prefer alternatives to a two-state solution, including a confederation, a binational state, or one single unified state.

Our goal is to replace Oslo's failed two-state plan with one that addresses the shortcomings of a negotiated two-state solution but allows the electorate to subsequently choose how they wish to be politically configured, without treating them as singular blocs of people on whose behalf representatives are authorized to make decisions. The International Court of Justice's opinion that Israel must end its illegal occupation and evacuate its settlers as rapidly as possible with no preconditions or negotiations is an important ruling buttressing the approach of the Blueprint. The court's opinion does not, however, set forward a plan for *how* to end occupation and apartheid or *how* to establish a democratic, rights-respecting process to determine the consequences of an end to occupation and apartheid, including allowing the electorate to determine whether they wish to see one, two, or more states emerge. We have drafted a plan for an interim democratic government because we believe it will be best equipped to allow the citizenry to choose their governance and to resolve outstanding issues of refugee rights, accountability, and reparations.

THE BLUEPRINT REQUIRES ISRAEL TO AGREE TO A
TRANSITIONAL GOVERNMENT. WHY DON'T YOU INCLUDE
A PLAN FOR HOW TO MAKE THAT HAPPEN?

The adoption and implementation of the Blueprint requires a sufficient degree of global and domestic pressure to lead Jewish Israelis—and, to a large degree, Palestinians—to conclude that survival and prosperity necessitate a new approach and to compel the government of Israel—and also the Palestinian Authority—to cede control to a transitional government. Such pressure could result from international state and civil society sanctions; boycott and divestment; Israeli economic isolation and decline; a deteriorating security situation; and domestic political changes that the existing regime in Israel cannot manage.

The Blueprint does not, however, articulate a specific plan for a global pressure campaign because numerous such plans exist and are underway. Countless Palestinian, Israeli, and international actors, including human rights organizations, governments, activists, academics, and advocacy groups, have worked for decades to advocate and advance such peaceful measures of international pressure that will help create the circumstances necessary for Jewish Israelis to choose an alternative to apartheid, occupation, and endless wars. Ongoing prosecutions against Israel and Israeli officials in the International Court of Justice and the International Criminal Court for genocide, war crimes, and crimes against humanity have created the political space for sanctions and accountability. In 2024, the International Court of Justice and UN General Assembly made clear that ending economic and political support for Israel and pressuring it to end its occupation and apartheid regimes is an obligation of every state. As a result, global civil society and government sanctions against Israel have dramatically escalated, particularly in the face of Israeli atrocities in Gaza.

The Blueprint aims to contribute to the success of these efforts by providing Israelis, Palestinians, and the international community with a tangible, practical, and comprehensive plan for a just resolution to the conflict, ending occupation and apartheid and allowing the people of the Territory to decide their future governance. The absence of such a plan has stymied many who otherwise wish to see Israeli crimes end and the conflict resolved but who have been unable to answer the question, "What comes next and how?," particularly from the perspective of those most concerned with Jewish Israeli security and sovereignty. We aim to provide this missing piece of the puzzle, encouraging and giving confidence that a just transition is not only necessary but possible with the positive, peaceful off-ramp that the Blueprint provides.

Of course this is not the only possible trajectory. It is also possible that Jewish Israelis choose a different, more violent, solution to the domestic and global pressures and isolation they increasingly find themselves facing. This could include the extermination or expulsion of all or most Palestinians from the OPT, with unwavering military support and political backing from the United States. We believe that scenario is less likely if there is a viable alternative plan for a peaceful transition to democratic rule that ensures the security and equality of Palestinians and Jewish Israelis alike. Avoiding such a catastrophic solution is exactly why we have created the Blueprint.

WHY DOES THE BLUEPRINT EXCLUDE AN IMMEDIATE RETURN OF ALL PALESTINIAN REFUGEES TO THE TERRITORY?

The focus of the Blueprint is narrowly limited to ending occupation and apartheid in the Territory and transitioning Israel-Palestine into a democratic, rights-respecting state that will have the legitimacy and mandate to address the myriad issues that require resolution. These issues include the return of refugees in accordance with international law. At the outset, the Blueprint plans for the Caretaker Government to publicly acknowledge the non-derogable rights of Palestinian refugees; allow refugees facing imminent harm or seeking family reunification to return to the Territory; directly support refugees outside the Territory in various ways; and start planning policy options for a future government to more fully realize their rights, including through return.

This is not an attempt to evade the question of return and refugee rights; it is a practical assessment that not everything can happen at once and that there is no single answer to the Palestinian refugee problem. The

Palestinian refugee population has increased tenfold since 1948 and transformed from a largely agrarian to a well-educated and mostly urban population. Today, it consists of many millions of people who have vastly different lived experiences, with some in refugee camps in war-torn countries, including Syria, Iraq, and Lebanon; a large population in Jordan; and others in cities in North and South America and Europe. The homes and towns they might wish to return to may no longer exist. Return, in other words, is not as simple as simply returning to one's literal home after seventy-five years—certainly not when compared to many successful refugee repatriation efforts in recent history. The Blueprint leaves decisions about how to implement a right of return to a future, democratically elected government or governments.

WHO IS THE TARGET AUDIENCE FOR THIS BOOK?

The Blueprint aims to persuade a broad audience of international policy professionals, as well as the general public engaged on the issue of Israel-Palestine, that there is indeed a feasible, positive alternative to the failed Oslo process that has served to entrench Israel's apartheid and occupation rule. We hope to reach policymakers who want to end the occupation and apartheid but who have a hard time envisioning how to do so peacefully, fairly, and justly. In doing so, we hope to give the global community a language to imagine—and develop and adopt—policies seeking different outcomes than those that leave Israeli apartheid and occupation in place while waiting for a perfectly negotiated political outcome.

We also hope to empower activists with alternative visions of the future, be they one-state advocates, those promoting the idea of confederation, or those pushing for a two-state outcome, by helping them fill in what's missing from nearly all of their plans: a viable blueprint for transformation. We hope to give them new ways to answer their critics who ask what success could look like. We hope to inspire others to draw up competing or alternative visions for transformation such that the question of how to end the occupation and apartheid becomes a debate instead of a way to end conversations.

DOES THE BLUEPRINT REQUIRE ISRAELIS TO GIVE UP ON ZIONISM?

Zionism has meant different things to different people over the years, and the authors of this book are not positioned to dictate—to Jews, Israelis, or Palestinians—which interpretations are more or less valid. The Blueprint does not demand that Israelis—or anyone else—abandon their aspirations for statehood and national self-determination. The Blueprint is, however, predicated on ending the Jewish supremacy and domination that has characterized Israeli rule for three-quarters of a century and building a transitional government predicated on equality and nondiscrimination. This includes dismantling and transforming institutions, laws, and movement regimes designed to create and maintain domination and supremacy of one group over another. We believe that the Blueprint offers a way for Jewish Israelis to continue to exercise their national rights, including cultural and linguistic autonomy and self-determination, and to enjoy the security of a homeland, alongside Palestinians who enjoy the same rights and the same relationship with the state. Whether Zionists accept our prescription as adequate to their ideological and national aspirations is not for us to decide.

WHY DOES THE BLUEPRINT SIDELINE THE STATE OF PALESTINE?

Recognition of the State of Palestine by 146 countries reflects growing global support for Palestinian liberation. In tangible terms, however, the State of Palestine has very limited status and authority—within UN bodies and on the ground. It does not control its borders, does not control the population registry of its own citizens, has limited authority to enter into bilateral agreements with other countries concerning trade and security, and does not have a monopoly on the use of force in its territory. The near-total invisibility and inability of the State of Palestine to halt the ongoing genocide in Gaza is merely one indication of its lack of state capacity. That is because Israel has declared its long-term intention—and forcefully acted—to prevent that state from exercising any meaningful control over any part of the Palestinian territory and to indefinitely maintain its apartheid and occupation regimes.

Just as the Palestinian Authority was never intended to be the government of the State of Palestine but rather a transitional body toward achieving statehood, folding its functions into the Caretaker Government does not preclude the subsequent emergence of a Palestinian state. The Blueprint puts the choice of governance under one, two, or more states in the hands of the people of the Territory, maximizing the democratic decision-making power of individual Palestinians and Israelis alike.

HOW DO YOU ADDRESS MILITANT SPOILERS WHO OPPOSE THE EXISTENCE OF AN ISRAELI OR PALESTINIAN STATE?

Every process of conflict transformation, resolution, and transition is forced to account for spoilers—those who oppose the process because it undermines their power, wealth, or ideology. The Palestinian Hamas movement, the Israeli Likud party and its closely aligned settler movement, and other ideological extremists may well include spoiler factions, even if some of their leaders agree to participate in the process. The Blueprint's overarching strategy for mitigating such spoilers is fostering inclusion and buy-in from as many potential parties as early in the process as possible. The groundwork for that inclusion takes place in the "pre-negotiation" stages, through the framework of a Conciliation Conference that precedes the creation of a transitional government. Much of the hard work of getting those parties to the table will have to be completed before the Transition itself begins, and such steps are in many ways largely congruent with the creation of the conditions necessary for the initiation and implementation of the Blueprint.

The Blueprint also includes prescriptions for spoiler management during the Transition based on the principle of maximum inclusion in the political process and clear guidelines for exclusion. Additionally, it spells out plans for integration and centralization of security forces in the Territory and processes for disarmament, demobilization, and reintegration of armed groups, but it leaves the design and implementation guidelines to local and international experts.

PART I

Chapter 1   International Law Framework

Like people anywhere in the world, the people of Israel-Palestine (the Territory) are entitled to the protections of global human rights laws. In addition, because of the ongoing conflict there, international humanitarian law, or the laws of war, also apply. When legal experts use the terms "illegal occupation" and "apartheid"—the two main problems the Blueprint aims to remedy—to characterize Israeli rule over various parts of the Territory, they are not mere observations about the facts on the ground but legal analysis based in the bodies of international law that define the requirements of military occupation and the crimes of apartheid and persecution. In July 2024, the International Court of Justice (ICJ) definitively weighed in on these legal questions in response to a request from the United Nations General Assembly (UNGA), opining that Israel's occupation is indeed illegal and characterized by criminal apartheid governance.

It's important to review the interplay of the relevant laws applicable to the Territory as a basis for understanding the approach and prescriptions of the Blueprint. The Blueprint represents a shift from conventional approaches to applying the various bodies of law applicable to the Territory, as well as a shift from prior approaches to conflict resolution that have prioritized political negotiations between Israelis and

Palestinians—or Palestinian economic and political development—ahead of resolving the crimes of apartheid and illegal occupation. The ICJ affirmed the Blueprint's approach of first focusing on ending Israeli crimes in its July 19, 2024, advisory opinion that concluded that the international community must take action to compel Israel to end its occupation unconditionally and as quickly as possible.[1]

THE INTERPLAY OF INTERNATIONAL HUMANITARIAN LAW AND HUMAN RIGHTS LAW IN THE OPT

The applicability of multiple bodies of law in the Territory, which do not overlap neatly and at times produce conflicting powers, rights, and remedies, is a product of unique historical circumstances. During its rule by the Ottoman Empire, Palestine, including its Muslim, Jewish, and Christian populations, was subject to Ottoman law, which in turn granted authority over personal status, family law, and certain property matters to the religious leadership of each community. Following the collapse of the empire, the League of Nations imposed "mandates" over the former territories of the Ottoman Empire, as well as certain former colonial states around the world, pursuant to Article 22 of the Covenant of the League of Nations.[2] The league assigned to the British government a mandate over Palestine's population, including all of the lands that today comprise the Territory, while maintaining certain Ottoman, Muslim, Christian, and Jewish legal orders over Palestine's diverse communities.

Following the Holocaust and the growth of the Jewish population in Palestine (primarily due to Jewish emigration from Europe), the UNGA pursued the idea put forward by Jewish Zionist immigrants to create a Jewish state. It recommended the division of the British Mandate over Palestine into two states—one Arab and one Jewish.[3] Instead, further conflict ensued and only one state was created in 1948—the State of Israel—over much of the land of Mandate Palestine. This was followed by decades of war with neighboring countries and Israel's eventual military occupation in 1967 of the lands that had been under Jordanian and Egyptian control following the partition plan's failure to create a Palestinian state. As a result, Israel maintained Egyptian law in Gaza and

Jordanian law in the West Bank and East Jerusalem, in addition to a continuation of religious law for family matters for each religious community. With the establishment of the Palestinian Authority following the Oslo Accords, itself intended as a temporary, transitional authority, it too introduced a host of laws in certain parts of the Occupied Palestinian Territory (OPT), layered on top of the existing Ottoman, Egyptian, Jordanian, and religious laws.

Since 1967, the international community has focused almost exclusively on critiquing Israel's violations of international humanitarian laws (the laws of war), with far less attention to human rights law, as related to the conduct of its military occupation and, at various intervals, the conduct of its intermittent wars in the OPT and Lebanon, where it has been in conflict with Palestinian and Lebanese armed groups seeking to liberate Palestinian and Lebanese lands.[4] The law of occupation is a part of the laws of war and can be found primarily in the Fourth Geneva Convention of 1949, the Hague Regulations of 1907, and customary international humanitarian law.[5] The Fourth Geneva Convention sets out the specific rules of what a military force occupying territory not its own and over which it does not have lawful sovereignty can and cannot do, and the ICJ has specifically ruled that the Fourth Geneva Convention applies to the OPT.[6] International human rights law is simultaneously applicable because it protects all people, including those living under military occupation, granting them broad civil and political rights and freedoms. When both human rights laws and the laws of war are applicable to a territory at the same time, however, the laws of war grant a state exceptional powers to suspend or curb many human rights, in particular civil and political rights, albeit only temporarily to preserve public safety and order.

The Fourth Geneva Convention explicitly recognizes a military occupation as a state of war, during which the occupying power can exercise exceptional powers reserved for emergencies; it allows an occupying force to impose military law; restrict freedom of speech, association, and movement; and take other steps to limit basic human rights, just as a government may restrict rights domestically during emergency rule. As former special rapporteur on the situation of human rights in the Palestinian territories John Dugard concluded, "Violations of human rights are a necessary consequence of military occupation."[7]

Like emergency rules, however, the laws of occupation anticipate a temporary suspension of rights for what is designed to be a temporary occupation. Accordingly, they explicitly restrict an occupying force from taking actions that would permanently alter or confiscate the territory, including usurping the land and resources of the occupied territory. They forbid making any changes to the occupied territory except in the interests of the occupied population, transferring its own civilian population to the occupied territory, and forcibly displacing members of the occupied population.

PROLONGED, ILLEGAL OCCUPATION

There is unanimity among UN bodies and global international law experts that Israel's military occupation has failed to abide by even the most basic requirements restricting the actions an occupying force can take in occupied territories.[8] In its July 2024 opinion, the ICJ joined that consensus, noting in particular the occupation's prolonged duration: "Israel's policies including expansion of settlements and associated infrastructure and exploitation of natural resources ... are designed to remain in place indefinitely. These policies amount to annexation of large parts of the Palestinian territories." Such policies have cumulatively turned the arguably *ab initio* lawful occupation into an unlawful one, the court reasoned, and ordered Israel to end its occupation and evacuate its settlers from the OPT "as rapidly as possible."

Over its nearly sixty-year occupation, Israel has confiscated vast swaths of Palestinian land for the use of its own population; used Palestinian agriculture, water, and natural resources for its own gain; settled nearly half a million of its civilians in "settlements" in the OPT; and forcibly displaced and expelled hundreds of thousands of Palestinians from the Territory. Its military occupation has also been accompanied by regular military incursions and full-scale wars in the OPT, during which time it has breached the most basic requirements of the laws of war, including the prohibitions on deliberate and indiscriminate targeting of civilians; extrajudicial executions; the use of civilians as shields; and the imposition of a siege and denial of items necessary to the survival of the civilian population. While the Gaza War may be exceptional in the scale of Israel's violations of the laws of war, including a widespread pattern of war crimes and crimes against humanity, there is nothing unique in how the Israel Defense Forces have prosecuted this war, albeit at smaller scales, compared to its prior wars and incursions into the OPT since 1967. For example, the International Criminal Court's (ICC) current investigation of crimes under the 1998 Rome Statute in the OPT by Israel and Palestinian armed groups emerged as a direct consequence of the atrocities carried out by Israel in its 2014 war in Gaza.[9]

As the ICJ confirmed in its July 2024 advisory opinion, Israel's military occupation, by now one of the world's longest military occupations, is not a temporary state of affairs and Israeli leaders have never had any intention of relinquishing the OPT. There has been growing understanding that the Israeli government's violations of the laws of occupation are not extraordinary or exceptional or the misdeeds of a few bad apples, but are part of a deliberate and systematic plan to ignore the laws of war and occupation for the specific purpose of permanently confiscating the OPT, installing its own civilian population, and driving out the indigenous Palestinian population. As Orna Ben-Neftali and colleagues conclude, "[F]rom a legal perspective, the Israeli government's actions actually constitute a greater violation of international law than that which would have been created by a straight-forward annexation, as they confer the benefits of annexation to the occupier without requiring it to incorporate the people under occupation to its polity, with its ensuing rights and privileges."[10]

As a result, many international experts have shifted away from merely examining individual incidents of abuse and violations of law to a review of the sum total of these violations over a long period of time. A review of the totality of evidence, including the compounding incidents and impacts of abuses, their systematic and widespread nature, and the evidence of long-held Israeli intent to permanently maintain the occupation and dominate the Palestinian population, has led various human rights and international law experts to conclude that Israel's occupation violates the rights of Palestinians to self-determination, that the occupation is itself illegal, and that it is accompanied by the crimes of apartheid and persecution.[11] This was exactly the approach of the ICJ in rendering its opinion on the illegality of the occupation.

For years, a similar recognition that Israel's occupation is not temporary, that its violations of occupation law are not inadvertent or exceptional, and that the extremely broad restrictions on Palestinian rights are no longer justifiable under the law has led others (including one of the authors of this book) to advocate ending deference to the restrictions that occupation law permits on the human rights of the Palestinian population in the OPT, albeit restrictions that were intended to be temporary.[12] Instead, they advocate prioritizing the requirements of human rights law, which permits no such broad derogations from basic civil and political rights. More than half a century later, whatever restrictions on human rights and basic freedoms occupation law might have permitted Israeli occupying forces—as a temporary measure for the purpose of public order and security—are no longer plausible or justifiable. Indeed, even occupation law imposes a heightened obligation to facilitate normal civil life and respect for fundamental rights with the passage of time. "The longer an occupation, the more military rule should resemble an ordinary governing system that respects the standards of international human rights law that apply at all times."[13] Human Rights Watch, in its seminal 2019 report analyzing Israeli restrictions on Palestinian rights and concluding that Israel is obligated to provide Palestinians in the OPT rights equal to Israelis, argued:

> The responsibilities of an occupying power toward the rights of the occupied population increase with the duration of the occupation. Israel remains principally in control of the West Bank, despite limited Palestinian Authority rule over certain areas, and yet has failed to provide the people living under its control with the rights they are due, including the right to equal treatment without regard to race, religion or national identity. It is long past time for Israel to fully respect the human rights of Palestinians, using as a benchmark the rights it grants Israeli citizens, an obligation that exists regardless of the political arrangement in the Occupied Palestinian Territory now or in the future.[14]

Increasingly, legal experts have also examined Israel's prolonged, illegal occupation from the broader framework of settler colonialism, assessing Israeli conduct as "that of an intentionally acquisitive, segregationist and repressive regime designed to prevent the realization of the Palestinian people's right to self-determination," "seizing land while subjugating and displacing its indigenous people and replacing them with its nationals."[15]

This has deprived Palestinians of their right to self-determination, most broadly defined as "a people's fundamental right to determine their political, social and economic status and develop as a people, free from foreign occupation, rule and exploitation."[16]

Alongside the conclusion that Israel's occupation of the OPT is illegal is the now-broad concurrence among world governments, legal experts, and human rights investigators that Israel is also committing the crimes of apartheid and persecution under the Apartheid Convention.[17] Both the Apartheid Convention and the Rome Statute to the ICC define apartheid as a crime against humanity consisting of three primary elements:[18]

1. an intent to maintain domination by one racial group over another;[19]

2. a context of systematic oppression by the dominant group over the marginalized group; and

3. inhumane acts, including "forcible transfer," "expropriation of landed property," "creation of separate reserves and ghettos," and denial of "the right to leave and to return to their country, [and] the right to a nationality."

The ICJ's July 2024 advisory opinion—albeit with an exclusive focus on the OPT—also concluded that Israeli policies amount to systemic discrimination, segregation, and apartheid, in violation of several treaties:

> The Court is of the view that the régime of comprehensive restrictions imposed by Israel on Palestinians in the Occupied Palestinian Territory constitutes systemic discrimination based on, inter alia, race, religion or ethnic origin, in violation of Articles 2, paragraph 1, and 26 of the ICCPR, Article 2, paragraph 2, of the ICESCR, and Article 2 of CERD.[20]
>
> [. . .]
>
> Article 3 of CERD provides as follows: "States Parties particularly condemn racial segregation and apartheid and undertake to prevent, prohibit and eradicate all practices of this nature in territories under their jurisdiction." This provision refers to two particularly severe forms of racial discrimination: racial segregation and apartheid.
>
> [. . .]
>
> The Court observes that Israel's legislation and measures impose and serve to maintain a near-complete separation in the West Bank and East Jerusalem between the settler and Palestinian communities. For this reason,

the Court considers that Israel's legislation and measures constitute a breach of Article 3 of CERD.

The ICJ's findings concurred with the findings of all of the leading Israeli, Palestinian, and global human rights law organizations, as well as university law clinics, that Israel is committing the crime of apartheid, following their comprehensive, detailed investigations on the ground in Israel and Palestine. While these findings have differing assessments of the extent to which all of the elements of the crime of apartheid are present in the entirety of Israel and the OPT, they have been unified in the unequivocal finding of "the present-day reality of a single authority, the Israeli government, ruling primarily over the area between the Jordan River and Mediterranean Sea, populated by two groups of roughly equal size, and methodologically privileging Jewish Israelis while repressing Palestinians, most severely in the occupied territory."[21]

REMEDIES FOR ILLEGAL OCCUPATION AND APARTHEID

International law prescribes mandatory remedies for certain violations of the law, requiring not only the party in violation to end and remedy its abuses but also the international community to take action to bring an end to the violations. "Under the law on State responsibility, the breach of an international obligation by a State gives rise to an internationally wrongful act, the commission of which requires first and foremost the State responsible to immediately cease the illegal act, ensure non-repetition and provide reparation for the damage done."[22] For the violations of international law that are the focus of the Blueprint—Israel's apartheid rule and illegal occupation—the prescribed remedies require, at minimum, an end to the Israeli practices and policies that undergird apartheid and occupation. The ICJ reaffirmed that obligation.

The Rome Statute identifies apartheid as a crime against humanity, described as crimes that "are particularly odious offenses in that they constitute a serious attack on human dignity or grave humiliation or a degradation of one or more human beings."[23] The prohibition of apartheid is a peremptory norm under international law, meaning that states have accepted a mandatory duty to prohibit it. The ICC's current investigation of violations under the Rome Statute should include a review of the crime of apartheid, for which it can find individual Israeli officials criminally liable. The Apartheid Convention calls on states that are party to the convention not only to prosecute those responsible for the crime of apartheid, but to prevent, suppress, and punish the crime itself.

The ICJ went further in defining the obligations of Israel to end the occupation, stating that Israel "has an obligation to bring an end to its presence in the Occupied Palestinian Territory as rapidly as possible." Israel is also under obligation to end its other unlawful acts resulting from its illegal occupation, it continued:

> Israel must immediately cease all new settlement activity. Israel also has an obligation to repeal all legislation and measures creating or maintaining the unlawful situation, including those which discriminate against the Palestinian people in the Occupied Palestinian Territory, as well as all measures aimed at modifying the demographic composition of any parts of the territory. Israel is also under an obligation to provide full reparation for the damage caused by its internationally wrongful acts to all natural or legal persons concerned.[24]

International law similarly imposes on states a duty to cooperate to bring such serious abuses to an end and to avoid recognizing the legality of, or aiding and abetting, the abuses themselves.[25] The ICJ advisory opinion affirmed this duty, writing that, together with the United Nations, all states have an obligation to help end Israel's occupation, as well as to help realize the Palestinian national right to self-determination:

> Taking note of the resolutions of the Security Council and General Assembly, the Court is of the view that Member States are under an obligation not to recognize any changes in the physical character or demographic composition, institutional structure or status of the territory occupied by Israel on 5 June 1967, including East Jerusalem, except as agreed by the parties through negotiations and to distinguish in their dealings with Israel between the territory of the State of Israel and the Palestinian territory occupied since 1967.

Specifically, that obligation, the ICJ writes, encompasses:

> the obligation to abstain from treaty relations with Israel in all cases in which it purports to act on behalf of the Occupied Palestinian Territory or a

part thereof on matters concerning the Occupied Palestinian Territory or a part of its territory; to abstain from entering into economic or trade dealings with Israel concerning the Occupied Palestinian Territory or parts thereof which may entrench its unlawful presence in the territory; to abstain, in the establishment and maintenance of diplomatic missions in Israel, from any recognition of its illegal presence in the Occupied Palestinian Territory; and to take steps to prevent trade or investment relations that assist in the maintenance of the illegal situation created by Israel in the Occupied Palestinian Territory. . . .

Moreover, the Court considers that, in view of the character and importance of the rights and obligations involved, all States are under an obligation not to recognize as legal the situation arising from the unlawful presence of Israel in the Occupied Palestinian Territory. They are also under an obligation not to render aid or assistance in maintaining the situation created by Israel's illegal presence in the Occupied Palestinian Territory. It is for all States, while respecting the Charter of the United Nations and international law, to ensure that any impediment resulting from the illegal presence of Israel in the Occupied Palestinian Territory to the exercise of the Palestinian people of its right to self-determination is brought to an end. In addition, all the States parties to the Fourth Geneva Convention have the obligation, while respecting the Charter of the United Nations and international law, to ensure compliance by Israel with international humanitarian law as embodied in that Convention.

The Blueprint takes cognizance of these legal conclusions—that Israel's prolonged military occupation is illegal, characterized by widespread war crimes and crimes against humanity; that Israel is committing the crimes of apartheid and persecution; that these crimes are causing immediate, severe harms to Palestinians; and that the international community has a duty to end them—in ordering its priorities and actions. We note as well the pending South African case before the ICJ charging Israel with breaching the Genocide Convention in Gaza in connection with the Gaza War. In its provisional order of January 26, 2024, the court found that there are facts and circumstances plausibly showing that Israel is committing the crime of genocide, or, in the language of the court:

In the Court's view, the facts and circumstances mentioned above are sufficient to conclude that at least some of the rights claimed by South Africa and for which it is seeking protection are plausible. This is the case with respect to the right of the Palestinians in Gaza to be protected from acts of genocide and related prohibited acts identified in Article III, and the right of South Africa to seek Israel's compliance with the latter's obligations under the [Apartheid] Convention.[26]

This was also the conclusion reached by a large number of genocide scholars and human rights experts that Israel has indeed met the thresholds of deed and intent for a finding that it is committing genocide against the Palestinian people in Gaza.[27] While the Blueprint focuses on addressing the long-standing problems of illegal occupation and apartheid, the authors are cognizant of the absolute urgency of ending the slaughter, siege, and famine underway in Gaza as of this writing and anticipate that the mass killings there will end when the war in Gaza ends.

When violations of international law cause extreme harm, including the loss of life, fundamental freedoms, and livelihood for a subjugated population, and in particular when the harms are compounded over decades, curbing the violations should be a matter of immediate priority and urgency. This is exactly why the ICJ ordered Israel to end its apartheid and occupation rule over Palestine as rapidly as possible. Accordingly, the Blueprint prioritizes ending the occupation and apartheid rule as matters of essential first order for Israel, Palestinians, and the international community. This approach departs from many years of (failed) international efforts to prioritize resolving what is described as the "conflict" between Israelis and Palestinians through a politically negotiated agreement. The conventional approach to conflict resolution in Israel-Palestine has assumed that there are two monolithic groups, one Israeli and one Palestinian, and demanded that they negotiate a political solution to their competing claims, based on land and statehood.

Most critically, the conventional political approach assumes that a political resolution between these two groups is a precondition to ending the *lesser* problems of apartheid, illegal occupation, and Palestinian human rights, including the right to self-determination. The United Nations has formally supported this approach, taking the position that

the end of Israel's prolonged occupation of the OPT must be contingent on the conclusion of negotiations between it and the [Palestine Liberation Organization]. This is a universally held position among each of the relevant five principal organs, and one that has been parroted throughout the UN system. Thus, the Security Council has since 1967 affirmed the need for Israel to withdraw from the OPT as part of a negotiated settlement under the land for peace formula.[28]

This approach also treats Palestinian rights, such as their non-derogable right to be free from illegal occupation, their right to self-determination, or the individual rights of refugees to return to their homeland, as negotiable. As Ardi Imseis has argued, making non-derogable rights conditional on negotiations creates a paradox:

> If realization of Palestinian self-determination in the OPT is a long-established right in the nature of a peremptory norm, derogation from which is not permitted, how can the culmination of this right be left to negotiation between an infinitely more powerful occupier and a beleaguered and vastly weaker occupied people? This is particularly so if the occupation itself is or has become illegal through the acts of a bad-faith occupant. . . . [29]

This was the overarching framework of the Oslo Accords, which

> framed the right to self-determination as the final objective of peacemaking after an interim self-rule . . . but merely recognized Palestinian autonomy in parts of the West Bank and the Gaza Strip and Palestinians' "legitimate and political rights" in the occupied Palestinian territory. In practice, the Accords left open the possibility that Palestinian self-rule short of independence could be extended in perpetuity.[30]

Such a political approach deprioritizes addressing the immediate harms caused by the Israeli government's crimes and violations against the individual Palestinians under its control, to whom it has legal duties and obligations. Furthermore, although the law mandates clear remedies to Israeli crimes and violations, as discussed above, the conventional approach demanding political negotiations as the first order of business wrongly demands we ignore the requirements of law and avoid seeking remedies and reparations in international courts for breaches of the law because they're "unhelpful" and "not constructive."[31] Even the concept of negotiating away the non-derogable rights of Palestinians is problematic: "It follows that a breach of international law should not be subjected to negotiations, as this would legitimize what is illegal. Therefore, because of the illegality of the Israeli occupation, owing to its prolonged, acquisitive and bad-faith nature, the obligation of cessation of the occupation cannot in any way be conditioned on negotiations."[32]

Indeed, over the years, Israel and its principal backer, the United States, have gone further and added additional preconditions even to the resumption of political negotiations, alternately imposing new benchmarks and demands on Palestinians before resuming a peace process. These have included demands that Palestinian leaders make declarations "recognizing the right of Israel to exist." At other times, Israel has insisted on waiting for a sufficiently unified Palestinian leadership such that negotiators can legitimately claim to be representatives. The peace process itself has conveniently become an elusive unicorn, forever on the horizon and forever out of reach.

It follows that prioritizing "peace negotiations" as a prerequisite to ending Israeli abuses is problematic not only because it is wrong as a matter of law and undermines the very laws on which the international rules-based order depends. It is wrong not only because it effectively permits severe Israeli harms against Palestinians to continue in perpetuity. It is wrong because this approach has been a complete failure for well over thirty years. While Israeli officials have admitted that such a state of perpetual, managed occupation with a mythical peace process forever on the horizon has largely suited Israeli interests, it has been catastrophic for Palestinians.[33]

The Blueprint addresses this by shifting the order of the problems it seeks to solve, first seeking to end Israel's illegal occupation and apartheid rule in the Territory—as prescribed by the ICJ in its July 2024 advisory opinion—before addressing questions of political solutions. The transition the Blueprint proposes aims to convert an undemocratic, abusive one-state reality into a democratic, one-state reality, albeit a transitional one. Only then, we believe, will the conditions be ripe for Israelis and Palestinians to address questions of political organization and statehood. Only then will they be able to do so in a democratic fashion, giving respect to the rights and voice to the wishes of every individual Palestinian, Israeli, and others who live in the Territory.

Chapter 2   When Will the Blueprint
             Be Relevant?

I look at my own body
With eyes no longer blind—
And I see that my own hands can make
The world that's in my mind.
Then let us hurry, comrades,
The road to find.

Langston Hughes, "I Look at the World"

There are three interrelated preconditions for the adoption and implementation of the Blueprint. The first condition is what scholars of conflict
resolution refer to as ripeness: the idea that parties to a conflict will reconsider compromises and proposals they once rejected if they find themselves in a costly and painful predicament from which they cannot
unilaterally extract themselves. The second condition, closely related to
the first, is buy-in of the plan itself—or at least the idea of it—by key stakeholders and power-holders in Israel-Palestine, including militant groups
and security forces; the changes the Blueprint requires simply cannot
happen without their active consent and participation. The third condition is the buy-in and active support of the international community for
the Blueprint's planning and implementation and seeking new regional
security arrangements meant to help mitigate the risks of renewed
military conflict.

These conditions do not exist today, in particular for Israelis who are
the group in power committing the crimes of occupation and apartheid.
There is currently nothing that is sufficiently causing—or forcing—the
vast majority of Israelis to reconsider the core values and interests that

have long defined their attachment to a Jewish state and concomitant majoritarian regime that privileges them. However, a reconsideration is possible; it is imaginable and, in some ways, even foreseeable. In this chapter, we review the current political consensus among Palestinians and Israelis, and the circumstances that may lead to ripeness for reconsideration about the status quo and buy-in and support for the Blueprint.

NO ISRAELI VISION BEYOND OCCUPATION AND APARTHEID

Over the past few decades, various Israeli politicians and writers have alternated between two visions for how to deal with Palestine: either "shrinking the conflict" to manage permanent occupation and apartheid rule with as little violence as possible, or mass, forced displacement of Palestinians and their outright extermination in the Occupied Palestinian Territory (OPT).[1] Even progressive Israeli politicians who remain theoretically committed to separation from Palestinians have migrated from a "two-state solution" toward the managed occupation plan, at best culminating in a "state minus" for Palestinians or, as former Defense Minister Benny Gantz described it, "a two-entity solution."[2]

Even excluding Palestinian noncitizens in the occupied territory, the very idea of an inclusive, liberal democracy for all citizens is well outside the acceptable political discourse for Jewish Israelis. Not even far-left Zionist parties are willing to use the phrase "a state of all its citizens," which in any other context would describe a liberal democracy. That phrase has become something of a slur in Israel, akin to treason.[3] The idea of Zionism, which once included different manifestations of national self-determination, has come to be defined by a belief that it can only exist in a nation-state that exclusively recognizes and privileges Jews.[4]

Of the few contemporary Israeli politicians who still openly support a two-state solution, none have proposed policies that could lead to, let alone create, two states. Not a single contender for the Israeli premiership in the past decade has run on a platform that includes a plan to end the occupation or apartheid rule, or otherwise meaningfully alter the undemocratic one-state reality between the Jordan River and Mediterranean Sea.

Benjamin Netanyahu's leadership has played an outsized role in shaping this dominant Israeli political outlook. By mid-2024, Netanyahu had been prime minister of Israel for thirteen out of the previous fifteen years, surpassing the country's mythological founding leader, David Ben-Gurion, as the longest-serving prime minister. During this time, he has vastly expanded Israel's settlements in the West Bank; challenged the Israeli judiciary's independence, including its ability to restrain the government's abuses in the OPT; authorized increasingly harsh and violent military control; shut down Palestinian human rights organizations; and of course, most recently, launched the unprecedented mass slaughter of Palestinians in Gaza.

To be sure, Netanyahu is not Israel, and he does not represent all Israelis—even those on the right of the political map. In Israel's parliamentary system, Netanyahu has never received more than 29 percent of the total vote count. As evidenced by the massive, weekly protests against his government in the months that preceded the October 7, 2023, attack, large portions of the Israeli public viciously opposed his rule. When it comes to Netanyahu's decades-long opposition to Palestinian statehood, however, most Israeli politicians have difficulty distinguishing themselves from him.[5] It would be a mistake, therefore, to treat him as an anomaly.

THE PALESTINIAN CONSENSUS AGAINST OCCUPATION AND APARTHEID

Palestinian views about the future of Palestinians and Israelis in the Territory are diverse, but they share one central, unifying feature: a universal consensus that Israel's occupation and apartheid rule over them must end. While some Palestinians, in particular official leaders, remain committed to a two-state solution as envisioned by the Oslo Accords, increasing numbers of Palestinians say they would prefer a single, democratic state for all of the people in the Territory.[6]

Palestine's current leadership, as officially represented by the undemocratic, two-decade rule of the Palestinian Authority (PA) under President Mahmoud Abbas, has formally endorsed an independent Palestinian state. The PA was itself created by the Oslo Accords as a Palestinian "government in waiting," and is the sole authority that Israel allows to carry weapons and exercise violence (exclusively against other Palestinians) in certain parts of the West Bank. The PA and the Palestine Liberation Organization (PLO), an umbrella organization of Palestinian political and liberation movements, appear to consider a negotiated two-state solution as the only manifestation of Palestinian self-determination they are willing to entertain.[7] From time to time, President Mahmoud Abbas and his PA deputies have threatened to resign and dissolve the PA, or have invoked a "one-state solution," though these have been mere rhetorical threats to Israel's intransigent apartheid rule.[8]

The PLO did briefly endorse a democratic one-state solution half a century ago, although it abandoned that position shortly thereafter. The Palestinian National Council, the PLO's legislative body, "voted unanimously in 1971 to support a resolution specifying that the goal of the national liberation struggle was the establishment of 'a democratic Palestinian state' in historic Palestine, where 'all [Muslims, Christians, and Jews] who wish will be able to live in peace there with the same rights and the same duties.'"[9] It is not unforeseeable, therefore, to imagine a world in which Palestinian leaders of the future adopt a rights-first strategy for liberation, either as a transitional measure as the Blueprint proposes or as a final destination.

Many observers, including many Palestinian analysts, attribute the PA's unwavering support for two states pursuant to the Oslo Accords as a product of corruption and self-interest, tied to the financial opportunities and privileges its leaders and bureaucrats have gleaned from holding power.[10] This includes their salaries, "VIP permits" from Israel that allow them to travel more easily through checkpoints and border crossings, and other privileges.[11] Furthermore, the Oslo process is what created the PA, and without the prospect of a negotiated two-state solution the PA would have no legitimacy, resulting in what several writers describe as the "sovereignty trap."[12] Together, all of this has led the Palestinian leadership to oppose steps that would abandon a two-state framework in favor of demanding that Israel instead give Palestinians their rights in a liberal, democratic, one-state solution.

Hamas, the only other significant Palestinian leadership, which has exercised limited control over Gaza since 2006, has also consented to a Palestinian state along the 1967 borders. In 2017, Hamas revised its charter and accepted a Palestinian state in Gaza and the West Bank, though it did not include specific recognition of the state of Israel.[13] In

April 2024, senior Hamas negotiator Khalil al-Hayya suggested that the group would "lay down its weapons and convert into a political party if an independent Palestinian state is established along pre-1967 borders."[14]

The Palestinian leadership did not exactly come about organically, however, an important point to remember in the context of Israel's insistence that it has no partner for peace. For the better part of the last one hundred years, Israel has used its military and intelligence services to actively foil the emergence of effective Palestinian leadership. It did so during its separate and unequal military government for Palestinian citizens of Israel between 1948 and 1966, initially using its intelligence and security services to stymie the development of Palestinian national identity through repressive control of politics, education, and movement.[15] When those same security services were tasked with overseeing the noncitizen Palestinian population in the territories captured in 1967, those efforts took on a clearer goal: "to defeat the Palestinian national struggle."[16]

In the occupied territories including East Jerusalem, the Israeli military and Shin Bet have always sought to control and decide the legitimacy of Palestinian leaders according to Israel's self-interest. At various points, Israel has intervened to stymie the emergence of Palestinian leadership through the use of deportation, assassination, imprisonment, and blackmail. Until just a few years before the Oslo Accords, even within the context of international peace efforts like the 1991 Madrid Conference, Israel refused to negotiate with the PLO, which the UN already had recognized as the sole representative of the Palestinian people for nearly two decades. After Israel finally accepted the legitimacy of the PLO in Oslo, it insisted on the creation of a parallel leadership in the PA as an attempt to sideline Yasser Arafat and the PLO's broader aspirations for liberation.

Until October 7, 2023, Israel proactively empowered and bolstered Hamas for similar reasons: "As far back as December 2012, Netanyahu told prominent Israeli journalist Dan Margalit that it was important to keep Hamas strong, as a counterweight to the Palestinian Authority in the West Bank."[17] In the West Bank as well, Israel arrests parliamentarians and candidates in local elections with the same aim. In a recent podcast interview, when former Shin Bet coordinator for East Jerusalem and the West Bank Arik Barbing was asked whether his job included preventing the emergence of new Palestinian leadership, he answered "unequivocally."[18]

The Palestinian public, however, has shifted in its own acceptance of Oslo's two-state framework, increasingly toward support for a single state across the Territory. This is likely primarily related to the failure of the Oslo process itself, the realization that ever-expanding Israeli settlements and fragmentation of Palestinian territory make two states impossible, and the discovery that Palestinian rule under the dictatorial PA or Hamas regimes has provided them no improved respect for their rights or freedoms, even within areas Palestinians are purported to have some measure of autonomy. A 2022 poll conducted by the Palestinian Center for Policy and Survey Research found that some 33 percent of Palestinians in the West Bank and Gaza Strip support one state for Israelis and Palestinians.[19] As a result, the majority of Palestinians and others advocating for a rights-first approach to ending apartheid and occupation find themselves at odds with the Palestinian leadership that remains committed to the "states-first" approach of Oslo.

THE EMERGENCE OF RIPENESS

Ripeness in conflict resolution is the idea, developed by William Zartman, that it is only possible to enter into productive negotiations when the main actors in a conflict perceive or acknowledge that they are in a mutually hurting stalemate and that they share the will to seek an alternative path out of that situation.[20] Such ripeness in Israel-Palestine can emerge with the confluence of two important and interrelated variables: domestic instability, probably accompanied by violence, and international pressure and isolation that will lead Israelis and Palestinians to conclude there are no unilateral pathways to mitigate, manage, or eliminate. Given the power disparities at play, what will truly matter is an Israeli conclusion that the price of staying the current course is too great.

DOMESTIC POLITICAL VIOLENCE

As mentioned, parties to a conflict will reconsider compromises and proposals they once rejected if they find themselves in a costly and painful predicament—typically the experience of violence and insecurity—from which they cannot unilaterally extract themselves. In Israel-Palestine, the levels of political violence experienced by Palestinians, particularly during the ongoing war in Gaza, may well have reached a level where they are prepared to accept a new alternative. Jewish Israelis have not reached a point where their personal experience of violence has led them to seriously consider alternative political visions, but continued war, disorder, and insecurity may.[21] This should not be interpreted as an endorsement of or invitation to violence, but a somber analysis.

Both Israelis and Palestinians have shown a high tolerance for suffering. They have built into their national ethos certain costs for survival. This can be seen in the prominence of the idea of *sumud*, or steadfastness, in the Palestinian national narrative and ethos following the Nakba of 1948, which canonized the idea of remaining on the land at any cost. Likewise, the centrality of the Holocaust in Israel's national narrative and ethos has resulted in a worldview in which painful losses are a built-in cost of survival and which must be achieved at any cost. "Both sides have folded the idea of 'no gain without pain' or 'it hurts but it's worth it' into their national myths to insulate them against the feelings of pain in their stalemate," Zartman writes, arguing that perceptions of pain and acceptable costs can be detrimental to reaching a situation of ripeness.[22]

In addition, both Israelis and Palestinians have sought to "win" the conflict using political violence, and indeed the state of Israel emerged following its military victory. The Israeli Right—and much of what can be described as the Israeli Center—has always subscribed to a theory, most popularly articulated by Ze'ev Jabotinsky in his essay "The Iron Wall," which argues Palestinians will only stop resisting Zionism when they come to the conclusion that they cannot emerge victorious and that the consequences of trying are too painful.[23] Israel's behavior in the Gaza War would seem to demonstrate that this theory of enforced submission still strongly motivates Israeli strategic thinking. As if to drive the point home, Israel named the military operation it launched in the West Bank in early

2025 "Iron Wall." Palestinian armed groups have long believed that only armed resistance, even if it violates the laws of war, will secure their liberation from oppression. Beyond casting the conflict as zero-sum, these national-political worldviews that violence can win have tended to make ripeness elusive, though they have, in fact, failed to bring any lasting peace and security for Israelis and certainly not Palestinians.

Even with intolerable suffering, the prospects of the current Palestinian leadership agreeing to cede its very limited autonomy and claims to statehood, even in exchange for an end to occupation and apartheid and the provision of democratic and human rights for all Palestinians in the Territory, may be difficult to imagine. However, given the shifts in Palestinian public opinion, it is not unforeseeable to imagine Palestinian leaders of the future adopting a rights-first strategy for liberation, either as a transitional measure like the Blueprint proposes or as a final destination. In a sad point of fact, the wishes of Palestinians, whether of their "leadership" or the vast majority, have had little impact on determining how Israel behaves. Palestinians living under occupation and apartheid already wish these crimes to end and have little means to make that happen, much less advance variations of a one- or two-state solution.

Likewise, a willingness to consider an alternative to occupation and apartheid rule can emerge if Israelis find themselves embroiled in domestic upheaval and violence sufficient to disturb their own security and stability and international sanctions and isolation that heighten their insecurity and instability. For that to represent a moment of "ripeness," it will require Jewish Israelis to reimagine and expand their thinking to include manifestations of national self-determination that are not mutually exclusive to Palestinian national self-determination. Jewish Israelis will likely only start to question that belief if they come to the conclusion that the Jewish state is no longer able to provide security, stability, and prosperity for Jews.

Even when outsiders might identify what Zartman calls a "mutually hurting stalemate" in conditions of escalating violence, the parties may either deny that fact or justify it as an unavoidable, zero-sum situation in which there is no choice but to continue.[24] Similarly, and with rich historical precedent in Israel-Palestine, when prior episodes of violence have reached intolerable levels, Israel has tended to find ways to "manage" the violence and keep it on a low boil. This is another reason why violence on its own will never be enough to create ripeness and why international pressure is also necessary.

INTERNATIONAL PRESSURE

International pressure will have to comprise the second pillar of whatever sequence of events leads to ripeness for the acceptance of the Blueprint among Israelis. The Israeli, Palestinian, and global human rights movement, and in particular the Boycott, Divestment, and Sanctions movement (BDS), have largely advocated for such international pressure to end Israeli abuses through boycotts, divestment, and sanctions by states, businesses, and civil society; accountability in global courts; and diplomatic isolation. These efforts have invited significant Israeli counter-initiatives to slow their success, such as securing the passage of laws in the United States and parts of Europe sanctioning citizens for advocating for boycotts of, or protesting against, Israel, and categorizing criticism of Israel as "anti-Semitic hate speech." Unprecedented restrictions on civil rights and free expression in the US and Europe have sadly been the casualties of these counter-initiatives.

By and large, while these international efforts to pressure Israel have resulted in few state-led repercussions against Israel, they have established the foundation for the global protests and significant state actions against Israel that have emerged since October 7 and the ensuing war in Gaza. Similarly, Israel's war in Gaza has expedited progress in international accountability against Israel led by the International Court of Justice and the International Criminal Court. As discussed in Chapter 1, the International Court of Justice recently concluded that Israel's occupation and apartheid regimes are illegal and that the international community has an obligation to see them brought to an end as rapidly as possible.[25] As of this writing, the International Criminal Court is seeking arrest warrants against Netanyahu and former Defense Minister Yoav Gallant for war crimes and crimes against humanity in Gaza as it proceeds with its investigation.

Each of these legal actions could strengthen international political will and significantly expand coordinated, multistate pressure toward Israel sufficient to impact Israeli calculations about the long-term viability of its apartheid and occupation rule. Similar to what the international community built to pressure South Africa's apartheid government, such actions can include state-led financial sanctions on individuals and entities or even entire industries; trade sanctions, ranging from revoking free trade agreements to full trade embargoes; and arms embargoes, which could include not only prohibitions on selling arms to Israel but also on importing Israeli arms. Sanctions can also include diplomatic measures akin to boycotts, like excluding Israel from the United Nations or international sports competitions, and implementing restrictive visa policies for Israeli nationals. They can also include civil society sanctions and boycotts, as proposed by the BDS movement, ending cross-border cooperation and partnerships with Israeli counterparts.

Albeit in a piecemeal fashion and without the critical endorsement of the UN Security Council, at the time of writing individual states have already begun implementing such sanctions. This includes states that have imposed arms embargoes on Israel; prohibitions on ships with weapons cargo for Israel from docking in their ports; trade embargoes; and sanctions on violent settlers and settlement entities in the West Bank. For two decades, the civil-society-led movement in support of BDS has established itself in forty countries.[26] In November 2024, over fifty countries asked the UN to impose an arms embargo on Israel.[27]

The biggest obstacle to the emergence of such international pressure has been and remains the United States, the world's superpower and Israel's staunchest ally. The US has effectively shielded Israel from accountability and granted it unparalleled military and political protection, allowing it to pursue its apartheid, occupation, and the ongoing war in Gaza with impunity. In recognition of this, in January 2025, our organization, DAWN, submitted a 172-page communication to the International Criminal Court urging it to prosecute President Joe Biden, Secretary of State Antony Blinken, and Secretary of Defense Lloyd Austin for their individual roles in aiding, abetting, and facilitating Israeli crimes in the Gaza War.[28] The Trump administration has deepened and strengthened the primary source of that impunity, expanding weapons transfers to Israel and taking no action to stop the Israeli starvation, siege, and deliberate and indiscriminate bombardment of Gaza that remains underway as of this writing; indeed, President Trump has proposed that the United States itself "take over" Gaza, encouraged Israel to displace the Palestinian population there, and envisioned building beach resorts in the area.[29]

The experience of global sanctions on South Africa and unified international pressure to force an end to apartheid there suggests the US will be the last to support efforts to punish and isolate Israel. Just as Israel has little incentive to change under the current conditions, the US will change its policies only when the political or economic costs of maintaining its support for Israel become too high, with too little return. Should sufficient international pressure emerge, it may have a greater impact on Israelis' sense of security than their pocketbooks. In South Africa, for example, the impact of economic and trade sanctions may have had "less to do with tipping an economic balance than with sanctions' psychological impact. The sanctions signaled the extent to which South Africa was isolated in the international community."[30]

It is plausible, however, that a combination of domestic violence and insecurity alongside international sanctions could trigger an economic crisis in Israel, also contributing to a willingness of Israelis to reconsider their allegiance to a regime committed to maintaining the status quo of apartheid and occupation.[31] Research shows that while there is a correlation between economic crisis and certain types of regime change, the resulting regime change is not necessarily democratic or liberalizing.[32] There are nevertheless ways that economic crises can contribute to changing political coalitions and power structures that can undermine the foundations of Israeli political consensus. As posited by the coalition theory of economic crisis and democratization, if support for the regime is dependent on its ability to provide economic incentives for various groups, it becomes vulnerable to collapse when it no longer has sufficient resources to sustain that political support.[33]

The Israeli state's long-standing arrangement with the ultra-Orthodox Jewish population, which it supports with immense financial subsidies and exemptions from military service, is a case in point. In recent decades, maintaining those benefits has become increasingly partisan, and it is foreseeable that the ultra-Orthodox population could dramatically change its political loyalties if its current patrons are unable to maintain that relationship. Similarly, the Jewish population of Israel writ large receives economic privileges and incentives not available to the Palestinian population. An economic crisis or severe instability triggered by domestic violence and international isolation could lead to new political coalitions and a willingness to support a dramatically different political path.

International pressure and isolation can also backfire. They could encourage the extremist Israeli government to accept its global isolation and choose to survive as a rogue state while it continues to pursue genocide and displacement of remaining Palestinians, but this is not a feasible outcome without US military and political protection. Such pressure could also undermine the viability of a successful democratic transition by creating an economic and political crisis and triggering mass intellectual and capital flight, primarily among Israelis. This could include an exodus of companies seeking to safeguard their businesses simply by leaving, or investors seeking to preserve the value of their capital, particularly if the Israeli currency suffers because of international sanctions and isolation. Business and capital are not only integral parts of the Israeli economy, they are also the primary source of income for the Israeli government. If the Israeli economy is irreparably crippled, the idea of building shared prosperity will become fanciful at best. If the state's coffers suffer beyond a certain degree, it will be difficult to carry out the Transition envisioned by the Blueprint successfully. Furthermore, the flight of educated elites could strip the Transition of a sufficient cadre of leaders and experts capable of implementing the plan. Finally, mass emigration could alter the demographic parity between Palestinians and Israelis such that the consociationalism envisioned as the basis for the Caretaker Government during the Transition will no longer accurately represent the population.

Early evidence from Israel suggests that such intellectual and capital flight may already be underway.[34] In late 2024, international credit ratings agencies downgraded Israel's credit rating and warned of a further drop to "junk" status.[35] This is partly due to the relative ease with which some dual-national and wealthy Israeli elites can leave and resettle whenever they want. Large swaths of Palestinian elites have fled or faced expulsion from the Territory for nearly a century. There may be no way to prevent the exit of Israeli intellectual and business elites who recognize that the status quo of occupation, apartheid, and war can't last; who don't want to endure international isolation and domestic instability; and who won't wait for a stable and secure future to emerge as part of a democratic transition. Ultimately, however, the long-term safety and security of the vast majority of Israelis and Palestinians in the Territory will require some form of resolution.

For international pressure and sanctions to be effective means toward such resolution, they must include clearly articulated, positive demands and a pathway to implement them. Without a viable pathway, neither Israelis nor Palestinians will be willing to entertain alternatives and compromises that could lead to a better future—together or apart. Movements like BDS, the One Democratic State Campaign, the Geneva Initiative, A Land for All, and others can develop compelling visions of what they want Israel-Palestine to look like, but without a credible plan for how to get from point A to point B, their ability to sell those visions to policymakers and create movement toward them will be very difficult if not impossible. The Blueprint aspires to articulate such a detailed plan for change and provide a clear off-ramp for Israel if it wants to see such sanctions lifted and rejoin the community of nations.

ISRAELI AND PALESTINIAN BUY-IN

Even if domestic violence and instability, coupled with international pressure, create the conditions necessary for the Blueprint to emerge as a viable exit ramp, the Blueprint will remain entirely dependent on the political will of a critical mass of Israelis and Palestinians and, more importantly, of their leaders. Conceptually, minimal public buy-in is a critical component of creating consent for any major societal and political transformation to have any chance of succeeding. Without consent there is no legitimacy (an idea we discuss at length in Section 1 of the Blueprint). A transitional government that is forcibly imposed without the consent of either the population or its leadership would be virtually indistinguishable from the lengthy history of colonialism that has shaped and fostered so many of the problems with which Israelis and Palestinians are grappling today. Would Israelis and Palestinians see a foreign caretaker government any differently than the legacy of the British Mandate, a supposedly transitional regime against which both peoples waged violent resistance?

The participation and engagement of the political and military elites in both societies is also critical. Political leaders must be willing participants because they will have to cede power to a caretaker government, even if they become members of it, and that cannot happen against their will. This participation is primarily achieved in the "pre-negotiation" stage, discussed in Section 1 of the Blueprint in the framework of a Conciliation Conference.

The Blueprint takes great pains to ensure continuity of state services and the maintenance of law and order during the Transition because transitions are by default vulnerable to chaos and disorder. To this end, political leaders will need to help ensure that the police, the judicial system, various government ministries, and municipal governments do not disband and that they continue to provide services to the people. Likewise, the Blueprint will require a massive restructuring of both Israeli and Palestinian security forces, including the disarmament and disbanding of many militant groups and official forces. That cannot happen without a high level of cooperation and consent. A scenario in which armed groups retain their strength and militancy and impose a constant threat of violent disruption of the transition as spoilers would likely cause the Blueprint to fail.

INTERNATIONAL SUPPORT AND BUY-IN

International support and buy-in also have an important role in the adoption and implementation of the Blueprint. The plan relies on the international community to provide technical expertise and support to the Transition in missions to establish the Caretaker Government and help with disarmament, security sector reform, and oversight to ensure the process doesn't get derailed. The Caretaker Government may well call on the international community to provide financial support for the Transition, particularly if there is an economic crisis. Ideally, international financial support should at least equal the amounts foreign governments have spent to finance Israel's occupation and apartheid, including repeated bills for humanitarian aid and reconstruction of destroyed Palestinian communities. Additionally, in light of long-standing Israeli and Palestinian fears and mistrust, the Blueprint envisions the international community supporting the Blueprint by providing international security guarantees to assuage fears regarding external threats.

CONCLUSION

Attempting to predict specifically when and how the conditions that will make the Blueprint relevant will emerge is foolish prophecy. The world is too unpredictable, as evidenced by the seismic changes that have taken place since the surprise Hamas attacks of October 7, Israel's untethered military response, and the world's flirtation with punishing Israel in the aftermath. Even when we are able to understand how world-changing events came to be in retrospect, like the fall of apartheid in South Africa and the Berlin Wall in Germany, the subsequent collapse of the Soviet Union, or the Arab uprisings of 2011, very few people actually saw them coming in real time.

With that in mind, the Blueprint starts with the world as it is today, modifying one critical variable: it presumes the existence of political will to end apartheid and occupation and transform an undemocratic, one-state reality into a democratic one. By building the Blueprint for a world that otherwise closely resembles the realities of today, we hope to make it accessible and comprehensible for policymakers and others who may have difficulty imagining alternative futures. Practically speaking, starting with today's reality also makes it much easier to identify the necessary changes to existing institutions, laws, and systems of governance, even if plans would need to be adjusted to match a different, future reality.

We recognize that some will be firm in their belief that the conditions for the Blueprint—including the existence of sufficient global pressure on Israelis to force them to rethink Zionism as a nonsupremacist political ideology; the reining in of violent, ideological extremists who want to expel or exterminate Palestinians; and the acceptance of the Blueprint as a way forward or the idea that militant Palestinian groups would accept a meaningful Jewish-Israeli political presence in Palestine—will never emerge. We hope that such readers will set aside their confidence in the long-term stability of the status quo in Israel-Palestine; the events of and since October 7 have made clear that nothing is beyond upheaval. The volatility of the current situation in Israel-Palestine and the genuine desire of the international community for a just resolution have certainly made it more likely that the conditions for the Blueprint may come to fruition sooner than anyone could have imagined when we started writing this book.

That said, a world in which the Blueprint gains acceptance will not be identical to the one we know today. We ask you to look past whatever those unpredictable differences may be and imagine what can be done differently today, or tomorrow, if policymakers decide to embark on a different path.

Chapter 3   The Day After the Blueprint

> I dream of white tulips, streets of song, a
>   house of light
> I need a kind heart, not a bullet.
> I need a bright day, not a mad, fascist
>   moment of triumph.
> I need a child to cherish a day of laughter,
>   not a weapon of war.
> I came to live for rising suns, not to witness
>   their setting.
>
> Mahmoud Darwish, "A Soldier Dreams of
>   White Tulips"

The aim of the Blueprint is to remedy the most urgent issues facing the Territory today—Israel's apartheid rule and illegal occupation—to create a rights-respecting state that provides all people of the Territory with equal political and civil rights. The Blueprint culminates and ends in the Territory's first democratic national elections in which both Israeli Jews and Palestinians participate to produce a truly democratic government. The second goal of the Blueprint is to prepare the ground for what follows: a sovereign decision by, and an expression of the self-determination of, the people of the Territory about the future governance of the Territory.

    The Blueprint deliberately remains agnostic on what form the governance of the Territory should take: remaining as one democratic state, separating into two sovereign states, reorganizing as a federal system with one central government, a confederal system with two governments closely cooperating, or any other system, so long as it guarantees democracy and equal rights to all people living between the Mediterranean Sea and the Jordan River. The most obvious way for the people to decide on new statehood and governance arrangements would be through some form of referendum. The Blueprint includes recommendations for the Caretaker Government to undertake extensive planning and preparation for such a referendum, but it does not take a position on what questions it should address, what form it should take, or when it should occur, nor does it mandate that a referendum be held. Those are decisions that elected officials and the citizens they represent must make, but not during a transition led by a Caretaker Government.

The national elections that mark the end of the Blueprint will take place no later than three years after the Caretaker Government assumes power. They will be preceded by local and municipal elections, which will occur within the Transition's first two years.

As described in Section 9, the Blueprint relies on consociationalism as a temporary necessity to ensure fair representation and power sharing in the formation of the Caretaker Government and in both municipal and national elections held during the Transition. The Blueprint mandates representational quotas for Jewish and Palestinian citizens, along with other minority groups, to promote collaboration and compromise and prevent any single group from dominating the political landscape.

A BETTER ONE-STATE REALITY

Some readers will judge the Blueprint as a thinly veiled attempt to create a permanent one-state solution. However, we believe that while our point of departure entails transforming the existing one-state apartheid reality into a democratic one-state reality, it does not and should not prejudice the possibility for alternative forms of governance and statehood. If anything, it makes deliberations about future governance more plausible and fairer. First, if, as the Oslo Accords envisioned, it is possible to transform the existing undemocratic state into two states then it should be no less possible to transform a democratic state into two states in various configurations. The Blueprint merely prioritizes ending the ongoing crimes of illegal apartheid and occupation over questions of governance. Such an approach both satisfies international law's unequivocal and urgent demand to end ongoing crimes and the need for decision-making that respects the principles of self-determination, sovereignty of the people, democracy, and equal rights. Without the distorted power dynamics created by occupation and apartheid, the people of the Territory would be much better placed to find such a solution collectively.

Second, the Blueprint's approach also seeks to manage the risks associated with any derailment that may emerge due to backsliding, stagnation, and spoilers. Once underway, it will be difficult to revert to the previous realities of occupation and apartheid. By extending citizenship, civilian rule, and guarantees of equal treatment on the first day of the Blueprint, would-be spoilers would have a much harder time reimposing an unjust, segregated regime. A consociational Caretaker Government will also be better positioned to peacefully manage and resolve violence, populist or nationalist movements, or various types of crises that may emerge, which we discuss in Chapter 4. One principle that guided much of the formation of the Blueprint is ensuring that if the Transition does come to a halt at any stage, it creates a better outcome than the one it found, from the current default of an undemocratic one-state reality to a new default of a more democratic one-state reality.

Similarly, if political deadlock or any other factor prevents a referendum, the people of Israel-Palestine will nevertheless be free of occupation and apartheid, enjoy freedom of movement, and have effective avenues for democratic political expression and representation.

A REFERENDUM AFTER THE TRANSITION

As detailed in Section 9, the Blueprint considers the possibility that whatever government emerges at the end of the Transition may wish to reconfigure as two or more states and suggests a referendum as the best way to manage that decision. Such a referendum in the current one-state reality of apartheid and occupation would lack democratic legitimacy. First, as long as Israel is the sole de facto sovereign over the Territory, it can veto or ignore the results, negating the facade of agency that a referendum today would theoretically give Palestinians.

Second, a referendum today would not be fair or free for Palestinians if their only choices are choosing a new state in which they have rights or the status quo in which they have none.[1] In contrast, a referendum under a post-Blueprint democratic state would give Palestinians a choice between two different systems of governance, either of which guarantees their rights.[2] Finally, a post-Transition government with a broad democratic mandate and legitimacy will be better placed to manage negotiations among its citizens about alternative forms of governance and statehood, including political disputes over borders and the return of refugees. As Fionnuala Ní Aoláin and Colm Campbell argue, it is helpful "to conceive of transitional situations not as involving one single transition, but in terms of at least two primary sets: a movement towards democracy (the 'democratic v. nondemocratic' antinomy) and that towards peace (a 'war v. peace' antinomy)," noting that "a sober recognition that some kind of conflict is an inevitable part of the human condition (and not necessarily one to be avoided) has focused less on the ending of conflict than on transformation from a violent to a nonviolent way of doing politics, one that can be expressed as a 'nonviolent conflict v. violent conflict' antinomy."[3]

The Blueprint does, however, mandate the Caretaker Government's Governance Committee to commence preparations and plans for a future referendum. The decision of whether, when, and what type of referendum to hold will be the sovereign prerogative of the first democratically elected government.

The committee can consider proposals for referendums for several different governance and state structure models. Three such models that a referendum could offer the people of the Territory are, in brief:

Two Independent States

Two independent states, Israel and Palestine, would be like the two-state vision proposed over decades of peacemaking efforts. This would likely require a process to negotiate borders and the relationship between the two states after they separate, for example, residency rights, restrictions on movement between the states, whether to maintain a single economic market, and other trade issues.

Confederation

In many ways, proposals for an Israeli-Palestinian confederation resemble a two-state solution, namely in that they are all predicated on the existence—or creation—of two states, one Palestinian and one Israeli. The main difference, explains Dahlia Scheindlin, is the rejection of separation and segregation as the basis for peace; instead, confederation "rests on limited shared institutions, borders designed for freedom of movement subject to security needs, residency rights on the 'other' side, and coordinating economic and security policy."[4] This approach has been detailed by A Land for All as well as a policy vision published by two former Israeli and Palestinian negotiators titled *The Holy Land Confederation as a Facilitator for the Two-State Solution.*[5]

Federalism in One State

Federalism retains a single central government with devolved powers to local governments. It emphasizes enhanced cooperation on shared resources and security while maintaining local governance and identity.[6] The decentralized nature of the government is the most unique and compelling feature of a federal model, as it balances power between central and local authorities, reducing conflict over control. Among other features, the central government is responsible for national defense and foreign policy, while constituent states are given broad autonomy to manage education, health care, and local law enforcement.

CONCLUSION

We believe the Blueprint can be complementary to any vision for a democratic future, be it a two-state solution, confederation, or federalism. By ending apartheid and occupation first, the Blueprint paves the way for genuine self-determination and sovereignty, which are crucial for any sustainable and just political solution.

While many have suggested that a one-state outcome is a negative to be avoided, or a default if all other efforts at conflict resolution fail—as has been leveled by Israeli and Palestinian leaders as a quasi threat—we believe that it presents more opportunities than dangers at this stage in history. Further, unlike some Israeli pundits' claims that Palestinian demands for a two-state solution are a mere stepping stone toward their ultimate goal of a one-state solution, we argue that the opposite could be true, if desired: a democratic one-state reality can make an equitable two-state solution possible.

None of the political visions discussed above can happen under the current dynamics, however, particularly in the absence of a political process with democratic legitimacy. By creating equal footing and mitigating the skewed power dynamics by ending apartheid and occupation, we believe that any of these democratic political outcomes become much more possible. Just as importantly, they would hold vastly increased legitimacy by virtue of being chosen democratically by all of the people of the Territory.

Chapter 4   The Challenge of Security, Violence, and Instability

There is no such thing as change without risk. Just as seemingly stable countries can face major unexpected crises and challenges to the established order, a transitional period is inescapably unstable. We have given serious attention and planning to identifying and mitigating the risks and pitfalls we anticipate the Blueprint may face, all of which pertain in some way to insecurity, violence, and instability. We have sought to balance the need for security during the Transition with the desire for freedom and justice. Because we believe that violence and insecurity are the gravest threats the Blueprint faces, we have prioritized ensuring security during the Transition though we know that this impinges on the most fulsome respect for freedom and rights. We believe this is necessary to enable the creation of a democratic state that will not need to make such severe compromises.

The instability inherent in transition creates a raft of opportunities that potential spoilers could exploit. Palestinian or Israeli armed groups who oppose the Transition could seek to derail the process or seize control of the state to prevent its implementation. There may be serious episodes of intercommunal violence or even a prolonged, organized insurgency. So-called lone-wolf armed individuals and irregular militias could carry out acts of vigilante violence, creating public disorder. Maintaining acceptable levels of public order is critical to the success of the Transition, without which it will be difficult to provide a sense of security for Jewish Israelis who must agree to cede the most power. There also exists the very real risk of a bloodless coup in which one party exploits instability to seize power of the new consolidated state and government.

In this chapter, we address how the Blueprint approaches these risks of violence and instability, and the policy prescriptions and choices the Blueprint proposes to mitigate them. We address the shortcomings in justice and freedom the Blueprint tolerates, particularly regarding past security force abuses, delayed transitional justice, and restrictions on movement. The Blueprint is less likely to be adopted without such security measures, and even if it is, without them, it will likely fail.

MILITANT SPOILERS

Armed groups are pervasive in Israel and Palestine and will likely seek to undermine or hijack the Transition. These include not only the Israel Defense Forces (the official armed forces of Israel) but also Palestinian armed groups and armed Israeli paramilitary settler forces. They may perceive regime change and the integration of the security forces as a threat to their own power and even safety. Ideally, the most powerful and largest Israeli and Palestinian militant groups will have consented to the Transition. Without their substantial buy-in, as detailed in Chapter 2, the Blueprint is simply not possible. The Blueprint mandates integrating and merging some of those sectarian security forces into national security forces— civilian police, military and organized militant groups, and intelligence services alike. It requires others to demobilize and disarm. Even with broad consent, however, the risk of spoilers emerging from these groups is real.

The first way the Blueprint addresses this threat is not by disbanding all of the Territory's armed groups but by keeping the major security and militant groups intact and then moving to integrate them. One of the worst decisions of the US-installed Coalition Provisional Authority in Iraq—though perhaps not the worst of the legendary failures of the US-imposed regime change—was the disbandment of the Iraqi military forces, leading to their reemergence as armed groups and to subsequent decades of civil war in the country.[1] Given the prevalence of violence in Israel-Palestine throughout the twentieth and twenty-first centuries, however, we anticipate that radical groups on both sides of the process may seek to use force to prevent—or end—security force integration.

The Blueprint draws on the successful model of South Africa's military integration, including shared command structures and extensive oversight mechanisms, following the end of apartheid.[2] Despite the strength of the South African state and the consent of the government to end apartheid, the White leadership of the South African Defence Forces attempted to retain its power by manipulating the integration process.[3] It is likely the Jewish leadership of the Israel Defense Forces, the national police, and intelligence services would attempt the same strategy, seeking to retain command even over Palestinians who join or merge into their ranks. One of the key strategies South Africa employed to mitigate this type of resistance was creating and implementing integrated advisory boards and commissions at every stage of integrating security forces.[4]

The Blueprint takes a similar approach, creating a number of independent commissions to monitor and assist in the integration, deployment, and transformation of security forces into bodies that serve the entire population in line with egalitarian, inclusive, democratic principles. As detailed in Appendix E, this includes creating and empowering a Transitional Justice Committee, Domestic Security Committee, Military Oversight Commission, and Free Movement Commission. The Blueprint also prescribes the creation of a new security doctrine that guides the integration process and the policies and practices of the new, integrated security forces, partially based on the various policing and intelligence white papers produced and implemented in South Africa and the *Chicago Principles of Post-Conflict Justice*.[5] Put simply, transitions from autocracy to democracy require "refocus[ing] the bureaucracy and the security and police forces from controlling subjects to serving citizens."[6]

The Blueprint also aims to mitigate the risk of violent spoilers through an internationally led disarmament, demobilization, and reintegration (DDR) program for armed groups that are not integrated into the new national bodies. In the first week of the Transition, the Blueprint mandates the Caretaker Government to appoint a Disarmament, Demobilization, and Reintegration Committee drawn from Palestinian and Israeli security experts, current and former combatants, civil society groups, and the government itself, to begin developing a DDR plan together with the UN Department of Peace Operations and any other international partners the Caretaker Government chooses to invite. We recommend that the DDR plan closely follow the UN's Integrated DDR Standards. DDR is not a quick process, and it requires comprehensive stabilization and economic and social programs that live long beyond the Transition. Starting it at the very beginning of the Transition, however, is an important step.

In a similar vein, the Blueprint does not include a comprehensive program for transitional justice for Palestinians, mostly because that should be designed and executed by a post-Transition government, but also as a concession to maintaining security and public order.[7] Such concessions during most transitions boil down to "assuring them that wholesale revenge against the former rulers and their main supporters would not be taken."[8] In South Africa this entailed truth and reconciliation commissions as an avenue to grant amnesty instead of prosecuting members of the security forces and their leaders, although truth and reconciliation certainly do not preclude prosecutions or retributive justice down the road. The Blueprint relies on international standards for lustration and other types of vetting (described in Sections 7 and 8) to ensure that the worst offenders do not remain in the new security forces, but it does not create a strict mandate to prosecute them. Such accountability and justice will have to wait for the post-Transition period.

These are not perfect processes and the compromises they entail will be painful, particularly for Palestinians who may rightfully prioritize achieving various measures of justice over maintaining elements of privilege and security for Jewish Israelis. We believe they are necessary compromises, and by virtue of the Blueprint being a plan for Transition and not one that dictates the future contours and policies of the state or states that come in its wake, they are neither absolute nor permanent.

PUBLIC DISORDER AND INTERCOMMUNAL VIOLENCE

Organized militant groups are not the only actors who can create massive insecurity and violence or sabotage a transition. One need look no further than the Oslo process to imagine how even sporadic violence by civilian actors can have an outsized impact. In 1994, an Israeli settler massacred twenty-nine Muslim worshippers in Hebron's Ibrahimi Mosque at the height of the Oslo Accords process. Following the attack, Palestinian militants carried out suicide bombings in Israel. The already divisive peace process never recovered.

Intercommunal violence verging on civil war also erupted in May 2021, in what Israelis refer to as "Operation Guardian of the Walls" and Palestinians as the "Unity Intifada," including "riots, stabbings, arson, attempted home invasions and shootings" in cities, towns, and highways across the country targeting both Jewish and Palestinian citizens of Israel.[9] Jewish mobs of armed Israeli settlers self-deployed to mixed, Palestinian-Jewish cities within Israel, raising the prospect of more organized violence.[10] At the time, Israeli security forces and officials spoke of these events as a warning of things to come, and they put into place preparations to quell future outbreaks of intercommunal violence.[11] In response, Israeli police, who were widely criticized for failing to protect Palestinian citizens of Israel targeted by mobs of Jewish Israelis, pushed forward plans to create a civilian paramilitary force called the Civilian Guard.[12]

These organized mobs and militias were, indeed, a harbinger of a dramatic rise in organized mob and militia violence by groups of Israelis largely composed of West Bank settlers. Following the Hamas attacks of October 7, 2023, groups of armed Israeli settlers terrorized and expelled dozens of Palestinian communities in the West Bank with almost no intervention by Israeli authorities.[13] Mobs of Jewish Israeli civilians also attacked Palestinian citizens of Israel.[14] Within weeks, Jewish settlers supported by Israeli security forces were blocking and violently attacking humanitarian aid convoys meant for civilians facing famine in Gaza.[15] These episodes, like the hundreds of Palestinian "lone-wolf" attacks against Israelis in recent years, provide a window into the type of intercommunal, civilian-led violence that could lead to a breakdown of the requisite public support and political will during the Transition.

The political, economic, and social changes intrinsic to regime change and transition also carry a specific set of risks when it comes to maintaining public order: "The changes usually result in high levels of crime and violence."[16] The Blueprint incorporates several strategies to minimize the eruption of public disorder and crime, relying primarily on regular civilian policing and law enforcement. As discussed at length in Section 7, dozens of Palestinian and Israeli security forces are currently tasked with various roles that can be described as maintaining public order, including the Israeli military, which has policing duties over Palestinians in the Occupied Palestinian Territory (OPT). The Blueprint creates a clear and hard distinction between military and civilian forces, revoking the military's jurisdiction to govern and police civilians. It subsequently integrates the Palestinian and Israeli police forces into a new national police force but keeps them in place geographically, policing their respective communities in the initial stages of the Transition, primarily for the sake of continuity and stability. As in South Africa, we believe a key to integrated policing success will be a joint command comprising Israeli and Palestinian police leaders. The Blueprint also incorporates lustration and other vetting procedures to ensure the integrity of the new police force and guides it with a new security doctrine.

In other transitions where the rule of law has prevailed, an important variable was whether the police leadership invested in "capacity building of their officers before and during the transitional period in the area of handling disorderliness that may erupt during transitional periods."[17] Accordingly, the Blueprint includes a two-year program for officers and commanders (regardless of which agency they served in previously) to align standard operating procedures, educate officers about relevant changes in the law, instruct them in the new security doctrine, train them in community policing, and teach them at least rudimentary, conversational Arabic and Hebrew and cross-cultural awareness and sensitivity.

The Blueprint also maintains the basic structures and personnel of the Israel Security Agency (ISA, or, the Shin Bet), changing its name to the Domestic Intelligence Agency (DIA) and integrating into it all ranks of the Palestinian Preventive Security (PPS). Like with civilian police and other security forces, these agencies will be subject to strict civilian oversight mechanisms, comprehensive lustration processes, and a two-year training program for all agents, regardless of their originating agency. Additionally, the Blueprint includes a strict, statutory, criminal prohibition on the use of torture—a prohibition that current Israeli law does not clearly articulate.

Maintaining these Israeli intelligence agencies is not something we take lightly; both the Shin Bet and the PPS agencies are responsible for some of the worst human rights abuses, and asking them to continue in similar roles, albeit with different rules and practices, risks the recurrence of many of those abuses.[18] The Caretaker Government and any subsequent democratically elected governments will slowly and systematically replace the personnel in these agencies with recruits and experienced experts who were not involved in the systemic abuses and torture carried out by the ISA and PPS. However, the risks of violence and spoilers seeking to disrupt or hijack the Transition require at least short-term continuity in domestic intelligence capabilities.

Finally, the Blueprint keeps internal checkpoints in place for up to three years to give law enforcement more tools to contain and preempt spoilers and armed groups. This, too, represents an uncomfortable compromise, in some ways maintaining the physical infrastructure of occupation and apartheid. To mitigate the harms posed by these checkpoints, the Blueprint prohibits categorical bans on movement and mandates passage of a Basic Law: Freedom of Movement, guaranteeing the right of every person to move freely throughout the Territory and through checkpoints, subject to physical security screening. The Blueprint also assigns responsibility for internal checkpoints to civilian police officers, requiring both an Israeli and Palestinian presence along with suggested international observers to ensure that checkpoints do not continue to violate basic rights.

"REGIME CHANGE FROM WITHIN"

The Transition can also be hijacked through political, nonviolent means. Legitimate actors in the Caretaker Government could try to take advantage of the instability and insecurity during the Transition to sabotage the process and reinstate apartheid and occupation. The literature offers ample warnings of illiberal "regime change from within" and suggests a correlation between economic crisis and illiberal regime change.[19] Even successful transitions to democracy correlate with a short-term deterioration in economic and other human development metrics.[20] Large-scale economic flight would probably take place prior to the Transition but may accelerate if economic and security conditions prove too unstable.

To mitigate these risks, the Blueprint adopts a consociational model of representative government. Consociationalism is, in its simplest form, a power-sharing arrangement among different groups designed to protect against majoritarianism and to mitigate mistrust. The Blueprint's model of consociationalism dictates representation quotas for Jews, Palestinians, and smaller minorities in the Caretaker Government and the first demo-cratically elected government so that no group has more power than another in the government. This is a particularly attractive option consid-ering there is currently near-parity in population size between Jewish and Palestinian residents of the Territory. With respect to political parties, this consociational system does not require Palestinians to vote for a Palestinian party or Jews to vote for a Jewish party; it may well be that Palestinians and Jews who share progressive values form a "Socialist" party, and those who share conservative or religious values form a "Conservative" party.

Another Blueprint safeguard establishes certain conditions for partici-pating in the Caretaker Government and democratic elections, in accordance with the Venice Commission Guidelines on Prohibition and Dissolution of Political Parties and the *Chicago Principles on Post-Conflict Justice*.[21] Importantly, the Blueprint requires political parties to commit to nonviolence, declare support for the democratic transition and rejec-tion of apartheid and occupation, and commit to dismantling or disarm-ing militant groups with which they may be associated.

CONCLUSION

Navigating the expected and unexpected pitfalls and challenges inherent in any democratic transition requires meticulous planning, the inclusion of major would-be spoilers, and a readiness to adapt to unforeseen cir-cumstances. The Blueprint recognizes these risks, particularly those related to violence and disorder, and seeks to manage and mitigate them as best as possible through the design of its various steps. The academic literature and lessons from historical case studies, such as South Africa's democratic transition, underscore the necessity of these measures for a transition to succeed.

Ultimately, we believe the viability of the Blueprint rests on the delicate balance between security and justice, a painful but not unique hurdle to overcome in any system of democratic governance. While some concessions are necessary to maintain stability and prevent violence, these compromises are not meant to be permanent, and the entire spectrum of transitional justice should be addressed more holistically once a democratic government is elected and, more likely, following a referendum on how the people of the Territory choose to shape their state or states.

PART II   The Blueprint

Establish a Caretaker Government

SUMMARY

The Blueprint is designed to transform a de facto undemocratic, one-state reality into a democratic one. It aims to democratize the one-state reality because ending apartheid, siege, and occupation can no longer wait—not for the prospect of a nonexistent diplomatic process, not for Palestinian politics to heal while Israel does everything in its power to maintain division, occupation, and apartheid rule, and not for the perfect leadership or nonviolent movement to emerge.

The Blueprint is a three-year plan to sufficiently democratize the entire territory of Israel-Palestine ("the Territory") such that all of its residents can participate equitably in permanent decision-making about how to relate to each other and the state—or states—in which they want to live as citizens, whether as one democratic state for all, a more traditional two-state solution, a confederation, a federation, or any other democratic configuration. To facilitate such democratic transition and decision-making, the Blueprint requires the creation of an interim Caretaker Government tasked with overseeing the Transition. This inherently means the suspension of Israel and Palestine as independent states during the Transition, replaced by the Caretaker Government that, as discussed in Section 5, could be called the State of Israel-Palestine, and the incorporation of the powers of the Palestinian Authority (PA) within the Caretaker Government. The end of the Transition will entail holding democratic elections, dissolving the Caretaker Government, and forming a new national government that can hold a referendum about the final form of the state or states that emerge.

The Caretaker Government itself will be a body that is organized with international support but selected by local representatives convened by a United Nations special envoy in a Conciliation Conference that can be thought of as a forum for pre-negotiations. While this is not itself a democratic process, it is a temporary necessity to peacefully and systematically bridge the transition from undemocratic to democratic rule. In addition, the Caretaker Government will itself be subject to checks and balances by a new High Court for the Transition and bound by a set of Guiding Principles that restricts its powers. The Conciliation Conference should comprise no more than fifty people living in Israel and Palestine. The conference will last no more than thirty days and serve a limited purpose: adopting the Blueprint, including its Guiding Principles and timeline, and appointing a Caretaker Government with the mandate to implement the plan.

To select Conciliation Conference participants, the special envoy will have to rely on flawed existing political maps while also taking steps to ensure that groups that have been excluded from politics and policymaking under the current systems of governance are also given a meaningful seat at the table. The exclusion of minorities and traditionally marginalized groups, including women, would be detrimental to the success of the Blueprint. Likewise, Palestinian refugees must be given a role, even if symbolic in some ways, from the beginning of the process. The selection methodology is detailed in Section 2.

Upon being appointed by the Conciliation Conference, the new ministers in the Caretaker Government will have thirty days to select a prime minister. If they are unable to do so, the special envoy will assume the role of acting prime minister. In its first weeks in office, the Caretaker Government will appoint a number of committees and commissions to guide and supervise the Transition. The committees and commissions are described in detail in the sections that follow, and a full list can be found in Appendix E.

APPOINTMENT AND STRUCTURE OF THE CARETAKER GOVERNMENT

The Caretaker Government shall consist of a cabinet selected by the Conciliation Conference and a special envoy authorized by the UN Security Council and chosen by the UN General Assembly.[1] The special envoy will be a permanent nonvoting member of the cabinet, except in the case that he or she assumes the role of prime minister. The special envoy's tasks will be mediating between parties, offering creative solutions, and facilitating international support for the Transition. Additionally, they will serve in a quasi-presidential role in which they will be required to sign any legislation before it can become law. They may exercise a veto only if they believe a law is gravely detrimental to the Transition or substantially contradicts any of the Guiding Principles. The special envoy's position as signer of laws will expire upon the swearing in of a new president following the first democratic national elections.

Some existing Israeli and PA ministries will convert with existing staff into the new transitional government, including the Defense, Foreign, Finance, Interior, Education, Health, Transportation, Taxation, Agriculture, Environmental Protection, Justice, and Tourism ministries. Senior staff and politicians shall be subject to a lustration process like the one described for members of the security forces in Section 7.

COMPOSITION OF THE CABINET

The cabinet shall be composed of seventeen ministers (including a prime minister) plus the special envoy. The cabinet should be selected as meritocratically as possible with an emphasis on selecting ministers with relevant experience or expertise. The makeup of the cabinet shall follow these criteria: eight of the cabinet members must represent Arab Palestinians, at least one of whom must be Christian; eight of the cabinet members must be Jewish Israelis, including at least one representing groups who do not identify as Jewish but who qualified for Israeli citizenship under the Israeli Law of Return; one cabinet member shall represent an ethnic minority not included above, such as Armenians, Druze, and Circassian citizens. At least one half of the ministers must be women, and the Palestinian and Jewish groups must include both religious and nonreligious parties or representatives. This is meant to ensure that the Caretaker Government is representative of major population groups in the Territory while preventing one group from dominating the others or seizing control of the process.

Once the cabinet is selected, the new cabinet members shall elect a prime minister from among themselves—by simple majority. If the new cabinet is unable to elect a prime minister within thirty days, the special envoy shall assume the role of acting prime minister until such a time as the cabinet is able to elect a prime minister or until the end of the Transition.

MISSION OF THE CARETAKER GOVERNMENT

The Caretaker Government has two primary missions. The first is to carry out the Transition itself. This includes implementing and executing the steps outlined in this plan to end the occupation of the territories captured by Israel in the 1967 war and to dismantle Israel's apartheid regime and usher that regime into the beginnings of a democracy. The second mission is to govern during the Transition and ensure as little disruption as possible to the daily lives of all residents, to maintain sound fiscal and economic policy in this period of uncertainty, build trust and support for the government, and normalize power sharing and cooperation within one state and within one government.

There are, however, many aspects of governance that will require longer-term, comprehensive plans to remedy the impacts of apartheid and more than five decades of occupation, but those aspects are beyond the scope of the Blueprint's mission. This means the Caretaker Government will not seek to make major changes or reforms on important issues such as women's rights, environmental concerns, economic redistribution, refugees, and transitional justice, to name just a few of the areas for which a democratically elected government will be responsible following the Transition.

THE STATE OF ISRAEL, THE PALESTINIAN AUTHORITY, AND THE STATE OF PALESTINE

The Blueprint envisions suspending the states of Israel and Palestine and merging the authorities and functions of various ministries and entities of the State of Israel and the Palestinian Authority into the Caretaker Government. If Israel were to simply withdraw—either because it is compelled or of its own volition—to the 1949 Armistice Lines and declare a two-state solution, that would, in our view, immediately dissolve into chaos and armed conflict because it would fail to address the vast power imbalances between two such states or provide a means to resolve the issues that are matters of collective concern and interest to Jewish Israelis and Palestinians alike. We believe that a Caretaker Government will be better suited to democratically resolve these issues and give all inhabitants of the Territory the opportunity to decide their future governance in one or more states, without assuming or predetermining what the ultimate configuration should look like.

It is important to consider that the State of Palestine remains largely a conceptual state with all the trappings of external affairs and functions—including, for example, the ratification of treaties—but almost none of those concerning internal affairs and functions, and of course it is entirely unable to exercise sovereignty. The PA is itself a transitional governing body created by the Oslo process but never endowed with the authorities and sovereignty of a state.[2] The Blueprint therefore envisions that the Conciliation Conference shall merge and transfer the powers of the State of Israel and the PA to the Caretaker Government upon its formation. The municipal functions and many of the offices and entities of the PA will continue to exist as local government bodies under the aegis of the Caretaker Government, as will most Israeli local government bodies and offices. This will, of course, require the consent of Israeli and Palestinian leadership in the pre-negotiation stage and would mean, at least temporarily, setting aside the nominal trappings of independent Palestinian statehood.

The reason for merging the two states' entities into the new, transitional state composed primarily of previously Israeli institutions—and, indeed, the state under the Caretaker Government will in many ways resemble the structures of the Israeli state—is first and foremost practical. As discussed at great length earlier in this book, as well as by prominent Palestinian, Israeli, and international scholars and political thinkers for decades, there exists today a one-state reality in Israel-Palestine and that reality is the Blueprint's practical point of departure. Neither the PA nor the State of Palestine controls its own borders or its population registry; has meaningful powers to enter into bilateral agreements with other countries concerning trade and security; controls its own natural resources; or has a monopoly on the use of force in its territory. These reasons alone, not to mention the dispersal of Palestinian and Israeli populations throughout the Territory, make it much more practical to merge the limited institutions of the PA into a Caretaker Government than to simply declare a Palestinian state into existence.

Second, simply declaring a Palestinian state into existence would undermine the imperative to tackle the already difficult issues of mutual concern to Israeli Jews and Palestinians alike, including transitional justice, restitution, the resolution of the Palestinian refugee problem, Israeli settlers who wish to remain in the Occupied Palestinian Territory (OPT), the status of annexed territories, the status of Jerusalem, or the status of land claims throughout the Territory. It would offer no answers to the elements of apartheid impacting Palestinian citizens of Israel, nor would it advance their right to self-determination. And it would be unlikely to overcome the power and resource differentials that would exist by default between the two states, making a just and equitable resolution of these issues nearly impossible.

Third, we do not assume that the right of and desire for self-determination—for Palestinians and Jewish Israelis alike—can only be reflected in two separate states. The historical predominance of that framework should also not foreclose the opportunity for the people of the Territory to decide how they wish to configure their governance. Increasing numbers of Palestinians and Israelis have expressed their support for one-state, binational, and confederation configurations.

We believe that a better way to resolve these issues and to maximally allow direct, democratic decision-making is to transform an undemocratic one-state reality into a transitional democratic state with universal suffrage, thereby allowing these citizens to decide their future governance. Far from precluding the establishment of two states—the State of Israel and the State of Palestine—we believe that by reforming the political and power dynamics that have blocked the emergence of a Palestinian state thus far, the Blueprint makes it more possible to establish a meaningful, sovereign State of Palestine alongside a State of Israel, should the entire electorate decide so.

BUILDING LEGITIMACY, PARTICIPATION, AND TRUST

A transitional government is highly irregular both in its essence and in form. This is perhaps most true in governments leading democratic transitions, which by virtue of transitioning to—and not from—democracies, are intrinsically undemocratic to varying degrees. A transitional government is therefore less bound by a broad social contract than it is driven by a singular purpose: the establishment of or transition to a democracy in place of an undemocratic system of government, while maintaining order and normal governance.

The questions of where a transitional government draws its legitimacy and who gives it its mandate to rule are among the most difficult of those irregularities to surmount. Without buy-in from Palestinians and a willingness to enter into a peaceful transition process, it is highly unlikely that Jewish Israelis would ever entertain a scenario that requires them to cede privilege, power, and a monopoly on the legitimate use of force. Likewise, without buy-in from Israelis that translates into a genuine willingness to dismantle apartheid, end the occupation, and create space for the expression of equal individual and national Palestinian rights, it is highly unlikely that Palestinians would participate broadly enough to bestow legitimacy on the Transition.

Achieving that buy-in requires overcoming deeply seated disparities in political representation among the different population groups living in the Territory. Israeli citizens, who are the majority of people living under

Israeli governance today, have high levels of democratic representation. Their existing elected representatives can provide consent and legitimacy to the Caretaker Government by virtue of having recently been elected. Roughly one-third of the population in the entire Territory, Palestinians without Israeli citizenship, have no national or broadly accepted leadership with a democratic mandate. The last Palestinian national elections took place in 2006.[3] Adding to that direct democratic deficit, over the years Israel has outlawed virtually every Palestinian political party active in the occupied territories and put strict limitations on the ideas and platforms of parties that represent Palestinian citizens of Israel within the Israeli system.[4] Palestinian refugees have virtually no democratic representation. As a result, while there are Palestinian political parties and politicians who at one point were elected, the Palestinian people have not had an opportunity to give a democratic mandate to any of them for nearly two decades, and certainly not enough of a mandate to cede power and agree to the formation of a Caretaker Government.

In practice, this means the special envoy must adhere to several principles. First, the Conciliation Conference must utilize consociationalism-based quotas to select conference members to prevent one group, or an alignment of groups and parties, from seeking to dominate the process. To that end, there should be roughly equal numbers of representatives from Jewish and Palestinian societies. In addition to representatives of political parties reflecting the most recent elections—for Palestinians, "recent" means the 2006 elections—the conference must also include members specifically representing oppressed and marginalized groups, such as women, smaller religious and ethnic groups, geographically peripheral areas, and civil society organizations from both Israeli and Palestinian society focusing on everything from human rights to religion, to agriculture and LGBTQ communities.

The Conciliation Conference must adopt the Blueprint because without it, there can be no legitimacy to the Caretaker Government's mandate and, by extension, the Transition itself. In other words, even if the path to reaching the requisite political will to embark on the Blueprint is one largely coerced by the international community, the Transition itself must be authorized and shaped by representatives of the people of the Territory. Without that sovereign approval, which in democracy is drawn directly from the people, the Blueprint would risk being little more than a modern-day mandate power at best, or an externally imposed regime at worst—both of which would be antithetical to the spirit of transforming an undemocratic regime into a democratic one.[5] Implementation of the Blueprint thus depends not only on support and pressure from the international community but also on sufficient domestic political will among both Palestinians and Israelis, or at the very least the support and buy-in of qualified leaders with enough legitimacy to bring a sufficient portion of the public with them.

At the same time, the existence or creation of political will does not automatically confer the requisite trust required for such a monumental change of course for the national aspirations of both the Palestinian and Israeli peoples as they have been most prominently expressed over the past century. Trust is built and earned, not given, and the transition process itself must play a central role in building and earning that trust for all peoples living in the Territory.[6] It must also have clear and agreed-upon values, guiding principles, and goals.

The Blueprint proposes four main strategies to address issues of legitimacy, participation, and trust in the Caretaker Government and the process itself: consent, representation, accountability, and clearly articulated expectations. The first two components stem directly from the right to self-determination, a peremptory norm of international law, which, among other things, requires that people consent to being ruled and have the right to determine their own political status and choose their own government.[7] The Blueprint envisions establishing such consent and representation prior to the establishment of a Caretaker Government through the Conciliation Conference discussed previously.

CONSENT

There are several ways that people can consent to a transitional government in a democratic transition process, but the most common is crafted in so-called pre-negotiations that design and shape the transition process itself. This is particularly true in states with existing elements of democracy, even those with democracy only for some—what are often categorized as "conflicted democracies."[8] In South Africa, years of secret negotiations between the apartheid government and the opposition African National Congress (ANC) legitimized the process that would end apartheid and transform the country into a democracy. The apartheid regime and its constituent class of White South Africans gained concessions in those negotiations, such as assurances on the perpetuation of a market economy, respect for White property rights, and nonprosecution as part of a truth and reconciliation process, that helped assuage fears of exclusion, revenge, dispossession, and prosecution. The ANC and Black South Africans gained concessions primarily in the release of prisoners and legalization of opposition and armed groups that ensured their legitimate participation in the process at an early stage.[9] The apartheid regime ultimately relied on a referendum that—successfully—sought the consent of White South Africans to continue down the path of ending apartheid, but even such a referendum would not have been possible without the political leadership's own consent to the process.[10]

Likewise, the Troubles in Northern Ireland, decades of violence between Irish Catholic nationalists and Protestant British loyalists marked by military occupation and terrorism, could not have ended without negotiations that led to the Good Friday Agreement.[11] It was only possible to reach that agreement four years after the major parties and armed groups negotiated a ceasefire in 1994. Despite their many, many flaws, even the Oslo Accords succeeded at creating productive dialogue to transform the relationship between Israel and the Palestinians living under its control— between legitimate representatives of the two peoples.[12] It's worth remembering that both the Irish Republican Army (IRA) and the Palestine Liberation Organization (PLO) were considered terrorist organizations by their respective interlocutors at the time. "The level of hatred [between the Unionists and IRA] was a shock to me," Bertie Ahern, the Irish taoiseach and a party to the Good Friday talks, recalled in an interview.[13] "I mean these people had never dealt with each other; they refused to share TV studios, radio studios, that they had no knowledge of each other."

The degree of consent necessary for the Blueprint is much greater than what was needed to negotiate a ceasefire in Northern Ireland or even a peace process for Israelis and Palestinians. The interim agreements in Northern Ireland were essentially talks designed to enable talks.[14] The

Blueprint demands a willingness not just to temporarily lay down one's arms or sit around the same table as one's enemy, but a willingness to fundamentally reevaluate and redefine the shape and goals of the national movements that have been so omnipresent in the war, apartheid, occupation, fear, and hatred of the past century. That is the significance of the type of consent the Blueprint demands, and the Conciliation Conference must give that consent before the process can begin.

PARTICIPATION

Participation is such an inextricable part of democracy that any democratic transition that maintains exclusionary norms and practices will not be capable of building popular buy-in, itself a driver of participation.[15] That is to say, democracy must not be delayed. The Blueprint aims to be as inclusive as possible while recognizing that transitions are fragile moments that can be undone or hijacked at many stages along the way. To that end, the only qualification required to participate in the Caretaker Government is a commitment to support the democratic transformation process and act in accordance with the Guiding Principles outlined below.

Fionnuala Ní Aoláin and Colm Campbell write of the importance and scope of inclusion:

> In a transitional society the concern about inclusiveness rests on the incorporation of the following problematic actors. First are minority or marginal communities hitherto excluded from a share in society's political functioning. Second are groups whose political identity is rooted in a commitment to destroy the state as it has hereto functioned, and thereby the privileges which define other groupings' sense of place within the social structure. Third are actors whose self-definition revolves around the use of violent means, where war is one of the threats and counter threats to be traded in the bargaining process of society's formation. Finally are groupings whose societal identity is constructed and perpetuated on hegemonic status, where any change to accommodate the other will inevitably produce a negative standing for themselves relative to their current position. Inclusiveness requires the bringing of all or some of these actors in tandem to the negotiation and accommodation table.[16]

Participation needs to happen in several ways and in several stages of the Blueprint and the processes that precede and follow. First, parties to the Conciliation Conference or any other negotiations that precede the Blueprint's adoption and implementation must be representative of the many different groups of people living in the Territory. Participants must be diverse and broadly representative of geographic regions, religious groups, genders, national groups, different socioeconomic strata and groups with different sources of power, and, of course, political views and affiliations. Such requisite participation and representation require the inclusion of elected representatives of active political parties in both societies, as well as civil society groups and others. The Conciliation Conference does not need to equally distribute decision-making power, but the voices and interests of all groups, particularly those who have been marginalized or politically excluded under the apartheid regime, must have a meaningful seat at the table in determining the shape and goals of the Transition.

Much has been written about the failures of the Oslo Accords, and there are many reasons the peace process that followed exploded into the Second Intifada. One of those reasons was the exclusion of significant political blocs of both populations, but particularly the Palestinian side—namely religiously and culturally conservative movements—from the process.[17] Israel, like countless other colonial regimes, has sought to choose its own Palestinian interlocutors in different territories at different times. The problem with undemocratic leadership, and even more so with leaders chosen or appointed by an outside power, is that even if they possess power, they lack legitimacy, which in turn translates to corrupt, ineffective leadership. Israel disposed of a good number of those chosen interlocutors of its own volition.[18]

Yitzhak Rabin was the first of very few Israeli leaders to speak honestly to Israelis on this point, famously saying of his decision to recognize the PLO as representative of the Palestinian people, "You don't make peace with friends. You make it with very unsavory enemies."[19] Yet, even then, Rabin's exchange of letters with Yasser Arafat that year marked the start of three decades in which Israel legitimized one Palestinian political stream (Fatah) and excluded another (Hamas), only to wind up strengthening the latter to weaken the former.[20] The Israeli and American insistence on the prima facie exclusion of Hamas—or any Palestinian faction—

from Palestinian governance, even in the post–October 7 world, remains a recipe for failure in any process and guarantees the inevitable resurgence of violence.[21]

The first key to ensuring participation, therefore, is inclusion, not only for outlawed political movements and parties, but more broadly of political groupings and values that aren't represented in the current political map.[22] Any transformation toward democracy and equality must include representatives and advocates of women's and LGBTQ organizations, labor unions, youth and grassroots political movements, religious values and groupings, and rural or peripheral geographic regions across the Territory. To fail to include them would not only rob the Transition of the legitimacy it requires, it would also include unavoidable blind spots to the consequences of its actions and the political viability of its policies, and ultimately it would perpetuate the vast political, economic, and security gulfs that separate most Palestinians and Israelis.

ACCOUNTABILITY TO DEMOCRATIC VALUES

The Conciliation Conference will ratify the Blueprint as a framework for the Transition—and its Guiding Principles, which enshrine the basic values of democratic, human, and civil rights—prior to the creation of a Caretaker Government. This ratification protects the process by codifying agreed-upon principles, values, and political objectives (such as ending apartheid), and designating bodies of international law as bodies of source law to guide the transitional authorities when they invariably face contentious issues and unexpected or challenging real-world developments.[23] A rapidly reformed judicial system, described at length in Section 4, will have limited but powerful judicial oversight powers over the Caretaker Government in adjudicating challenges to transitional policies or legislation or resolving conflicts of law.

In a conflict where the best or most desired resolution is far from clear, it is not the place of a not-yet-democratic transitional authority—or of the authors of this plan—to begin shaping or even envisioning a constitution on an artificial timeline.[24] Much like the path taken in South Africa in its own transition from apartheid to democracy, the Blueprint clarifies and codifies a set of principles, values, and, where appropriate, rights, but leaves the job of negotiating and drafting a constitution until after the first inclusive democratic election. This accomplishes three important things: it creates a quasi-constitutional framework to keep the Caretaker Government accountable to its raison d'être of ending the occupation, dismantling apartheid, and transforming an undemocratic one-state reality into a democratic one; it moves the process forward by agreeing on principles with which everyone can live rather than holding out for more gains or fewer concessions; and it establishes a new reality in which it is progressively harder to derail or reverse the Transition. In other words, it creates facts on the ground.

CLEAR EXPECTATIONS

Another critical component of maximizing the chances of popular buy-in for the Transition and the Caretaker Government is managing the public's expectations of it. Prior to diving into its mandate, the Caretaker Government will need to spend significant resources on articulating not only the democratic vision it is pursuing but also communicating the limits of its role, and which changes regular citizens can expect to see and experience at loosely specified intervals of time. Managing expectations is a major component of building and maintaining trust, and proactive and clear communication strategies will go a long way in mitigating frustrations that can lead to abandoning or, worse, sabotaging the process.[25] This is one of several reasons we believe it is so important to attach a timeline to the Transition.

Section 2   End Military Rule and Revoke Emergency Laws

SUMMARY

This section focuses on reforming the governing legal systems for the Territory, in particular the laws, policies, and regulations that have been central to maintaining the systems of apartheid and occupation. Central to these legal reforms is ending military rule over the territories and establishing and implementing a single civilian legal system for the entire Territory, which the Caretaker Government shall undertake in week 1. This will result in an immediate end to the practice of trying civilians in military courts and will formally transfer control of military prisons in the Occupied Palestinian Territory (OPT) to civilian authorities.

The steps outlined in this section will also abolish the separate and unequal legal systems that discriminate against different population groups in the same geographic region of the Territory.[1] Creating uniformity or, more realistically, some form of congruence or interoperability in those different legal systems is a task beyond the scope of the Blueprint. Some parts of that job, however, cannot wait.

As an interim measure, the Blueprint recommends the application of existing Israeli criminal and labor laws and travel regulations to all persons in the Territory. This is necessary to quickly ensure that the state treats all people equally before the law on matters of liberty and livelihood. The choice to apply existing Israeli criminal law instead of Palestinian criminal law is based on an assessment that the former offers more protections for its citizens, which will immediately extend to Palestinians.[2] In addition, much of the laws used in the OPT are themselves fragmented and outdated relics of earlier rulers, including Ottoman law, British law, Egyptian law, and Jordanian law, which Palestinian authorities have not replaced with unified codes.[3]

Another step necessary to erase more technical means of discrimination and segregation is the careful consolidation of the Territory's population registries. Currently, Israel maintains—and controls—population registries for Israeli citizens and residents, as well as the Palestinian population registry for the West Bank and Gaza Strip.[4] Which registry somebody is included in often forms the basis of differentiating between different classes of citizenship and residency and determines whether the state grants or restricts various basic rights.[5]

It will neither be possible—nor will it be desirable in many ways—to carry out a wholesale unification of all areas of law in the same sweeping manner we propose for the laws undergirding occupation and apartheid. In particular, we are wary of disrupting municipal government services and areas of civil law that regulate local economic and civic activities, such as local traffic, building, and health and safety regulations. We therefore propose keeping most municipal and other local government bodies and laws as is, including ensuring they retain their existing budgets, authorities, and the means to provide services to residents.

The Caretaker Government can accomplish these goals in the following legislative steps:

On day 1:

- extend civilian law and the protection of all rights to people in all areas of the Territory;
- revoke all emergency laws, which will, among other things, rescind the military's authority to govern the OPT; announce end to buffer zones; and
- rescind the jurisdiction of military courts over civilians regardless of nationality.

In week 2:

- instruct the Interior Ministry to consolidate the Israeli and Palestinian population registries.

FORMAL APARTHEID: DUAL LEGAL SYSTEMS

Israel's unique regime of apartheid in many ways overlaps with, but is nevertheless not entirely congruent with, its military occupation. Most clearly demonstrating this point is the fact that for decades prior to the occupation of the OPT in 1967, Israel created and maintained an apartheid regime within its sovereign borders.[6] In those years, between Israel's establishment in May 1948 until December 1966, Israel ruled over its Jewish citizens with a civilian government and over its Palestinian citizens with a parallel military government.[7] Israeli governments—and, in many cases, Israeli courts—dismantled much of that system of apartheid, but many elements of it remain for Palestinian citizens of Israel to this day, as detailed by Amnesty International in its report *Israel's Apartheid Against Palestinians*.[8] After Israel occupied the West Bank in 1967, apartheid became so interwoven into the fabric of occupation that over time the two have become both inextricable and occasionally indistinguishable. Occupation and apartheid take on different forms in other areas of the Territory, be it illegal annexation in East Jerusalem, the distinct regime of cruelty created in the besieged Gaza Strip, and in Israel's attempts at ongoing ethnic cleansing of Bedouin and other Palestinians in the Negev/Naqab, Masafer Yatta, and Jordan Valley.[9]

All of these regimes that comprise Israeli apartheid and occupation have in common legal systems and tools designed to differentiate between populations based on their identities. Israel's various regimes also have in common that they carefully carve out exceptions for Jewish Israelis, granting them access to norms and protections usually associated with liberal democracy.[10] It is this experience as the privileged group, of living in what is for them a liberal democratic regime, that best defines what life is like for most Jewish Israelis under apartheid. It is almost impossible, therefore, to approach a process of dismantling the occupation, Israeli apartheid, or in our case both, without first dismantling their most manifest and recognizable feature: separate legal systems for Jews and Palestinians in the occupied territories. These dual legal systems, military for Palestinians in the Territory and civilian for Jews, must be eradicated at the very outset of the Transition. The easiest way to do that is to eradicate the military rule—including its authorities specific to governing civilian populations—to which Israel subjects OPT Palestinians.

At the start of the occupation of 1967 there were no separate legal systems for different groups of people in the OPT. Israel decided almost immediately that it would treat the territories as occupied and therefore placed them under the control of the military commander who would serve as a temporary stand-in for a sovereign power in line with the international law of belligerent occupation, part of what is known as international humanitarian law (IHL).[11] For the first few years after 1967, Palestinians and Jewish Israelis present in the OPT were subject to the laws created by the Israeli military; Israeli settlers were even tried for criminal offenses in Israeli military courts. The problem was that those courts were designed for a so-called enemy population, and Israeli settlers were not "the enemy." To ensure Jewish Israeli settlers could live under the same laws as their compatriots inside Israel, the Israeli parliament "passed a law granting Israeli courts and authorities jurisdiction over any Israeli national accused of committing a crime that violates Israeli law, even if the alleged crime was committed within the OPT."[12] That temporary law, a so-called emergency regulation, has been renewed every few years to this day.

Dual legal systems that are applied based on the ethnic, racial, religious, or national identity of a person are patently unfair, unequal, and by design create a system in which one population has more rights than others. While the parallel civilian and military systems are apparent in myriad aspects of life, from health care to taxation to freedom of movement and even building and planning rights, the injustice of it is most brazen in Israel's dual criminal justice systems in the West Bank, where "[t]he national identity of a suspect or defendant determines which law will apply to them and who will have legal authority over them. In every stage of the legal proceedings—from the initial detention to the trial to the verdict—Palestinians are discriminated against when compared to Israelis."[13]

Whereas a Jewish Israeli protesting in the occupied territory carries with him the right to free assembly and expression granted to him under Israel's Basic Law: Human Dignity and Liberty, a Palestinian protesting in the exact same spot could be arrested and subject to military prosecution because most acts of protest are illegal for Palestinians under Israeli military law. Ending martial law and the military occupation, therefore, is a critical first step in conferring upon Palestinians all of the civil rights and protections that Jewish Israelis enjoy in the same geographic spaces.

Eradicating military rule and the provision of military law in the Territory would also end the military court system Israel created to exercise jurisdiction over Palestinian civilians. Israel designed its system of martial law—especially its military courts—to prioritize the political interests of one ethno-religious group, Jews, over the basic human and civil rights of every other group in the Territory. "Every legal apparatus, in fact, is designed and intended to serve a political project. Since the political project put forward by the Israeli military-legal system is one of unlawfully prolonged occupation, toward permanent territorial control, the courts' central role will remain that to serve as agency of dispossession of both basic human rights and territory of the Palestinian population, advancing Israel's 'creeping' annexation."[14] The system of martial law and military courts has also allowed Israel to layer a veneer of legality and legitimacy on top of its illegal and illegitimate practices of conflating its political, ideological, and economic interests with security needs. From outlawing almost all civil protest, to declaring that human rights organizations and political parties are terrorist groups, to creating the legal infrastructure for land confiscation, such security justifications have been a central method of oppression under the Israeli apartheid and occupation regimes.

REVOKE EMERGENCY LAWS

A less manifest legal cornerstone of apartheid under occupation is Israel's use of emergency regulations, a British colonial trademark that the leaders of the nascent Israeli state decided to retain upon independence.[15] Emergency regulations, designed to carve out exceptions to norms, laws, and values to maintain the domination of one group over another, are a hallmark of—but not unique to—Israeli apartheid.[16] Both because of their role in maintaining the dual legal systems in the occupied territories but also as an always available tool to bypass legal protections and basic rights in the territory writ large, the Caretaker Government must dismantle them at the outset of the Transition. Doing so also serves to protect the Transition process by instituting badly needed restraints on the state and its various arms, ending some of the most egregious forms of discrimination such as a ban on family reunification visas for Palestinians and most other Arabs, and signaling that equality before the law is an immutable principle.[17]

Ending emergency laws also would end the use of administrative detention, which allows for indefinite imprisonment without conviction or public evidence. Under existing Israeli law, Israeli authorities can arrest anyone "preventatively" without having to prove they committed any crime, without giving them the chance to defend themselves, often without telling them of what they are accused, for periods of several months at a time that can be renewed indefinitely. At the time of writing, Israel was holding 3,661 Palestinians in administrative detention—without charge or trial—including two hundred minors and seventy women.[18] All Palestinian administrative detainees and most Palestinian prisoners and detainees are designated as "security detainees" upon entry into the Israeli prison system if a senior prison guard determines that the crime they are suspected of committing had "nationalist motivations," or if they are suspected of a list of crimes ranging from espionage to belonging to an outlawed organization.[19] Ending emergency laws would also mandate the end of "security" vs. "criminal" classifications of prisoners, the former of which is used as a stand-in designation for political prisoners but also forms the basis of the ethno-national segregation of prisoners, which itself inherently leads to and is used as a justification for discriminatory treatment. "Administrative detainees and prisoners serving life sentences, prisoners sentenced for organizing or participating in demonstrations, for being active in political movements declared 'illegal' by the occupying forces, for possessing ammunition, and for planning suicide bombing: all are categorized, *en bloc*, as 'security prisoners,' as threats."[20]

Concomitantly, Israel's 2016 Prevention of Terrorism Act, which the government legislated to codify a great number of policies and practices that previously existed only in emergency regulations, will also need to be revoked at the outset of the process. The law was a limited attempt to formally legislate practices that had previously been allowed only under emergency regulations, taking informal practices and permanently codifying them. The law "gives security forces overly broad surveillance powers, and gives full discretion to Israel's Minister of Defense to designate a group as a 'terror organization,' even when the group is not involved in any illegal actions such as 'terror acts' as defined in the Counter-Terrorism Law. The law does not provide clear norms to limit this discretion, and it uses overbroad and vague terms."[21] Revoking the 2016 law, therefore, would effectively revoke Israel's domestic terrorist designations of groups and individuals, which it has used to outlaw human rights and civil society organizations and to control and constrain Palestinian political and social organizing.

WHAT TO DO

On day 1, the Caretaker Government will:

REVOKE "LAW TO EXTEND THE EMERGENCY REGULATIONS (JUDEA AND SAMARIA—JURISDICTION AND LEGAL AID 5727-1967)" AND REPLACE WITH "LAW TO EXTEND ISRAELI LAW TO ALL AREAS AND PERSONS LIVING IN THE TERRITORY"

The emergency regulation gives broad jurisdiction to the Israeli courts and legal system over Israeli nationals present in the occupied territories, including criminal law, tort law, national insurance and health rights, debt collection and the enforcement of judgments, rules of evidence, and many other areas.[22] The distinction created is foundational to the discriminatory, dual legal systems of the apartheid regime.

The new legislation should ensure that all laws are applied equally to all persons in all areas of the Territory, and similarly guarantee all rights and protections to the aforementioned. If a phased approach is determined to be appropriate, it is of urgency to extend criminal law and labor law, laws and regulations regarding entry and exit to the entire territory, and laws and regulations pertaining to free movement and association.

FORBID MILITARY COURTS FROM EXERCISING JURISDICTION OVER CIVILIANS OF ANY LEGAL STATUS IN ANY LOCATION

Rescind the jurisdiction of military courts over civilians in the OPT by revoking IDF Military Order 1651, "a consolidated version of many orders issued since 1967 and related to the arrest, detention and prosecution of an individual. . . . [I]t replaced a total of 20 military orders issued between 1967 and 2005, including Military Order 378, which established the creation of Israeli military courts in occupied territory, provides the basis for arrest and detention by the Israeli army and defines charges under military law."[23] Revoking Order 1651 will thus disband all military courts that serve any function other than courts-martial and tribunals for serving members of the military. This will have already occurred in practice with the revocation of Military Order 1.

GUARANTEE THAT MUNICIPALITIES CONTINUE TO RECEIVE THEIR EXISTING BUDGETS

Ensuring continuity of government services, in particular those provided by local governments, such as trash collection and other utilities, education, traffic and code enforcement, and local zoning, is critical for maintaining public support for the Transition.[24] If the Caretaker Government is perceived to be ineffective at providing basic services, people will lose trust in its ability to carry out far more complex tasks. The Caretaker Government, while assuming the powers of the Palestinian Authority (PA) and Israeli government, will aim to maintain as much autonomy and local control over the municipal and other local governments that previously fell under PA and Israeli control.

The most important aspect of this local governance continuity is guaranteeing that municipalities and local government institutions continue to receive their existing budgets, in full, which the Caretaker Government will ensure for a period of one year. Concurrently, the Caretaker Government shall task its new Governance Committee with identifying and remedying gaps, inequities, and discrepancies in the provision of budgets, municipal services, and any other social or health services that are provided and budgeted at a municipal or regional level. As the committee identifies gaps, the Caretaker Government shall increase budgets and the provision of services in underserved and underbudgeted communities and municipalities to more universal standards. The Caretaker Government must ensure that the provision of government services is fundamentally the same in rural and urban locales, and in predominantly Jewish and Palestinian cities or regions. At the start of year 2 of the Transition, the Caretaker Government will undertake a more systematic effort to fairly and equitably distribute funds to local government bodies.

MAINTAIN MUNICIPAL AUTONOMY

Local and municipal governments shall retain a level of autonomy in certain areas, including family law, zoning and some urban planning, education, determining the day(s) of rest for municipal services and schools, and determining certain hyperlocal regulations and ordinances such as neighborhood or street-level traffic or zoning regulations. This is as much about maintaining public order and some level of autonomy as it is about fostering a new relationship between military subjects turned citizens. "[T]o bridge the local-national gap, communities have to be integrated into the process of institution building, where they live and at higher levels, in order to foster a sense of identification with the greater whole and a feeling of ownership of the alternative structure. . . . This sort of realignment is assuredly an arduous and lengthy undertaking, and yet it must start at the very beginning of an intervention."[25]

Starting in month 6, the Governance Committee shall review municipal and local government regulations and ordinances to ensure they do not directly or indirectly perpetuate, maintain, create, or aggravate segregation or discrimination or violate the rights of any individual or group, irrespective of their past, current, or future residency in said locality, based on their race and recommend any amendments to the Caretaker Government by the end of year 2. If the Caretaker Government does not implement these amendments, the Governance Committee will have standing to ask the new High Court to order them.

EXTEND TAX LAWS TO ENCOMPASS THE ENTIRE TERRITORY

Existing Israeli tax laws will remain in place for the duration of the Transition, and the Caretaker Government will in week 1 apply them across the Territory to all people in the new population registry. This is necessary to ensure the Caretaker Government has the resources to govern and carry out its mission and will be accomplished by modifying Basic Law: The State Economy.

REVOKE ALL EMERGENCY LAWS AND REGULATIONS, INCLUDING:

- Order for the Extension of the Validity of Emergency Regulations (annual extension and expansion of emergency regulations);
- the Emergency Powers (Detention) Law (authorizes administrative detention in Israel);
- the Prevention of Terrorism Ordinance (2016) (gives police and other state bodies broad authorities to outlaw organizations, restrict movement, restrict protest, suspend and deny due process rights, and more);
- Defense Regulations (Times of Emergency), Regulation 125 (authorizes declaring "closed military zones," which Israel uses to confiscate Palestinian land and exclude Palestinians from certain spaces);
- the Emergency State Search Authorities Law (permits searches of persons and private property without a judicial warrant);
- the State of Emergency Land Appropriation Administration Law (authorizes the seizure of private property for various purposes); and
- the Prevention of Infiltration (Offences and Jurisdiction) Law (criminalizes the entry and presence of Palestinian refugees and other noncitizens).

REVOKE TERRORIST DESIGNATIONS

- Immediately revoke all designations of illegal associations, outlawed organizations, terrorist organizations, and any other classifications that outlaw or restrict freedom of association.
- Revoke laws, clauses, or subsections of laws or regulations that create different tracks and punishments for the same crime based on determinations of political or nationalist intent, circumstances, or determinations. This includes "security" classifications of persons, crimes, prison conditions, and segregation.
- Revoke any regulations, laws, or any clauses and subsections thereof that give security agencies additional powers based on such designations or classifications of associations and organizations or population categories or regions that are not explicitly granted to them by legislation passed by the Basic Law: The Transition.

In week 2, the Caretaker Government will:

CONSOLIDATE THE ISRAELI AND PALESTINIAN
POPULATION REGISTRIES INTO A SINGLE DATABASE

Israel currently maintains ownership and ultimate control over the Palestinian population registry in addition to its own.[26] The Interior Ministry will need to consolidate those registries, in as much as they are separate, to allow the Caretaker Government and any subsequent government to manage and effectively govern the entire population. "By late 1949, the Ministry of Minorities, seeking to prevent Palestinians from claiming citizenship, initiated the amendment of the Population Registry Ordinance—a colonial law that outlined procedures for the registration of the population—to enable the distribution of temporary permits instead of ID cards to certain Palestinians deemed less desirable as potential citizens. Over time, the permit regime evolved into a massive surveillance mechanism that classified people under a range of categories of suspicion and collaboration, effectively wiping out the option of being considered loyal citizens."[27]

The population registry is a particularly sensitive bureaucratic tool that the British and later the Israeli apartheid regime used to classify and either grant privileges to or oppress individuals and various groups in the Territory. When Israel occupied the West Bank, including East Jerusalem and the Gaza Strip, in 1967, it carried out a new census, the results of which it used to create a new Palestinian population registry. "Israel's administration of the Palestinian population registry is the basis of its control of freedom of movement, immigration, residency and nationality of the occupied territory's Palestinian residents. A person must be included in the population registry to obtain travel documents, which in turn enable movement both internally and abroad and determine access to a range of movement-dependent rights, such as the rights to work, education and medical care."[28]

Therefore, the Interior Ministry must take great care in redesigning the population registry and clearly defining and restraining the ways the state can use it. The Blueprint recommends the following:

- Assign new identity numbers from which national, ethnic, or religious identities cannot be deduced or categorized. To achieve this, it should randomize the sequencing of identity numbers themselves.

- In the new, consolidated database, remove any official fields or unofficial indicators of any type, including notes added by civil servants or security services, that were or could be used to categorize an individual or group of individuals by national, ethnic, or religious identity, or level of suspicion or threat, be it security or political.
- All names should appear in all official languages (Arabic, Hebrew, and English).
- A copy of the previous population registries should be maintained for the exclusive use of the newly created Refugees and Restitution Ministry in order to assess eligibility for special state benefits that it might offer to refugees, internally displaced persons, people who lost property, people who were discriminated against, people who were political prisoners, or whatever category of persons might become eligible for affirmative action, reparations, or any other benefits the legislature tasks it with assessing eligibility for or disbursing in any possible justice program that a post–Caretaker Government decides to undertake.

Starting in month 6 of the Transition, the newly merged Court Administration (Section 4) will publish official translations into Arabic, Hebrew, and English of the following laws, regulations, and decisions:

- all new, retained, and modified primary legislation and statutes;
- all new, retained, and modified regulations and secondary legislation;
- the Guiding Principles for the Transition;
- all human rights treaties referenced and incorporated by the Guiding Principles;
- all appellate decisions from all appellate courts in the Territory, including the Supreme Court(s); and
- all High Court decisions, hearings, and other officially published documents or rulings.

Restore Freedom of Movement

SUMMARY

The Blueprint requires an end to all restrictions on travel within the Territory, which means creating a new movement regime that guarantees the right of all people living in the Territory to live in and travel freely between all other areas. Civilian police will be responsible for enforcing security measures or checks to facilitate free movement inside the Territory, but they will be forbidden from restricting any individual's movement or residency on any other basis, including ethnic, religious, national identity, or political affiliation.

The Caretaker Government will have ended most restrictions on movement immediately in all areas by virtue of the abolition of emergency regulations and military orders described in other parts of the Blueprint. Some restrictions will remain in place and will require more time for reform and are detailed in this section. Most notably, while the new Basic Law: Freedom of Movement will define the criteria for passing through existing checkpoints to reflect the nondiscrimination and equality tenets of the Guiding Principles, many of those checkpoints will remain in place. Among others, we envision this being the case for the checkpoints surrounding the Gaza Strip, and Jewish settlements in the West Bank with a history of violence, for a period of no more than three years.

In addition to the changes impacting freedom of movement described elsewhere in the Blueprint, the Caretaker Government shall implement the following to create a new movement regime:

- In weeks 1 through 4, deploy civilian police at checkpoints instead of the military, possibly including international observers.
- In weeks 1 through 4, define police powers to restrict movement in accordance with the new security doctrine detailed in Section 7.
- By the end of year 1, the Free Movement Commission will start reviewing the necessity of remaining internal checkpoints.
- In month 6 of year 1, the Free Movement Commission will start planning to remove the wall/separation barrier.

BACKGROUND

Restrictions on movement are one of the central tools the apartheid regime used to manage the Palestinian population—inside the territory that became Israel, in and between different parts of the Territory, and refugees or any Palestinian who was outside of the Territory on a few key dates or for certain periods of time. These restrictions prohibit not only where people can travel within the Territory but also where they may reside and work or with whom they can cohabitate or marry.

During and after the 1948 war, Palestinians remaining in cities like Jaffa and Lydd (Lod in Hebrew) were forced into literal ghettos surrounded by barbed wire fences.[1] Entire villages were declared closed military zones to prevent the return of internally displaced persons, or IDPs.[2] For the first nineteen years after Israel's establishment, it ruled nearly all of the Palestinians who remained under a military regime, while Israel's Jewish citizens lived under civilian rule and government. The military governor forced Palestinian citizens to seek permits in order to travel outside their villages, to work, to receive health care, and more.[3] This, like nearly all policies restricting movement, was done under the guise of security—but security, then as today, was driven by plans for demographic design, preventing the return of refugees and IDPs, and to facilitate the seizure of land and resources.[4]

Half a year after Israel lifted military rule from its Palestinian citizens in 1966, it conquered and imposed a nearly identical movement regime in the West Bank and East Jerusalem, the Gaza Strip, as well the Sinai Peninsula and Golan Heights. Israel never disbanded the institutions of the 1948–66 military government; it simply regrouped and refocused them on their new mission several months later, following the June 1967 war.[5] In the newly occupied territories, just as it did inside the 1949 Armistice Lines until December 1966, Israel used restrictions on movement to force Palestinians off their land, stymie political and popular resistance against the nascent occupation, and prevent refugees from returning to their homes.[6]

Additionally, in the post-1967 era but particularly since the early 1990s and later aggravated by the new reality created by the Oslo agreements, Israel has used restrictions on movement to limit the development of the Palestinian economy, to restrict freedom of occupation, to seize and maintain control over natural resources, to attempt to sever ties between Palestinians in different areas of the Territory, to stymie the development of Palestinian political parties, political unity, and political institutions, and as a tool for compelling individuals to collaborate with the apartheid regime—all in the name of security.[7]

Today, restrictions on movement within the Territory are all undergirded by emergency regulations, cabinet decisions, and military orders. For instance, the restriction on Palestinians entering Israel from the occupied West Bank and requiring them to acquire a military permit to enter or exit is based on the "closed military zone" military order that Israel imposed on the Occupied Palestinian Territory (OPT) starting in 1967 (Military Orders 1 and 34, applying to the Gaza Strip and West Bank, respectively).[8] Israel also uses this order to justify its control over where Palestinians can live and work within the West Bank. Likewise, this order is the legal justification for barring Israeli citizens from entering Area A of the West Bank today.

Israel has used a similar legal basis for restrictions on Palestinian movement in and out of the Gaza Strip, although a 2007 government designation of Gaza as a "hostile territory" added new restrictions on the movement of people and goods.[9] The Caretaker Government will revoke this designation in week 9, upon assuming power. Furthermore, the Caretaker Government shall publicly announce that it is revoking any remaining "buffer zone" adjacent to the Gaza separation barrier, although it will not technically be necessary due to the cancellation of both the "closed military zone" for Gaza, its designation as "hostile territory," and the revocation of the military's jurisdiction within the Territory, as described in Section 2.

Israel has at times given security justifications for imposing categorical restrictions on movement for Palestinians, starting with the ghettos and military rule inside Israel in the years after 1948 and through the construction of the separation wall and imposing the siege on Gaza. Experts differ in their assessment of the efficacy of those measures in improving measurable security for Israelis, and for Jewish Israelis in particular, but many agree that at the very least these measures' success is often limited to curtailing one type of violence in the short term.[10] Restricting the movement and entry of Palestinians in the OPT may reduce the likelihood of certain types of attacks in the short term, but they unjustifiably impede Palestinians' human rights to freedom of movement.[11] However, the deployment of Israeli security forces in Palestinian areas, a necessary component of restricting movement, creates points of friction that are often the scene of violence by Israelis against Palestinians as well as by Palestinians against Israelis.[12]

Despite bona fide security concerns, the methods and systems for achieving security that the Israeli apartheid regime has chosen to implement over the years are meant to serve—and have been accountable only to—Jewish Israelis and Jewish Israeli political and economic interests. As detailed in Section 7 on building national security forces, particularly in the subsection on a new security doctrine, any new approach to security must give equal weight to the personal security and rights to freedom of movement of all residents of the Territory. Likewise, state security must protect the principles of equality, the transformation from apartheid to democracy, and eventually to protecting that democracy.

To be clear, separation and restrictions on movement have provided incremental returns on security for Israelis but at the cost of ever-heightened captivity and oppression for Palestinians. The persistence of attacks against civilians inside Israel proper should be evidence enough that checkpoints, walls, and restrictions on movement—even at the unacceptable cost of one group's security over another's basic freedoms—are not a sustainable or particularly effective approach. Hamas's shift from suicide bombings to rockets as a way of overcoming physical barriers provides more evidence that the security benefits of barriers and restrictions on movement are limited. Additionally, Israel's systems of apartheid and separation have created security vacuums in areas of East Jerusalem and the West Bank, where Israeli police do not operate and Palestinian police are forbidden. These lawless areas create acute insecurity for Palestinians living there and contribute to broader insecurity for Israelis and Palestinians alike.[13] The Gaza Strip represents an even more extreme example.

Additionally, and as addressed in Section 7, it is imperative for the Caretaker Government to educate the populace and security forces that freedom of movement is more than a right in and of itself—freedom of movement is also a foundational precondition for restoring and realizing many other rights and equality writ large. This includes the right to reside anywhere in the Territory, to receive equal social and medical benefits regardless of where in the Territory one resides, to work in all areas of the Territory, and others. While the practical steps for restoring the right to free movement fall largely in the realm of lifting and reforming security infrastructures and systems, the imperative for its realization should be understood in that larger context. Without it, the rest of the transformation simply cannot take place. For that reason, the Caretaker Government must restore the right to free movement at the start of the Transition.

IMPLEMENTATION AND RATIONALE

Restoring freedom of movement in the Territory will take place gradually throughout the Transition. Initially, the Caretaker Government will terminate the vast majority of rules and regulations that restrict free movement when it ends military rule and revokes emergency regulations. However, the Caretaker Government will maintain existing checkpoints, albeit in a nondiscriminatory manner, to give police the tools to maintain security in what may be a volatile period, as discussed in further detail below. The Caretaker Government also should develop a plan to demolish the wall/separation barrier in an environmentally sound manner to comply with the 2004 International Court of Justice advisory opinion that found it to be illegal.[14]

Israeli law currently imposes a second category of restrictions on movement for its external borders. Policies regarding immigration and refugee rights are sovereign decisions that should be made by a duly elected sovereign power—not a caretaker government. Therefore, the Caretaker Government will freeze all immigration not tied to family reunification, including rights of return for refugees, but it will reform nonimmigration entry and exit policies to ensure nondiscrimination.

Internal Movement: Checkpoints

WHY KEEP INTERNAL CHECKPOINTS

In an ideal world, it would be possible to remove all the Territory's internal checkpoints within a short period of time. Transitions, however, are volatile periods, and it is likely that armed individuals and spoiler groups will seek to oppose the removal of checkpoints or gain control through the use of violence. The design and placement of checkpoints in the Territory today reflect the needs and interests of the apartheid and occupation regimes, namely the separation of different population groups and granting greater privileges and freedom of movement to one group over another.

The Blueprint does not take lightly its recommendation of leaving these relics of apartheid and occupation in place for any longer than absolutely necessary, but it does recognize their utility. Checkpoints, as problematic as they are, represent infrastructure that is already in place that police can use—in ways that comply with the Guiding Principles and human rights standards—to prevent the movement of weapons and wanted individuals between different parts of the Territory. At least in the early stages of the Transition, when security and stability have not yet been secured and disarmament efforts only begun, it will be necessary to leave most internal checkpoints (between areas inside the Territory) in place under the conditions detailed in this section.

REPLACE MILITARY PERSONNEL WITH CIVILIAN POLICE AT ALL INTERNAL CHECKPOINTS WITHIN THE TERRITORY

In week 1, the Caretaker Government will transfer responsibility for any remaining checkpoints from the military to the newly created civilian national police force, as discussed in Section 7. Checkpoints will be manned by officers of both Jewish Israeli and Palestinian identity.

The Blueprint recommends that the Caretaker Government request the special envoy to seek the temporary deployment of an international police training and observer force, as described in Section 7, which can maintain a presence at all internal checkpoints to protect against abusive or discriminatory practices and support the integration of police. The international force can also provide the Free Movement Commission regular reports on the implementation of free movement. Inviting international forces into the Territory, however, is a decision the Caretaker Government will have to make, and it will require the approval of third countries and the United Nations.

ARTICULATE MANDATE OF POLICE AND CHECKPOINTS TO FACILITATE, NOT IMPEDE, MOVEMENT

In line with the Guiding Principles of the Blueprint and the new security doctrine, the Caretaker Government will mandate security forces to facilitate free movement (Section 7). This is a very different role than security forces stationed at checkpoints under the apartheid regime currently play, using checkpoints and other barriers to enforce separation. The new role of police at checkpoints, like checkpoints in other cities, is to prevent the transport of weapons or other contraband or detain wanted persons—and not to control the movement of entire segments of the population.

CHECKPOINT LOCATIONS

The Blueprint advocates the maintenance of internal checkpoints, including some of the most notorious ones like the Qalandiya checkpoint separating Jerusalem and Ramallah. This is potentially problematic given the practical and symbolic role of these checkpoints in confining and discriminating against the Palestinian population in violation of their fundamental human rights. Within one year, the Free Movement Commission will evaluate the addition or removal of checkpoints throughout the Territory to maximize freedom of movement and ensure nondiscrimination while taking into consideration the needs of legitimate policing activity.

REMOVING THE SEPARATION BARRIER

Starting in month 6, the Caretaker Government shall task the Free Movement Commission with developing a plan to dismantle the separation barrier/wall in accordance with the International Court of Justice's 2004 advisory opinion.[15] The commission must finish drafting the plan by the start of year 3, at which point the Planning and Development Ministry will begin the process of dismantling the barrier.

SUNSET CLAUSE

The Caretaker Government must make every effort to end the use of internal checkpoints and supervised crossings by the end of year 3 of the Transition. This is of paramount importance considering how the Israeli government adopted temporary emergency regulations created by the British Mandate government and turned them into permanent features of its apartheid and occupation regimes.[16] This is addressed further in Section 7 on the integration of security forces.

External Borders

Immigration, visas, and other international entry policies fall under the category of issues that a sovereign government should address after the Transition. Nevertheless, the Caretaker Government will need to update entry policies in the interim. The apartheid regime uses both internal and external restrictions on movement to manipulate the country's demographic makeup, to seize control of valuable land and other natural resources, to prevent the return of refugees, to gerrymander citizenship and suffrage, as well as to punish and exert leverage over individuals and groups it deems political threats.[17] "Between 1967 and 1994, in the West Bank alone, Israel excluded a total of 130,000 individuals from the registry, and provided no procedure by which they could appeal against their effective exclusion from the territory—denying them the right to reside in their homeland permanently, and making it impossible for many of them even to re-enter."[18] Therefore, the Caretaker Government will need to repair the previous regime's border policy as detailed below to avoid creating new injustices and inequalities.

This will be accomplished with a reform to the Entry into Israel Law of 1952, as described in Section 5 and Appendix B, which shall reflect the following immigration policies:

- No person shall be excluded prima facie from eligibility for entry into or movement within the Territory as a tourist during the duration of his/her visa.

- Despite the suspension of immigration during the Transition, the Caretaker Government will create a family unification process, allowing permanent residency—and a pathway to citizenship—for first-degree relatives of citizens of the Territory. The Caretaker Government will revoke all individual and categorical entry or exit bans.

- Suspicion of intention to permanently settle in the Territory shall not be sufficient reason to deny entry to an individual attempting to enter on a short-term or tourist visa, given its wide-scale abuse by Israeli officials over many decades to deny entry to Palestinian nationals of third countries. Other criteria in the law shall remain.

- No group shall receive special privileges regarding entry during the Transition based on ethnic, religious, or national grounds, and the border doctrine shall be driven largely by principles of nondiscrimination.

- All citizens or residents of the Territory shall have the irrevocable and unconditional right to exit and enter the Territory freely.

Section 4   The Courts

SUMMARY

There are three main reasons why the court systems in the Territory must be overhauled at the start of the Transition process: to reflect the consolidation of several legal systems and ensure their function during the Transition; to create a trusted judicial institution capable of acting as a check on the unavoidably undemocratic nature of the Caretaker Government; and to ensure that state bodies and individuals of the Caretaker Government, new and existing legislation, and lower courts are acting in compliance with—or, in some cases, toward implementing—the basic human rights and democratic principles outlined in the Blueprint.

To do so, the Caretaker Government will in week 1 enact the new Basic Law: The Judiciary, which defines and delineates the jurisdictions of the Israeli and Palestinian Supreme Courts, disbands the Israeli High Court of Justice and replaces it with a new High Court for the Transition, creates a unified criminal court system across the Territory, and creates the legal framework for the continued operation of the various existing civil and family courts.

BACKGROUND

Extending one system of laws across the entire Territory, as detailed in Section 1, requires reconciling many of the structural and legal differences between the existing Israeli and Palestinian systems, including their respective judicial institutions. Within pre-1967 Israel, for instance, in both the magistrate and district court levels, there are courts pertaining to criminal and civil affairs, labor, family law, youth, local affairs, small claims, traffic, military affairs, and administrative affairs, in addition to religious courts for family law matters for all officially recognized religions.[1] The Palestinian Authority's court system in the West Bank is similarly composed of a court of first instance, a court of conciliation, a court of appeals, an electoral court, religious courts, and military courts.[2] In the Gaza Strip there exists a judicial system and structure largely parallel to the West Bank system. Sitting atop these systems are supreme and constitutional courts with varying structures that serve as a final court of appeal as well as separate chambers or courts that hear constitutional challenges to government actions, policies, and legislation.

ONE JUDICIAL SYSTEM OUT OF MANY

One of the most complicated tasks in the creation of a transitional court system, although not the most difficult by any stretch of the imagination, will be overseeing the staged and partial integration of at least two dozen court systems and functions from across the Territory. This will entail ensuring that sitting judges—those who remain on their respective benches, as detailed below—and new appointees are familiar with the laws they are tasked with adjudicating, including all updates and amendments made by the Caretaker Government. As addressed in Section 2, the Caretaker Government will mandate the immediate official translation of legislation, regulations, and all appellate decisions into Arabic, Hebrew, and English. While some laws and regulations have been translated from Hebrew to Arabic and English, it has never been a quick or comprehensive process, and relevant Palestinian legislation and case law have never been comprehensively translated to Hebrew or English. With multiple judicial functions and courts, Israeli and Palestinian, that continue functioning with separate civil laws, the Caretaker Government will need to draft and implement appeals procedures and pathways, including diversifying and adapting the Supreme Court as the final court of appeals. There will also be smaller procedural issues that are no less critical to a functioning legal system that the Caretaker Government or the courts will need to decide, such as how to prevent abusive forum shopping between civil courts in different regions of the Territory, for which extensive model legislation undoubtedly exists in abundance.

The second reason it is imperative to quickly design and implement a transitional court system is to help mitigate distrust toward the Caretaker Government, which at various times all parties are bound to view with suspicion. One indirect but vital function of the Caretaker Government is to develop the institutions of, and build public faith in, an inclusive, transitional democracy and its nascent—if temporary—institutions. It is critical, therefore, that the public perception from day one be that nobody is above the law and that effective avenues for judicial recourse are a built-in feature of the system, from which it gains a healthy portion of its legitimacy.

Drawing on the experience of Northern Ireland and South Africa, Fionnuala Ní Aoláin and Colm Campbell explain the importance of legal and judicial reform as part of a democratic transition, particularly to build "the legitimacy of law and legal institutions" in states where the previous regime self-identified as a democracy, which they call "conflicted democracies":

> In the ideal type liberal democracy, law's legitimacy is axiomatic. But, in the conflicted democracy, the law's complicity in human rights abuses (whether through the facilitation of abuse, or in its failure to provide redress), can create a situation where communities at the sharp end of violent conflict, confidence in law and in legal institutions collapses. The result (in a sociological sense) is a loss of legal legitimacy.
>
> The conflicted democracy may therefore evidence a legitimation paradox to add to the others. In a normative ("ought") sense, the state's adherence to democratic standards (for instance its employment of regular elections) may be taken to guarantee the legitimacy of its laws and institutions, but in a sociological ("is") sense, there may be a pronounced loss of legal and institutional legitimacy within communities most affected by the violence.

Transition requires that these various paradoxes be addressed: specifically it requires the building or rebuilding of the legitimacy of the law across sites of profound societal alienation.[3]

THE HIGH COURT FOR THE TRANSITION (HCT)

The Caretaker Government will appoint a transitional Judicial Appointments Committee in week 1. The committee will appoint a new High Court for the Transition (HCT) no later than week 6 to replace the Israeli High Court of Justice, which is currently a part of the Israeli Supreme Court.[4] The HCT will safeguard the Transition process and ensure all legislation, regulations, state actions, and lower court decisions comply with the Guiding Principles as well as the international human rights instruments it references and from which it draws its authorities.

The HCT will be composed of six Palestinian, six Israeli, and three international justices, similar to the effective arrangement following the transition in Bosnia and Herzegovina.[5] The initial terms of the justices shall be for the duration of the Transition or until a new high court—or high courts, if more than one state emerges—is appointed following the first democratic elections.

The Judicial Appointments Committee will be composed of: ranking members of the Israeli and Palestinian bar associations; Israeli and Palestinian law professors from within the Territory as well as without; sitting judges on the Palestinian and Israeli courts at the district or Supreme Court level; representatives of Palestinian and Israeli civil society organizations; and representatives of major Palestinian and Israeli political parties that have endorsed the Transition and its democratic goals. The international judges will be selected by a special session (referred by the UN Security Council) of the International Court of Justice and approved by a simple majority of the Judicial Appointments Committee. The committee may formulate additional criteria to establish qualifications for judgeship. For example, the constitution in Tunisia after its 2011 revolution mandated that two-thirds of the new high court's members be magistrates, a majority of whom are elected by their peers.[6]

The HCT will also adjudicate disputes between different branches and strata of government (local government as opposed to the central, Caretaker Government) as well as disputes arising from differences of law in different parts of the Territory. The HCT will have original jurisdiction to hear challenges to legislation, government policies, and state actions that violate the spirit or letter of the Guiding Principles.

WHY REPLACE THE HIGH COURT OF JUSTICE

Despite the Israeli High Court of Justice's historical recognition for its professional jurisprudence, legal scholars have critiqued its role in legitimizing and thereby perpetuating the apartheid and occupation regime.[7] It has for decades legalized, or refused to sanction, policies that violate international human rights and humanitarian laws, and upheld the maintenance of Israel as a Jewish supremacist state.[8] Illustrating the universality of that belief, retired vice president of the Israeli Supreme Court Elyakim Rubinstein once *described* the court as "a Zionist institution."[9] Replacing the High Court of Justice with the new High Court for the Transition will represent a major step toward reinventing the judicial system to better support democratic principles and eliminate perceptions of bias inherent in the current structure. As Ruti Teitel argues: "Transitions imply paradigm shifts in the conception of justice; thus, law's function is deeply and inherently paradoxical. In its ordinary social function, law provides order and stability, but in extraordinary periods of political upheaval, law maintains order even as it enables transformation. Accordingly, in transition, the ordinary intuitions and predicates about law simply do not apply. In dynamic periods of political flux, legal responses generate a sui generis paradigm of transformative law."[10]

The Caretaker Government must therefore put in place a court whose raison d'être is ensuring the development, survival, and success of democracy for all in the Territory. Without reinventing the institutions and role of the judicial system, particularly as it relates to questions of government policy and constitutionality, even a best-intentioned constitutional court with an equal number of Israelis and Palestinians would continue to be seen as an organ of the apartheid regime. That lack of trust would be catastrophic for the prospects of a successful democratic transformation.

MAINTAINING ISRAELI AND PALESTINIAN JUDICIARIES BELOW THE HCT

Beyond the creation of the High Court for the Transition, the Blueprint strives to maintain as much continuity as possible in the judicial systems in place across the Territory. All lower-level civil (district and magistrate) courts will remain in place, as will family, labor, and religious courts. The Palestinian and Israeli Supreme Courts will remain in place as final courts of appeal. All of these courts will come under the administration of the unified Courts Administration, and all will fall under the supervision of the Judicial Oversight Commission. Criminal courts will remain largely in their current structure, but the Courts Administration will closely supervise and help restructure them to reflect the new, unified criminal code across the Territory.

WHAT TO DO

CREATE HIGH COURT FOR THE TRANSITION

- Abolish the High Court of Justice chamber of the Israeli Supreme Court.
- The head of the Caretaker Government, or an individual to whom he or she has delegated that authority, shall convene a transitional Judicial Appointments Committee. The committee shall consist of:
  - two senior members of the Israeli Bar Association;
  - two senior members of the Palestinian Bar Association;
  - three senior Palestinian law professors, including one who has taught for more than five years at a distinguished law school in a foreign democratic country;
  - three senior Israeli law professors, including one who has taught for more than five years at a distinguished law school in a foreign democratic country;
  - two representatives of Palestinian civil society organizations with expertise in law and the judiciary;
  - two representatives of Israeli civil society organizations with expertise in law and the judiciary; and
  - the head of the Caretaker Government or their representative.

- The Caretaker Government will amend Basic Law: The Judiciary to establish a new High Court for the Transition.
- The transitional Judicial Appointments Committee will select and appoint justices to the High Court for the Transition, composed of:
  - Six Palestinian judges
    - including at least one Christian judge;
    - including representation from at least four regions of the Territory,[11] two of which must be part of the territories occupied by Israel in 1967; and
    - at least three women.
  - Six Israeli (Jewish) judges
    - including at least one religiously Orthodox judge;
    - including representation from at least four regions of the Territory;[12]
    - at least three women.
  - Three international judges
    - The international judges shall be nominated by the International Court of Justice and must be approved by the transitional Judicial Appointments Committee.
- The initial terms of the justices for the duration of the Transition or until a new high court—or high courts, if more than one state emerges—is appointed following the first democratic elections.
- The High Court for the Transition may hear challenges referred to it by:
  - the head of the Caretaker Government or his/her delegees;
  - one or more municipal council(s), when the matter is a conflict of authority or powers;
  - any district court judge; or
  - two-thirds of members of any of the oversight commissions created in Section 1. This is meant to indirectly create enforcement mechanisms for the commissions, which will not independently have such powers.
- The High Court for the Transition will have the power to:
  - annul legislation it determines to be in contradiction of or detrimental to the Guiding Principles;
  - order state agencies to cease carrying out an activity or policy that violates the Guiding Principles;

○ declare a public servant unfit for office due to credible allegations of human rights abuses or grave crimes; and

○ resolve disputes related to the powers of the different branches and organs of government, as well as disputes of law among different jurisdictions within the Territory.

WHO REMAINS ON THE BENCH

To maintain a functioning legal system during the Transition, all magistrate-level judges across the Territory, whether serving in Israeli or Palestinian courts, will remain on the bench, conditioned on their willingness to take a new oath of office to uphold and protect the Guiding Principles.

Sitting appellate court judges (district courts) will remain on the bench for one year conditional on a review of their role in violations of human rights and international humanitarian laws either as part of their judgeship or in some other capacity. The Judicial Oversight Commission shall complete this review in year 1.

The Judicial Appointments Committee will appoint new appellate judges on a rolling basis.

RETRAINING JUDGES

Starting in month 6, the Judiciary Committee will prepare and implement a training program for judges whom it will require take and pass courses in:

- human rights and the protection of the individual;
- the Guiding Principles;
- new unified criminal laws; and
- new court procedures, including common rules of evidence.

The Judiciary Committee will merge Israel's Courts Administration with the West Bank and Gaza courts administrations. The newly merged Courts Administration will conduct continuing education for judges. The Caretaker Government will task the Courts Administration—with the support of foreign-trained Israeli and Palestinian lawyers and judges, and international bodies experienced in training judges in transitional democracies—with writing a curriculum for these courses, recruiting staff to conduct the courses, and writing and publishing regulations for participation and successful completion of the trainings.

MAINTAINING ISRAELI AND PALESTINIAN SUPREME APPELLATE COURTS

The Israeli and Palestinian Supreme Courts will continue to serve as the highest courts of appeals in their respective jurisdictions. In situations where rulings conflict, each respective Supreme Court or a district court where such a conflict arises may refer the matter to the High Court for the Transition.

Section 5   # Revoke Racist, Discriminatory Laws

SUMMARY

This section outlines the legislative reforms specifically necessary to dismantle the apartheid system across the Territory. Israel's apartheid regime is supported by a complex array of laws, practices, and norms that enforce domination, segregation, and inequality across various domains, including political representation, free expression, land use, ownership rights, and access to resources. These laws exist both as explicit tools of apartheid and as seemingly neutral regulations that nonetheless perpetuate discrimination.

Most of these discriminatory practices are rooted in the emergency laws Israel adopted from the British Mandate period when it declared independence, addressed in detail in Section 2. In this section, we detail a host of racist and discriminatory legislation that the Caretaker Government will also need to reform or revoke to align with democratic principles and international human rights standards, starting in week 9 of the Transition. Further details on each law and recommended changes are listed in Appendix B. The Legislative Committee, established by the Caretaker Government in week 9, will guide this process, including by prioritizing laws for remediation and continuously assessing others to ensure legislation upholds equality and justice for all people in the Territory.

DISCUSSION

As discussed elsewhere, the goal of the Blueprint is to design the process for dismantling Israel's military occupation of the Occupied Palestinian Territory (OPT) and dismantling its regime of apartheid. Israel's apartheid regime predates the 1967 occupation, exists in varying degrees on both sides of the pre-1967 lines, and, in many ways, functions independently of the military occupation.[1] Discriminatory apartheid rule is buttressed by an entire system of laws, practices, and norms that creates and maintains a system of domination. These laws impact: political representation and organization; free expression; land use, ownership, zoning, and other property-related matters; immigration; personal legal status, including family law; access to natural and economic resources; the provision of state services and benefits; policing and security; institutionalized distrust and permanent suspicion of non-Jewish citizens and residents and others. Simply ending the occupation and extending the existing Israeli legal framework to the occupied territories, therefore, is wholly insufficient for the aim of dismantling apartheid.[2]

The bedrock of the apartheid regime on all sides of pre-1967 borders is the state of emergency and the concomitant emergency regulations that the nascent Israeli government chose to inherit from the British Mandate government when it declared independence in May 1948 and in several instances codified into its own new emergency laws.[3] The bulk of the most egregious laws that serve the apartheid regime are dependent on this declared state of emergency, and every Israeli government has renewed the state of emergency to this day.[4] These emergency laws allow Israel to exercise authority in the OPT and include restrictions on movement, the seizure of land, restrictions on speech, assembly, and association, and family unification.[5]

Emergency laws are not the only source of discriminatory apartheid legislation, however. Starting around the turn of the millennium, the Israeli Justice Ministry and the Knesset codified many emergency regulations into regular laws that do not depend on a declared state of emergency to remain in effect.[6] The most prominent and consequential example is the 2016 Counter-Terrorism Law, applicable within Israel, which codified broad, discretionary, administrative powers, previously only available in times of emergency, to restrict speech, assembly, movement, and political expression and to override or limit many protections of criminal suspects, detainees, and prisoners, and outlaw civil society organizations.[7]

Within the territories Israel treats as sovereign today (the area within Israel's pre-1967 borders, the Golan Heights, and East Jerusalem) are laws that may even appear to be neutral at first glance but are discriminatory in impact and intent and wholly inconsistent with the Guiding Principles and international human rights law. Adalah, a civil rights organization focusing on protecting Palestinian citizens of Israel, maintains a comprehensive list of legislation that may not be discriminatory at first glance but has discriminatory impact and intent.[8] This list, which has been widely cited by academics, leading human rights experts, and UN bodies, can serve as a starting point and important resource for a dedicated effort to identify and rescind or amend such legislation. Elsewhere, lawmakers and other policymakers have been far more explicit about the true intentions of their legislative efforts—in media appearances, party platforms, coalition agreements, and papers written for think tanks and policy groups.[9] All of these can serve as resources for identifying legislation that requires revoking or amending.

The Caretaker Government also will need to address secondary legislation that gives bureaucrats the discretion to uphold and even create discriminatory policies beyond what the law prescribes. These include the discriminatory and segregationist criteria for implementing and making determinations regarding personal status, planning and zoning, social and economic benefits, policing and the use of force, the functioning and powers of intelligence agencies, and even freedom of movement.[10]

Reforming laws that regulate land and property rights also will require a more comprehensive plan that can be started during the Transition, but this will take much longer to complete and should take place in a post-Transition, transitional justice process. Some of these laws only allow property sales to, and acquisitions by, Israeli citizens or noncitizen Jews.[11] Historically, Israel has partly implemented these discriminatory restrictions by depositing large swaths of land with organizations and institutions that only sell to Jews or Israeli citizens. "The gradual normalization of this seizure began almost immediately [after 1948], with the repeated reclassification of the land, first as 'abandoned land,' then as 'absentee land,' and finally as 'Israel Lands,'" Geremy Forman and Alexandre Kedar explain, a process that "was part and parcel of this drive towards Jewish domination of Israel's sovereign territory."[12] Other laws in the OPT restrict land sales only to Palestinians.[13]

The Caretaker Government can reform overtly discriminatory land practices without waiting for a transitional justice process, specifically: laws limiting who can buy or sell land based on religion or nationality; revoking or amending planning and zoning laws, laws designed to encourage Jewish settlement, laws permitting housing discrimination, and others in relatively straightforward ways to end active discrimination and apartheid. The Caretaker Government can also simply dismantle other mechanisms that Israel designed to seize or maintain control of land and then put those lands under the administration of a new state land authority that will be bound by the Guiding Principles, a future constitution, and a sovereign transitional justice program. What such transitional justice entails is beyond the scope of the Blueprint's goals to end occupation and apartheid and create the conditions for democratic decisions about governance, which we discuss at length in Section 8.

Lastly, as discussed below, there are laws that define the symbols and identity of the state itself.[14] If Israel is going to transform itself into a state that treats all of its citizens equally, it will need to reckon with how those symbols serve or detract from that goal and the principles of the Transition.

A gradual process to remedy apartheid laws is not unique to Israel-Palestine. In South Africa, several different official bodies pored over decades of legislation—and continue to do so—to weed out laws and regulations designed to foster or result in policies of apartheid.[15] In our case, after immediate revocations of overtly discriminatory laws, the Legislative Committee will carry out this deeper review process, with roles for the High Court for the Transition and the Caretaker Government. A post-Transition government may need to conduct further review and amendment of legislation and regulations.

WHAT TO DO

The Caretaker Government will carry out the vast majority of legal reforms to end apartheid rule within the first six months of the Transition, as detailed in the timeline in Appendix C. Appendix B includes a list of laws and suggested amendments, where relevant, that the Caretaker Government can immediately change to delete discriminatory provisions or rescind entirely in week 1 of the Transition.

The remainder of legal reforms will require a deeper examination of existing laws to identify those that indirectly support, maintain, or create discrimination, apartheid, or supremacy. It will also require careful consideration of the consequences of amending or rescinding such laws, including a case-by-case assessment of whether changing a particular law is in the best interests of the Transition or is better left for a sovereign, post-Transition, legislative, constitutional, or transitional justice process.

At the start of the Transition, the Caretaker Government will establish a Legislative Committee, the composition of which is detailed in Section 1, to examine other laws and regulations that may be discriminatory. It will assess whether the Caretaker Government should reform them or defer them to a post-Transition process on a case-by-case basis. For laws the committee decides should be addressed during the Transition, it will formulate amendments and recommend revocation or re-legislation to the Caretaker Government, or, if it deems it necessary, refer the legislation to the High Court for the Transition for judicial review. The High Court may exercise judicial review over, and by a majority reverse, a decision by the Caretaker Government not to amend or rescind a law referred to it by the Legislative Committee. In addition, civil society groups, local governments, the High Court, or the Caretaker Government itself may refer laws and regulations to the committee for review.

A Special Review of Land Laws

The land registration and ownership regime in the Territory is particularly complicated because it is an amalgamation of Ottoman, British, Jordanian, Egyptian, and Israeli land laws. A post-apartheid land regime will also have to account for tens of thousands, if not hundreds of thousands, of ownership disputes among current residents, refugees, and others whose property Israel seized through various mechanisms over the decades. The land regime designed and implemented by Israel includes mandates to maintain Jewish control of large swaths of land through institutions such as the Jewish National Fund, the Custodian of Absentee Property, the Israel Land Authority, the military's Civil Administration, and various planning authorities.[16] Control over land is one of the biggest root causes of conflict on a national level and a major pillar of the apartheid regime. Laws in the OPT, some of which predate the 1967 occupation, also restrict the purchase or sale of land by non-Palestinians.[17]

Ideally, questions about how to dismantle apartheid or other discriminatory laws in the land regime would be left to a sovereign, transitional justice process and not a transitional government. However, there are many aspects of existing law regarding land ownership, planning and zoning, historical rights, and the ability to acquire and sell land that, in addition to perpetuating historical injustices, could also be exploited to maintain apartheid and continue discrimination in land ownership, planning, and use. The primary task during the Transition when it comes to land reform should, therefore, be revoking laws that discriminate on the basis of race or national origin, including Israeli laws that restrict land sales to non-Jews and Israelis, or Palestinian laws that restrict land sales to non-Palestinians. The approach must be cautious, however, as removing national and religious restrictions on land transactions and allowing any citizen of the Territory to buy land anywhere could create new inequities in land ownership in light of disparate levels of wealth and resources between Palestinian and Jewish communities, preclude a meaningful transitional justice process, and complicate a decision of the post-Transition electorate to separate into two or more states. To prevent large-scale transfers of land in ways that prejudice political and transitional justice outcomes, we recommend a freeze on outright property sales and transfers of ownership— or leases longer than twenty years—for the duration of the Transition. While this might be seen as antithetical to most conceptions of liberal property rights, we believe it is a temporary and necessary step.

The Legislative Committee shall appoint a subcommittee, the Land Laws Subcommittee, to launch an in-depth review of land laws in the Territory at the start of year 2 of the Transition. Over the following six months, it should identify land laws, regulations, and practices not already revoked or amended that contravene the values and principles of the Transition. The subcommittee should prioritize reforming by the end of year 3 of the Transition the laws, regulations, and practices that harm or discriminate against individuals and communities targeted by the apartheid regime. Structural matters, including systems of land registration, historical rights, and refugee rights, should—to the greatest extent possible—be left to a post-Transition process for resolution. The Land Laws Subcommittee should include and consult with land law experts and community representatives reflective of the national, religious, socioeconomic, and geographic diversity of the Territory.

Settlers in the OPT

Under both the Geneva Conventions and the Rome Statute, the transfer by an occupying force of its civilian population to settle in occupied territory is a war crime.[18] The absolute prohibition on settlements under international law is intended to prevent efforts to change the demographic composition of occupied territory or to otherwise attempt to permanently occupy territory. "According to the final report of the UN Special Rapporteur on the Human Rights Dimensions of Population Transfer, including the Implantation of Settlers and Settlements, the implantation of settlers is unlawful and engages State responsibility and the criminal responsibility of individuals."[19] The International Court of Justice's 2024 opinion on the illegality of Israel's occupation was clear that "the State of Israel is under an obligation to cease immediately all new settlement activities, and to evacuate all settlers from the Occupied Palestinian Territory."[20] This opinion is presumably premised on an undefined two-state solution that would theoretically emerge as the de facto remnant of Israeli withdrawal to its 1967 borders, but the opinion does not contain a plan for how to do this in an orderly and peaceful fashion.

Because the Blueprint's Transition plan dismantles the occupation and erases the legal distinction of the 1949 Armistice Lines, however, international humanitarian law and the legal status of both the Geneva Conventions governing military occupation and the settlers residing in illegal settlements will no longer be the guiding legal framework.[21]

Instead, it allows the people of the Territory to decide whether they wish to separate into two states, or not, at the end of the Transition. The Blueprint therefore does not contain an immediate requirement for settlers to move out of the settlements in which they live. Those settlements, along with all other land in the Territory, will no longer be restricted to Jewish Israelis or subject to exceptional security rules that regulate who can enter the settlements. To the extent that there are pending claims disputing ownership of the land on which the settlers live or farm, courts will adjudicate them like any other property conflicts, as discussed in Section 4. The status of the rightful ownership of the lands on which settlements currently exist, and the larger question of settlement and restitution itself, will be resolved as part of the longer-term transitional justice process, as described in Section 8.

State Symbols

The symbols of the Israeli state are, by design, replete with its presentation as a Jewish state for all Jewish people around the world and are therefore felt to be exclusionary to non-Jewish citizens, particularly given their association with the previous apartheid regime.[22] These symbols include the name of the state itself, Israel, the Star of David flag, the national anthem, and the state seal of the menorah. Abolishing the flags and symbols of abusive regimes during a transition is a common undertaking. For example, as the Anti-Defamation League explains, "after the end of apartheid, South Africa adopted a new national flag in 1994, as the previous flag had come to symbolize the apartheid regime."[23]

The success of the Transition will depend on the participation of historically excluded groups, and so, in an ideal situation, a Caretaker Government would find a compromise on interim state symbols that feel inclusive to Palestinians and Jews at the start of the Transition. Such a compromise would go a long way in building trust and buy-in from the communities and individuals victimized by apartheid and occupation or who feel excluded by the existing Jewish symbols of the state. It would also advance the idea that the Caretaker Government does not serve or accord privileged status to one community or group over another.

However, the chances of reaching a compromise that does not threaten to derail progress in more critical areas of the Blueprint are low and unnecessary for the Transition's success. Furthermore, avoiding the prescription of changes to state symbols during the Transition leaves open the possibility for a referendum to form two states or a confederation that may wish to retain the existing symbols in one form or another. As a result, the Blueprint does not prescribe changes to these symbols during the Transition. Instead, it proposes temporarily renaming the transitional state as "Israel-Palestine" and suspending the official use of both Israeli and Palestinian national symbols, including the flag, the anthem, and the state seal, until a post-Transition electorate can determine their ultimate system of governance in one, two, or more states. For similar reasons, the Blueprint also proposes retaining the use of the existing Israeli currency during the Transition, as it is already the primary currency used across the Territory.[24]

Laws to Revoke and Amend

Appendix B provides a more detailed list of all laws that must be revoked or amended, along with suggested amendments or replacements for many.

FULLY REVOKE:

- Trading with the Enemy Act, 1939;
- Absentee Property Law, 1950;
- the Law of Return, 1950;
- Citizenship Law, 1952;
- World Zionist Organization–Jewish Agency Law, 1952;
- Jewish National Fund Law, 1953;
- Jewish Religious Services Law, 1971;
- Basic Law: Jerusalem, Capital of Israel, 1980;
- Temporary Order: Citizenship and Entry to Israel, 2003;
- Negev Development Authority Law, 1991;
- Revoking [Pension] Disbursements to Members of Knesset and Former Members of Knesset for Crimes, 2011;

- Counter-Terrorism Law, 2016;
- Admissions Committees Law: Amendment to the Cooperative Societies Ordinance;
- Anti-Boycott Law (2011) and Boycott Entry Law (2017);
- Tax Deductible Donations for "Settlement": Income Tax Code, Amendment 191, 2012;
- Limitations of Civil Liability for Military Acts, Amendment No. 8 to Civil Wrongs Law, 2012; and
- Palestinian laws forbidding the sale of property to foreigners.

SIMPLE AMENDMENTS:

- State Education Law, 1953;
- Broadcast Authority Law, 1953;
- Interpretation Law, 1981;
- Use of the Hebrew Date Law, 1998;
- Political Parties Law, 1992;
- Entry into Israel Law, 1952; and
- Budgets Foundations Law ("Nakba Law" Amendment of 2011).

Section 6   Citizenship and Voting Rights

SUMMARY

Extending full citizenship rights to all residents of the Territory during the Transition is a crucial step toward transforming the undemocratic one-state reality into a more democratic one. With citizenship comes voting rights and irrevocable rights to be in and enter the country, but more importantly, citizenship signals belonging, both legally and politically. A citizen is, by definition, a member of a state; in a democracy, a state should also belong to all of its citizens. Although citizens will not vote until the end of the Transition, the extension of citizenship to Palestinians whom Israel considers residents of the Territory living under military occupation will confer critical protections and privileges as well as a sense of rightfully shared ownership of their polity. As prescribed in Section 2, after consolidating the population registry, the Caretaker Government will extend full citizenship and voting rights to all adults that appear in the new registry.

DISCUSSION

The right to vote is perhaps the most critical element of any democratic system, but elections alone do not make a democracy. Israel's current regime has been described in many ways, from democracy to ethnocracy to apartheid state and more.[1] Indeed, Israel maintains multiple regimes in the Territory, with some of the people in any given geographic space subject to one system of rules and governance while another group of people, even within the same geographic space, is subject to a different system of rules and governance.[2]

Within the 1949 Armistice Lines, Jewish Israelis enjoy full citizenship, and immigrating Jews can obtain automatic citizenship. They can elect representative officials to government, receive exclusive benefits from the state, enjoy economic opportunities, and benefit from the most permissive and liberal relationship with the state of any other group in the Territory.[3] Palestinian citizens of Israel have citizenship, but their citizenship is unequal to the rights and privileges of Jewish Israelis. "Palestinian citizens of Israel are denied a nationality, establishing a legal differentiation from Jewish Israelis," Amnesty International describes in its 2022 report on apartheid.[4] Israel, somewhat perplexingly, does not recognize an Israeli nationality that would ostensibly include all citizens, instead defining its Jewish citizens as Jewish nationals and Palestinian citizens as either Muslim or Christian.[5] At the same time, Israel defines itself as the nation-state of the Jewish people.

On paper, Palestinian citizens of Israel can elect representatives to the Israeli parliament. But because Israel bars political parties and candidates that reject Israel as an exclusively Jewish state, in practice Israel limits which parties and politicians can serve in government and what they can say, therefore limiting true democratic representation. Palestinian citizens are denied many of the economic benefits and opportunities the state provides to Jewish Israeli citizens, including, for example, land distribution, advanced job training, and benefits related to military service. Palestinian citizens are also subject to de facto, state-sanctioned discrimination in nearly every facet of life, including the availability of credit, housing, and employment. Civil rights organizations have extensively documented how Israeli law enforcement and domestic intelligence agencies treat Palestinian towns and cities much more aggressively than Israeli Jews, use more invasive and violent tactics, subject them to more extensive surveillance, and regularly violate Palestinian civil rights in ways they do not to Jewish citizens and towns.[6] Any of these discriminatory and racist practices and policies would fail even basic civil rights judicial scrutiny in the United States or other democracies.

Israel formally annexed occupied East Jerusalem in 1980, but the international community does not recognize this annexation. Despite annexing the land of East Jerusalem, Israel did not grant the Palestinians living there citizenship; instead, it classified the vast majority of East Jerusalem Palestinians as "permanent residents."[7] Even this status has not been permanent, however, as Israeli authorities have stripped Palestinians of their Jerusalem residencies on the slightest of ever-expanding pretexts in a deliberate effort to increase the Jewish demographics of the city.[8] Israel does not allow Palestinian permanent residents to vote in national elections, and existing law allows Israeli authorities to revoke their residency—and has done so to more than fourteen thousand Palestinian residents of East Jerusalem since 1967—for a number of reasons, ranging from breach of loyalty to living abroad for too long or even acquiring citizenship from a state other than Israel.[9] Palestinian permanent residents are permitted to apply for Israeli citizenship, but few do. And even for those who do apply, citizenship is not automatic; between 1967 and 2022, Israeli authorities approved only one-third of those citizenship applications.[10] As a result, only 5 percent of East Jerusalem Palestinians hold Israeli citizenship today. On paper, Israel permits East Jerusalem Palestinian permanent residents to vote in municipal elections, but Israeli officials have openly conspired to limit their electoral power for decades, ensuring Jerusalem remains a Jewish-controlled city.[11]

In the occupied West Bank, Palestinians have neither Israeli citizenship nor Israeli residency.[12] Israel treats them as an "occupied population" pursuant to the Geneva Conventions, although it does not formally or officially recognize them as such.[13] The apartheid nature of Israeli governance is most starkly apparent in the West Bank, where Israeli Jewish settlers and Palestinians live in the same territory but the settlers are entitled to superior laws, rights, protections, and resources.[14]

Unlike Palestinians, Israeli settlers in the West Bank have the right to vote in Israeli elections—elections that often hinge on policy questions related to the Occupied Palestinian Territory (OPT).[15] Israeli settlers serve in all levels of the Israeli military and police. Palestinians in the West Bank have no democratic avenues for affecting the policies or governance that most impact their lives. On paper, Palestinians in the West Bank can elect the parliament of the Palestinian Authority (PA), but it has little more than municipal powers over items like sanitation, policing, education, family law matters, and traffic control, as described in Section 1.[16] And even there, the PA has refused to hold parliamentary elections since 2006. Israel also regularly interferes with local Palestinian city and town elections in the West Bank, severely limits the autonomy of Palestinian institutions, and regularly arrests and arbitrarily imprisons elected Palestinian representatives on patently political charges.[17]

Palestinians in Gaza technically have the same rights to elect local representation as their countrymen in the West Bank, but in practice, much like Palestinian refugees, they have no meaningful democratic representation. In 2006, Palestinians in Gaza and the West Bank held elections for the PA parliament, won by Hamas, but Mahmoud Abbas's Fatah party ousted the Hamas government following pressure from the United States and Europe.[18] After months of clashes and a failed Fatah attempt to assassinate Hamas Prime Minister Ismail Haniyeh, Hamas expelled Fatah officials from the Gaza Strip in 2007.[19] Since then, Hamas had established its own civilian and military government in Gaza, while Fatah, through the PA, had established its own civilian and military government in the West Bank, though in both cases with extremely limited powers and authority. As a result of the schism between the Fatah-dominated PA and Hamas, there has been no unified leadership and no democratic elections for the OPT since.

In Gaza as in the West Bank, Israel has continued to maintain control over movement, the economy, the population registry, maritime rights, airspace, and even access to some types of medical care. It remains the occupying power over Gaza despite its 2005 "disengagement," when it removed some twelve thousand Jewish settlers from the territory along with the troops deployed to protect them.[20] In 2023, Israel reinstalled its troops in Gaza as part of its military campaign there, and as of this writing, it remains in physical control of most of the area, the vast majority of which appears to be unfit for human habitation as a result of Israel's widescale physical destruction.[21]

Like Palestinians in the West Bank and most in East Jerusalem, Palestinians in Gaza have no democratic avenues to influence the Israeli authorities who regulate where and with whom they can live, what they can import and export, where they can travel, where they can study, and even what medical care they can receive. Israel, with cooperation from Egypt, has imposed a blockade on Gaza since 2006, strictly limiting and often completely prohibiting Palestinians in Gaza from exiting the territory or internationals from entering.[22] Israel has also restricted, and during the Gaza War completely shut down, the flow of water, electricity, food, medicine, and fuel to Gaza, for which the Office of the Prosecutor of the International Criminal Court sought arrest warrants for Israeli Prime Minister Benjamin Netanyahu and former Defense Minister Yoav Gallant.[23] While it was not clear at the time of this writing what Israel's occupation of Gaza would look like following the war, Israeli leaders have been clear that they intend to maintain permanent military control over the territory.[24]

Thus, while approximately half of the people in the Territory enjoy living under Israeli democracy, the other half experience Israeli governance as a military dictatorship. The easiest and quickest way to begin to remedy that democratic deficit is for the Caretaker Government to extend equal citizenship to all adult residents of the Territory. The practical result of this step will be the enfranchisement of the entire population, as detailed below.

LIMITATIONS

While extending full citizenship to all residents of the Territory is indeed a remedy that dismantles a pivotal piece of Israel's apartheid and occupation regimes, the type of sweeping enfranchisement envisioned in this section is not an end in itself. In fact, one of the dangers of a broad and sudden change, particularly like the extension of full equality and democratic rights to all people living in the Territory, is that such a change would be mistaken for a durable solution.[25] The Israeli apartheid regime defines citizenship in an exclusionary manner to maintain the domination of one group over another.[26] This section merely seeks to neutralize citizenship as a tool of domination.

Questions on how to comprehensively define citizenship, particularly questions regarding the inclusion of Palestinian refugees living outside the Territory, go beyond the scope of the problems the Blueprint seeks to address—Israeli occupation and apartheid. How to fulfill the rights of refugees outside the Territory is a question that should be answered democratically and in line with international law in a post-Transition government. This means that while the Blueprint explicitly recognizes the rights of Palestinian refugees, as discussed in Section 8, it does not dictate what resolution or return might look like in the vast majority of cases.

WHAT TO DO

After the Caretaker Government consolidates the Israeli and Palestinian population registries, as described in Section 2, it will automatically grant citizenship to all adults over the age of eighteen who are listed as permanent residents or citizens in the consolidated registry. The Caretaker Government will also automatically confer citizenship on anyone who was listed in the population registry since June 6, 1967, but whose citizenship or residency the Israeli government revoked for any reason. As explored in Chapter 2, Israel has revoked the residency of hundreds of thousands of Palestinian residents of the West Bank and Gaza since 1967.[27]

Security Forces and Disarmament

SUMMARY

There is no escaping the fact that transitions are times of turbulence that, if not managed successfully, run the risk of leading to a security breakdown. They are fertile ground for the growth of armed groups and militias and create legitimate fears of chaos for the people living through them. Some of these risks are unavoidable, but transitional state institutions can mitigate them to minimize their potentially destabilizing impact. Security is not just a matter of concern for the period during the Transition but critical to its ultimate success in transforming a one-state undemocratic reality into a more democratic one.

With the dismantling of occupation and apartheid and the end of armed conflict among organized armed groups, there will be no need for national military forces to carry out ordinary policing functions as they do currently, and no need for irregular armed groups and militias to resist them. Instead, the Caretaker Government will need to create unified domestic security forces responsible for policing crime, and national security forces responsible for protecting the Territory from external threats.

To achieve the appropriate, sustainable level of security for all residents of the Territory while maximizing previously denied freedoms, we propose five baskets of reforms:

1. Create a hard separation between domestic and external security forces, authorizing only civilian police to handle domestic security in the Territory, subject to civilian oversight and accountability mechanisms.
2. Integrate existing Israeli and Palestinian police forces into a new national police force.
3. Embark upon a comprehensive and holistic effort toward the disarmament, demobilization, and reintegration of disbanded members of armed groups and security forces.
4. Create a new and inclusive security doctrine that strives to provide and guarantee equal levels of security for all persons and peoples of the Territory.
5. Create an international and regional framework of external security guarantees, including a program of nuclear disarmament led by the International Atomic Energy Agency.

DISCUSSION

Reforming and reorganizing security forces is politically and logistically difficult partly due to deep-seated fears among Israeli Jews and Palestinians alike about their respective security at the hands of the "other side's" security forces and armed groups. Without guarantees for a democratic transition, it would be impossible to convince Palestinian armed groups to lay down their weapons or to avoid the emergence of new groups. Without guarantees for Jewish Israelis' security, it would be impossible to convince the Israel Defense Forces (IDF) and various other security apparatus to make difficult changes, namely integrating Palestinians into restructured joint forces or, in some cases, disbanding. From a logistical standpoint, the idea of disarming militant groups in the Gaza Strip might have seemed delusional to many prior to October 7, 2023, when Palestinian militant groups were much more entrenched—and literally underground.[1] As discussed in Chapter 1, a disarmament process in Gaza is tragically easier to imagine following the Gaza War, which will likely result in the near-total disarmament of Hamas and other armed groups in Gaza.

Although vastly different in scale and types of dangers, Israelis and Palestinians, like all people living in the Territory today, lack full security. The indiscriminate and deliberate attacks on Israeli civilians of October 7, 2023, demonstrated the fragility of both physical security and a more cognitive sense of security for Jewish Israelis, hundreds of thousands of whom were forcibly displaced for months on end. The year-plus of Israeli attacks in Gaza that followed October 7 has resulted, as of this writing, in over 47,000 recorded deaths, the majority being those of women, children, and the elderly, although the actual death toll is likely to be vastly greater as bodies under rubble are recovered and those injured or unable to obtain medical care succumb.[2] There are more than 110,000 injuries, damage to over 60 percent of Palestinian housing units and other structures, and mass food insecurity and dire predictions of imminent famine, all of which should underscore beyond any doubt the absolute physical insecurity of Palestinians.[3]

Among Jewish Israelis, seeking and maintaining security is the most central political issue and the justification for many of Israel's abusive and undemocratic policies.[4] For Palestinians, meanwhile, the absence of security and safety living under occupation has been reflected in the glaring disparity of the deaths and injuries they have suffered at the hands of Israeli security forces for decades. Likewise, for Palestinians, Israel's concept of security has become synonymous with its means of oppression, in particular with the enforcement of military occupation and apartheid rule.

Even in times of less intense violence than the current Gaza war, these dynamics have bolstered the idea that security is inescapably zero-sum. Changing this perception will be just as important as the provision of more tangible security.

SEPARATING INTERNAL AND EXTERNAL SECURITY ROLES

Traditional security arrangements around the world involve three primary sets of security actors: domestic police forces for the enforcement of domestic criminal laws, national military forces for the protection of the nation from external threats, and domestic and foreign intelligence agencies tasked with dealing with national security threats. In most democratic countries, national military and intelligence forces rarely undertake domestic policing activities unless there's some sort of emergency. However, Israel treats the Occupied Palestinian Territory (OPT) as a hybrid space, both domestic and foreign, intentionally blurring internal and external security within the same territory. It treats the OPT as a "domestic" concern, providing civilian Israeli policing and security to the hundreds of thousands of Israeli citizens there, while it treats millions of Palestinian noncitizens living alongside them as a foreign concern, subjecting them to IDF military control.

While the Palestinian Authority exercises domestic policing in Area A of the West Bank, Israeli military forces carry out regular incursions there.[5] In addition, there are domestic police forces operating under the control of the Hamas-led government in Gaza, as well as armed groups in Gaza, some of which are part of Hamas's military wing, while others are independent. Finally, the West Bank has smaller armed groups operating independently of the Palestinian Authority. Detailed descriptions of the major armed groups and security forces operating throughout the Territory—Israeli and Palestinian—can be found in Appendix D, along with recommendations for integration or dismantlement of each.

One of the key components of Israel's current apartheid regime is the system of different classifications for individuals and groups, slicing them along the lines of religion, ethnicity, and citizenship.[6] These classifications determine the jurisdiction of different security agencies and even legal systems over people in the same territory. This is a major structural driver of inequality, as discussed at length in Section 2.

The Caretaker Government can begin to remedy this inequality, integrate the civilian forces, and limit military forces to external threats by creating a uniform legal system and redrawing the jurisdictions of security and law enforcement agencies in three stages.

First, upon its formation (Section 1), the Domestic Security Committee of the Caretaker Government will need to undertake significant changes within the structure and composition of the civilian police forces across the Territory. This sequencing and integration plan ensures that there is no policing vacuum: Israeli police will continue to patrol in Israel and

Areas B and C; and Palestinian police will continue to patrol in Gaza and Area A, but they will all be integrated into a single civilian force. Full integration of Palestinians and Israeli Jews is necessary in the long term, but that does not mean that different localities with distinct ethnic, religious, or cultural characteristics cannot have officers that represent that community as a major element of the local police force.

The changes include:

- changing the name of the Israel Police to the National Police (day 1);
- rapidly integrating all ranks of Palestinian police into the National Police, with identical, new uniforms for all (weeks 1–4);
- appointing a combined Jewish-Palestinian leadership of the police force for the duration of the Transition period (weeks 1–4); and
- commencing a two-year education and training for officers and commanders, regardless of which agency they served in previously, designed to align standard operating procedures, educate about relevant changes in the law, teach the Internal Security Doctrine (as described below), including a strong emphasis on community policing, and teach both Arabic and Hebrew languages (month 6).

Second, in week 1 the Caretaker Government also will issue an order limiting the jurisdictional authority for all domestic security—vis-à-vis citizens, residents, and any other person present in the Territory—exclusively to civilian policing and government bodies. The order will limit the jurisdiction of the military to external threats, which may maintain bases within the Territory, but without any law enforcement or governance powers. This will correspond with handing over internal security responsibility, including responsibility for all internal checkpoints, to civilian police.

In week 1, the Domestic Security Committee will order Israeli civilian police to replace soldiers and other security officers at all internal checkpoints consistent with the new movement regime (Section 3) and security doctrine outlined below. When the integration of Palestinian police begins in week 4, police should ensure that both Palestinian and Israeli officers are stationed at all checkpoints.

Third, the Caretaker Government will subject the Israel Security Agency (Shin Bet), Israel's domestic intelligence service, to strict civilian and judicial oversight, forbidding it from discriminating in its treatment of different population groups, and integrating the Palestinian Preventive Security force, including its senior leadership. This process will not be quick, but it must begin week 1 with the Caretaker Government amending the Shin Bet Law, including:

- changing the name of the Shin Bet to the Domestic Intelligence Agency (DIA) (week 1);
- rapidly integrating all ranks of Palestinian intelligence agents into the DIA (weeks 12–20);
- appointing a combined Jewish-Palestinian leadership of the DIA for the duration of the Transition period (week 12); and
- commencing a two-year education and training for intelligence agents, regardless of which agency they served in previously, designed to align standard operating procedures, educate about relevant changes in the law, teach the Internal Security Doctrine (as described below), including a strong emphasis on community policing, and teach both Arabic and Hebrew languages (month 6).

A NEW SECURITY DOCTRINE

Israelis and Palestinians have vastly different lived experiences of security, which create vastly different expectations of what type of security to expect from the state. However, on that broad spectrum of different experiences, all people living in the Territory today lack security—both physically and in a more cognitive sense.

Among other things, a security doctrine is what contextualizes and defines the role, objectives, practices, and authority of security forces.[7] Israeli security forces are today loyal to the state. But because Israel has crafted the definition of the state, including in the Jewish Nation-State Law of 2018, as belonging exclusively to and preferentially serving the Jewish people, the current approach of prioritizing Jewish security is not appropriate for a state that treats all of its citizens equally. Likewise, the Palestinian security forces effectively have no security doctrine (particularly since the Fatah-Hamas schism), and, as evidenced in the most recent Gaza war, no ability whatsoever to protect the security of Palestinians.[8] Internal political schisms and questions about cooperation with Israeli forces have further muddled the identity and purpose of Palestinian police and other security forces.

A security doctrine translates the values and goals of the state into operational and even structural guidance for the security forces tasked with achieving and maintaining them. The Transition asks members of existing security forces to perform new roles, change the way they treat entire categories of people, and discard the perception that security is a zero-sum equation. These types of changes are difficult, and a security doctrine is an important tool for those forces to succeed in their changing political context. A security doctrine can guide individual officers and commanders alike when facing situations without clear answers in legislation and other legal orders. It is, in a sense, a constitution for the security forces.

Reform and integration of the Territory's security forces are critically important for ensuring that the state and its organs provide security to all residents of the Territory on an equitable and nondiscriminatory basis. As reflected in the *Chicago Principles on Post-Conflict Justice*, the creation of a new security doctrine forms an important part of security sector reform and establishing public trust in those institutions.[9] This section provides recommendations for the doctrinal pillars and principles for internal security.

Recommended Doctrinal Pillars

1. The security of all citizens and residents of the Territory will be provided on an equitable and nondiscriminatory basis and will ensure territorial integrity, including critical infrastructure. This includes ensuring that all people feel safe.

2. In enforcing the law and upholding the rule of law, the security forces will center the protection of the values of equality, democracy, human rights, and freedom from threats both domestic and extraterritorial.

3. Security forces will ensure the integrity of the transition to democracy from apartheid and occupation.

4. The security forces will build public trust in policing and the rule of law through transparency and accountability, strong community policing foundations, and recognition that security achieved through political means is far more durable than security achieved through the use of force alone.

5. Recognizing that policing is only one "part of an integrated criminal justice system that is demilitarized, professional and community-centric,"[10] the new National Police will take a holistic approach to crime prevention that includes cooperation with economic actors, social welfare officials, and community leaders.

Implementation

1. Internalize and operationalize the core tenet that law enforcement officials in the Territory will abide by the UN Code of Conduct for Law Enforcement Officials and the UN Basic Principles on the Use of Force and Firearms by Law Enforcement Officials, including using force only when strictly necessary and to the extent required for the performance of their duty.[11]

2. Police will treat all matters of internal security under civilian criminal laws and not militarily or extrajudicially.[12]

3. Security forces will take an oath of loyalty to the rule of law and the Guiding Principles of the Transition.

4. During the Transition, the Caretaker Government will require that security forces become demographically representative of the various communities and population groups in the Territory generally, and specifically of the communities they are assigned to serve and protect.

These doctrinal pillars and principles must form the foundations of security practices, the education of security forces, and guidance in the formation of security policies. It is also critical to proactively prioritize doctrinal pillars and principles so that inevitable conflicts can be easily resolved as they arise.

DISARMAMENT, DEMOBILIZATION, AND REINTEGRATION

It bears repeating that disarming and demobilizing militant groups, including the integration of some of their fighters into official security forces, is only possible with the agreement of their respective military and political leadership. This is one of the reasons why there must be a Conciliation Conference that precedes the Blueprint—to establish consent and political will. Without it, attempts to disarm and demobilize armed and paramilitary groups and to integrate Palestinian and Israeli security forces would be indistinguishable from current Israeli military operations aimed at destroying Palestinian armed groups.

There is no single formula for disarmament, demobilization, and reintegration (DDR). Decades of experience and scholarship have demonstrated that to have a chance of success, while disarmament must be undertaken as soon as possible, the manner in which DDR takes place should be flexible, context-specific, and inclusive of a broad spectrum of local and international actors.[13] What the Blueprint proposes, therefore, is that at the start of the Transition, in week 1, the Caretaker Government appoint a Disarmament, Demobilization, and Reintegration Committee drawn from Palestinian and Israeli security experts, current and former combatants, civil society groups, and the government itself, to begin developing a DDR plan together with the UN Department of Peace Operations.

The DDR plan should closely follow the UN's Integrated DDR Standards.[14] DDR is not a quick process, and it cannot be carried out without more comprehensive stabilization and economic and social programs, but it is imperative that the process be part and parcel of the Transition. In particular, the work to reintegrate former combatants into civilian life will likely outlive the Transition.

The attacks on October 7, 2023, and the war Israel launched in response had stark consequences on both Palestinian and Israeli conceptions of security. For some Israelis, it undermined the idea that force alone can create or maintain security, while for others, it reinforced the belief that only greater security measures would protect them. For Palestinians and much of the world, the stakes and urgency of ensuring Palestinian security became clear in previously unthinkable ways.

As of this writing, it is not clear which Palestinian armed groups will remain standing at the end of this war, including whether Israel will succeed in its goal of eliminating Hamas's ability to threaten it from Gaza. Without justifying the actions Israel has taken in the name of that objective, the widespread destruction Israel has wrought on Gaza thus far makes disarmament in Gaza seemingly more feasible and practical than it would have been before October 7. If nothing else, the destruction of the network of tunnels in Gaza will likely make it harder for armed groups to maintain or replenish their armaments.

The Blueprint proposes that the DDR Committee undertake disarmament of all irregular forces, along with several official security institutions, starting week 1 of the Transition. Disarmament includes Hamas and Palestinian Islamic Jihad militants in the Gaza Strip, as well as the Israel Border Police and settler paramilitary forces. The same goes for Palestinian and Israeli security forces that are not integrated into either the transitional or new law enforcement agency. A list of these groups and whether they are to be integrated or disbanded can be found in Appendix D.

The DDR Committee will need to collect large numbers of weapons from civilians of all stripes, from armed Palestinian militants and settlers in the West Bank and Gaza, from Israeli rapid response paramilitaries, and from other civilians holding both licensed and unlicensed firearms, and should seek to complete the vast majority of this process within the first three months of the Transition. Failure to do so would create powerful spoilers with the means to disrupt or sabotage the Transition. The experience with disarmament and demobilization of security forces and armed groups in other transitions has demonstrated—most recently in Libya, Iraq, and Somalia—that without prompt disarmament, a transition to democratic, civilian rule will fail because it will fail to establish security under the authority of a single government. Holding that monopoly on the use of violence is a central ingredient of effective state sovereignty and certainly of a government's ability to maintain peace and order.

But merely demanding the disarmament of former group members will not succeed on its own. Such a demand must be coupled with alternatives and incentives for disarmament, including employment and education opportunities, to succeed in securing the cooperation of the armed groups.[15] The Blueprint does not propose exactly what a package of disarmament and reintegration should look like because decades of scholarship have demonstrated that to succeed, DDR processes must be locally led and be flexible toward dynamic circumstances.[16]

Lustration of the security forces is another challenging topic. Deciding who can and cannot continue to serve in security roles touches on several aspects of the Transition: transitional justice, building public trust in new state institutions, and institutional reforms meant to prevent the recurrence of human rights violations. The Blueprint does not prescribe a specific transitional justice program, as discussed in Section 8, so we do not detail whether, if, and how members of security forces suspected of involvement in serious violations of human rights and humanitarian law should be granted amnesty or face prosecution.

However, to build trust in the security forces, the DDR Committee will need to develop a process to identify, vet, and exclude individual members of security forces responsible for the worst offenses from the ability to exercise force under the color of law.[17] Numerous international guidelines discuss who should be excluded from continuing to serve in security forces during and following a democratic transition. The US Department of State defines lustration as a policy "to remove from public institutions personnel who have been implicated in activities that call into [question] their integrity and professionalism, such as human rights violations or abuses, violations of international humanitarian law (IHL), or related crimes, as a way to build confidence in the public sector."[18]

United Nations guidelines on vetting security forces personnel in democratic transition offer comprehensive guidance in the design and execution of this type of process. It is important to note that in addition to questions of individual integrity, any vetting process must also assess—and in some cases require compromise between competing interests of—individual competence and the organizational needs of each security body moving forward.[19]

Regarding integrity vetting specifically, the UN guidelines note that certain past actions should automatically preclude someone from continuing to serve in or be recruited to public service. Specifically, these include serious international crimes and grave violations of human rights: "genocide, war crimes, crimes against humanity, extrajudicial execution, torture and similar cruel, inhuman and degrading treatment, enforced disappearance and slavery."[20] For lesser violations and crimes, however, automatic disqualification is not recommended because a single action does not—or should not—necessarily define an individual's integrity in perpetuity.

To screen existing security personnel and vet potential recruits, the DDR Committee will need to formulate standardized criteria. The questions that should shape those criteria, as outlined in the UN guidelines, are:

- What was the specific nature of the abuse or misconduct and what was the context?

- Was it a generalized institutional practice (e.g., a generally corrupt professional milieu)?
- Has the act of abuse or misconduct concluded or is it continuous?
- If concluded, has the act been acknowledged? Has the record improved?
- Has the act fundamentally affected civic trust? If so, will it be possible to regain civic trust? Under what conditions?[21]

The answers to these questions can help the DDR Committee assess an individual's integrity and determine the consequences that should follow: continued service, suspension, or exclusion (at least for a period of time). For example, certain past actions might permanently disqualify someone from a security role, while others might only result in temporary disqualification. Other determinations might simply limit what roles an individual can fill. Others might require the DDR Committee to refer certain cases for examination by a prosecutor as part of a broader transitional justice process.

In addition, vetting and lustration processes in democratic transition should follow standards of due process. To accomplish that, the DDR Committee must formulate and publish the criteria that will define and guide the process. While standards of evidence and due process do not need to follow criminal law per se, they should guarantee fairness akin to the protections afforded by administrative law, including avenues to appeal decisions.

The DDR Committee should commence this process in week 4, at the same time the integration of different security bodies begins, and complete the review and vetting of serving members of the security forces by the end of month 6. These lustration processes should also guide recruitment and hiring standards moving forward.

EXTERNAL SECURITY AND ISRAEL'S NUCLEAR WEAPONS

Critical for successful security reforms is the imposition of clear and hard separations between internal and external security, with the former moving exclusively to the realm of civilian policing and law enforcement and the latter remaining a traditional security force responsible for securing against external threats. Because the Israeli military is such a powerful actor and because it is so symbolic of the occupation and apartheid regimes, we believe the international community will need to play an important and active role in shaping the external security policy of the Territory during the Transition.

The international role, as we envision it, is rooted in two assumptions. First, the Blueprint cannot reasonably come to fruition as long as Jewish Israelis fear that abdicating their exclusive control over military force, including nuclear weapons, is likely to be exploited by hostile regional actors.[22] This will require commitments from traditionally hostile regional actors like Lebanon and Syria, guaranteed by more powerful actors with influence over them, which the Foreign Ministry will seek to secure in year 1 of the Transition.

Second, the new National Defense Forces will need to retain many personnel currently serving in the IDF, at least in the officers' corps and for highly specialized professional roles like pilots. The Defense Ministry will eventually need to fully integrate military ranks such that they represent and are immutably committed to the protection of all citizens from external threats, but that process will take time—far longer than the Transition's timeline.

The steps that should be taken with respect to the Territory's military forces are as follows:

1. The Caretaker Government, as the acting sovereign of the Territory during the Transition, shall become the civilian leadership of the military immediately upon taking power in week 1.

2. The Caretaker Government shall abolish mandatory conscription in week 1 and order the military to develop a recruitment process to diversify new enlistees to reflect the population of the Territory. While this diversification process will certainly involve the integration of some members of Palestinian security forces, primarily the National Security Forces, the National Defense Forces should strictly avoid the creation or maintenance of segregated units or branches of the military. Ethnically or nationally segregated armed forces branches or units are a danger to the cohesiveness of the force. Segregated forces face the risk of tensions forming between them, including over nonpolitical issues like funding and pay, as was the case in East Timor.[23]

3. The Caretaker Government shall task its Foreign Ministry with seeking out regional security guarantees and if possible, enter into mutual defense treaties to reduce the risk of military confrontation, which the ministry will work to secure in year 1.

4. The Caretaker Government shall, starting in week 1, appoint a Military Oversight Commission composed of retired officers from both the IDF and Palestinian National Security Forces (NSF), retired Israeli and Palestinian judges, international experts, and representatives of the Caretaker Government to oversee the process of integration and subordination to the new regime. This will be necessary to prevent elements of the security forces from subverting the integration process to maintain undue control or from acting as spoilers in other ways, as was seen in South Africa.[24]

5. The Caretaker Government will task the foreign minister to begin the process of joining the Non-Proliferation Treaty and working with the International Atomic Energy Agency (IAEA) to commence dismantling the Territory's existing nuclear weapons program and ensure any civilian program complies with the Non-Proliferation Treaty and IAEA standards and obligations in year 1.

Section 8   Restorative Justice, Prisoners, and Refugees

SUMMARY

The three topics of this section—restorative justice, prisoners, and refugees—all pertain to vital processes of truth, justice, and reconciliation. The people of the Territory should design, develop, and implement those processes democratically—after the Transition—for a chance at meaningful success.

The predominant wisdom among experts in the field is that most aspects of transitional justice should be designed and led by local actors to ensure that they address the specific historical, social, and political context of a transition but also center the needs and desires of victims.[1] Transitional justice and rule of law reforms that emerge from national dialogue are, as UN Secretary-General António Guterres summarized, "more likely than those imposed from outside to secure sustainable justice for the future, in accordance with international standards, domestic legal traditions and national aspirations."[2] For instance, the compromises and concessions of a truth and reconciliation process that emerge from a peaceful transition are ones that outside observers may reject or judge to be imperfect, but they are compromises and concessions that the collective population is making together. They are also starkly different from a process imposed as part of a victors' justice that may satisfy all of the demands for accountability and reparations by one group but result in long-standing grievances by the group held accountable, thereby undermining the ultimate goal of peace, stability, and communal cohesion. As summarized by Dustin Sharp, "Peace processes and justice mechanisms not embraced by those who have to live with them are unlikely to be successful in the long term," and local design is a central element of that.[3] At the same time, transitional justice must take place within the normative framework of international law—which is clear about the necessity of reparations, among other aspects of transitional justice—and the experiences and lessons drawn from other contexts, which can create tensions with the need for local ownership.[4] It is important to note that the International Court of Justice's 2024 advisory opinion on Israel's occupation determined not only that Israel should end its illegal occupation but that it must pay reparations to its victims.

In the aggregate, the Blueprint represents one pillar of transitional justice: institutional reforms. It does not comprehensively address other elements of transitional justice, such as reparations (property restitution, compensation for damages, the realization of refugee rights, etc.), which we recommend take place after the Transition as part of a truly democratic decision-making process. "While specific strategies may be successfully implemented on their own, the larger objectives of post-conflict justice are best served through a coordinated, coherent, and comprehensive approach," states the *Chicago Principles on Post-Conflict Justice*, which represents the most authoritative guidance and consensus on the matter.[5] The Blueprint does not attempt to undertake the entirety of that comprehensive transitional justice program; such a comprehensive program is outside its mandate to end apartheid and occupation and to lay the groundwork for democratic governance and beyond its competency as a transitional but not truly democratic government.

Yet the Blueprint does undertake partial remedies and preparatory steps on restorative justice, prisoners, and refugees that are essential for their ultimate resolution and that are the topic of this section.

PRISONERS

- In week 6, the Justice Ministry will initiate the release of administrative detainees and several other categories of prisoners, providing a time-limited but reasonable opportunity to press formal charges where fitting.
- In week 16, the Justice Ministry will initiate the phased and supervised release of political prisoners, as described below. This includes those convicted of violent crimes who are members of a party that has committed to abandoning armed activities and participating in the new political system.

RESTORATIVE JUSTICE AND REFUGEES

For the restorative justice and refugee steps, the Caretaker Government will establish a Refugee and Restitution Ministry (RRM) in week 1. The ministry will:

- In week 1, take control of all property currently under the control of the Israeli Custodian of Absentee Property and begin developing a menu of policy proposals for reparations and compensation.
- In month 9, roll out mechanisms for the return of movable property.
- In month 10, roll out mechanisms for the reclamation of unused immovable property.
- No later than month 6, publish a searchable database of all records of seized, abandoned, and other types of property transfers from Palestinians against their will or under contested circumstances.

To address the refugee problem, the RRM will:

- In week 4, permit refugees who make a credible claim of imminent risk to their lives in their current place of residence to return immediately to the Territory with a short pathway to full citizenship. Simultaneously, process applications for family unification, granting them permanent residency and a process to gain citizenship in the Territory.
- Beginning in month 6, develop and implement a program for creating connections with and gaining a comprehensive assessment of the needs of different refugee populations and begin providing certain services to them in their current locations.

- Beginning in year 2, build a menu of policy options for a post-Transition government to consider regarding the fulfillment of refugee rights, including the right of return.

DISCUSSION

Transitional justice should not be understood as a goal in and of itself but rather as a tool—or requisite element—for carrying out a societal or political transformation.[6] In other words, community approaches, design, and implementation of transitional justice should serve the political goal of reconciliation and building a durable polity in a postconflict situation.[7] "[P]ervasive structural inequality and normalized collective and political wrongdoing are tightly interconnected," Colleen Murphy argues, writing that, "dealing with the consequences of wrongdoing for victims often requires dealing with pervasive structural inequality. In addition, with the future of a community deeply ambiguous, the way that wrongs are dealt with can have broader implications for the future direction of a community."[8] More specifically, Nadim Khoury highlights how a comprehensive transitional justice process differs from previous attempts to address historical injustices and how that can help build buy-in:

> The primary appeal of applying transitional justice mechanisms to Palestine/Israel lies in their capacity to deal with historical and enduring injustices. To appreciate how this differs from the approach of the Oslo peace process, one could contrast the monetary compensation offered to the refugees at the Taba negotiations in 2001 to the reparations that transitional justice could potentially offer in the future.
>
> [. . .]
>
> The only way forward, [proponents of transitional justice] insist, is for Israel to reckon with its past through a host of transitional justice mechanisms. These include material remedies such as return, restitution, and compensation, as well as symbolic reparations like apologies. Had Israel issued an apology when it recognized the Palestine Liberation Organization (PLO), notes Meron Benvenisti, the peace process would have been placed on an entirely different footing. "A sincere Israeli apology," writes George Bisharat, "would be a milestone toward reconciliation that no Palestinian could ignore." Both recommend that Israel follow the example of other governments that have issued apologies for crimes of mass violence, such as

ethnic cleansing, internment, slavery, and apartheid. Of course, apologies can be cheap. However, if they acknowledge responsibility, expresses [*sic*] remorse, and are supported by a host of legal and material remedies, they can be meaningful and consequential.[9]

Transitional justice is generally understood to include five main elements, as described in the 2023 report of the UN special rapporteur on the promotion of truth, justice, reparation, and guarantees of nonrecurrence, Fabián Salvioli, and summarized here.

1. **Accountability:** It encompasses the pursuit of legal accountability through judicial mechanisms, focusing on the prosecution of individuals responsible for significant human rights violations. This process aims to uphold the rule of law and restore faith in the justice system by ensuring that perpetrators are held accountable.

2. **Truth:** This pillar involves establishing the truth regarding past abuses through thorough and impartial investigations. It includes the rights of victims and their families to understand the full extent of the violations against them. Truth commissions play a central role in documenting and acknowledging these abuses, facilitating a collective understanding and acknowledgment of past wrongs.

3. **Reparation:** Reparations address the harm suffered by victims, tailored to reflect the severity and nature of the violations. This component is multifaceted, including restitution, compensation, rehabilitation, satisfaction, and guarantees of nonrepetition, aimed at restoring victims' dignity and alleviating the consequences of the abuses.

4. **Memorialization:** Recognizing the importance of memory, this aspect focuses on preserving and honoring the memory of the violations and their victims. It involves creating memorials, renaming public spaces, and incorporating the history of these violations into educational curricula to ensure that the abuses are not forgotten and to educate future generations.

5. **Institutional Reforms and Guarantees of Nonrecurrence:** This preventive measure involves reforming institutions, laws, and practices to prevent future abuses. It includes ensuring effective civilian control of the military and security forces, protecting human rights, and fostering a culture of respect for the rule of law.[10]

All of these elements are necessary for a successful transition from apartheid and occupation rule. The Blueprint addresses only urgent matters of transitional justice while building a foundation for future remedies according to these priorities: halt present (at the time of implementation) and future injustices and harms; create conditions for success and do the groundwork for a more comprehensive transitional justice program to be undertaken by a post-Transition government, including the recognition and realization of refugee rights; and where there are remedies (primarily restitution of unused property) that the framework of existing laws can undertake without creating new harms, begin the process of restitution and some other elements of restorative justice.

RESTORATIVE JUSTICE AND REPARATIONS

While the conflict of many decades between Israelis and Palestinians is very much a national conflict, it is also a conflict over land and control over that land. Even a casual observer of the conflict likely understands the central role of land in attempts to resolve the conflict. The paradigm of a two-state solution—a process most famously attempted in the various undertakings of the Oslo era—primarily addressed the drawing of new borders, commonly discussed in the framework of the 1949 Armistice Lines, or Green Line. This type of land dispute is not relevant for the Blueprint because the delineation of boundaries separating different parts of the Territory will become much less impactful on citizens in their day-to-day lives.

What the Blueprint does partially address is private property that Israeli authorities seized, classified as abandoned, or otherwise made unusable to its rightful owners. This includes: land owned by individuals or communal entities; movable property like books and other tangible property, including money; and nontangible property like businesses and intellectual property. In many cases where Israel seized or took ownership of Palestinian property, it made the property available to, gave it to, or sold it to Jewish citizens or Jewish-controlled entities. The Blueprint does not address restitution in cases where Jewish citizens and others remain in or have gained legal ownership over such property because immediate and full restitution would create new harms and grievances and should instead be a part of a post-Transition, democratic process for restitution.

Where the Blueprint does offer immediate, prescriptive steps is for the relatively smaller fraction of seized Palestinian properties that are not currently occupied or where restitution can be carried out without creating new or additional harms and grievances. In these cases, such as empty land and homes and immovable property that can be returned, the Caretaker Government should not wait for a fully sovereign transitional justice program and should take steps toward full restitution.

What to Do

ESTABLISH A REFUGEE AND RESTITUTION MINISTRY

In week 1, the Caretaker Government shall create the RRM, which will be responsible for matters of property restitution and refugees. Upon the creation of the ministry, the Caretaker Government will transfer all property and assets currently under the control of the Israeli Custodian of Absentee Property. Additionally, the RRM will provide need-based humanitarian and diplomatic support for internally displaced Palestinians and refugees, wherever they may be in the world. The RRM will permit Palestinian refugees who present credible claims of imminent danger to their lives in their current place of residence to return immediately to the Territory and obtain citizenship.

FACILITATE THE RETURN OF MOVABLE PROPERTY

The Refugee and Restitution Ministry will compile and publish a list of movable property and funds it confiscates from the Custodian of Absentee Property, along with any information it holds about the original owners of each item. Simultaneously, it shall form a team of archivists, historians, lawyers, and investigators to proactively identify and contact owners or legal heirs of all absentee property in its custody.

For property and assets transferred from the Custodian of Absentee Property that are not currently in the possession or ownership of other individuals or private entities, the RRM will restore full property rights to the rightful owners if there is no contested ownership. In cases where rightful ownership is unclear or contested, the ministry shall refer the matter to probate courts.

PREPARE POLICY OPTIONS FOR RESTITUTION, COMPENSATION
FOR IMMOVABLE PROPERTY

The RRM will develop a menu of policy options for the restitution and compensation of immovable property that Israel has appropriated from Palestinian refugees since May 14, 1948. The ministry will compile and make publicly accessible all land records, surveys, and any other documentation that can be used to make a claim for restitution. It shall develop an accessible way for refugees and their heirs to file claims for lost or stolen property, and it shall securely store those claims such that a future government—or governments—can implement a chosen policy or refer them to relevant legal or judicial bodies. For this, the RRM should model the claims mechanism upon the methodology and practices developed over the years by the Conference on Jewish Material Claims Against Germany (the Claims Conference).[11]

PRISONERS

Political prisoners hold an important place in Palestinian society and the Palestinian national struggle as it has been defined for decades.[12] The Caretaker Government will need to remedy the issue of prisoners if there is any chance of attaining adequate Palestinian buy-in for the Blueprint to succeed. Nearly every Palestinian family has been affected by Israeli carceral policies. Since 1967, Israel has incarcerated nearly one million Palestinians, including roughly one hundred thousand during the First Intifada and seventy thousand in the Second Intifada.[13] As of May 2024, Israel was holding 865 Palestinians from Gaza as "unlawful combatants," in addition to 3,424 Palestinians from the West Bank under administrative detention.[14]

The penal system that has produced the arbitrary incarceration of hundreds of thousands of Palestinians is part and parcel of Israeli apartheid and occupation.[15] There is little to no justice to be found in military courts, where judges and prosecutors literally wear the same uniform and conviction rates are 96 percent.[16] Additionally, Israeli prisons and detention centers are epicenters of abuse, where conditions have particularly worsened since the election of the extremist government in 2023 and the war in Gaza, including grave violations of human rights such as torture.[17]

"While a Palestinian may actually threaten safety and public order in the occupied territory, Israel's all-encompassing criminalization shows that the military legislation, rather than safeguarding security, renders every single Palestinian potentially subject to imprisonment for ordinary acts of life," wrote Francesca Albanese, the UN special rapporteur on the situation of human rights in the Palestinian territories occupied since 1967, in her report to the 53rd session of the Human Rights Council.[18] Combined with the fact that most Israeli arrests of Palestinians in the Occupied Palestinian Territory (OPT) are related in some way or another to resisting the occupation and Israeli apartheid regimes, including non-violent resistance, it should be no surprise that most Palestinians consider "political prisoners" what Israel calls "security prisoners."[19]

There are also legitimate objections to releasing all perceived political prisoners, particularly those who were convicted of crimes involving violence directed at civilians. Doing so could undermine Jewish support for the Transition if safeguards aren't implemented to ensure that released prisoners do not contribute to the resumption of violence. After the completion of the Transition, a democratically elected, representative body should produce a comprehensive prisoner release scheme.

What to Do

Despite the limitations discussed above, there are actions the Caretaker Government can take. This includes releasing the following categories of prisoners and detainees, regardless of national identity, in week 6:

- administrative detainees, defined as persons detained by Israeli courts under the Emergency Powers and Counterterrorism Laws;
- prisoners convicted of crimes under laws that the Caretaker Government has revoked, that is, membership in or support of a banned movement, party, or organization; crimes relating to the permit regime or based on one's presence in a geographic area; crimes relating to being a resident or citizen of, being in contact with a resident or citizen of, or visiting or being in, a previously designated enemy state or enemy territory;
- prisoners convicted of patently political and nonviolent crimes, such as incitement, organizing or participating in a protest (including ancillary or stand-in charges like obstructing a police officer or soldier, insulting a

public servant, throwing stones, etc.), and any charge related to speech or publications in online, broadcast, print, or social media; and

- prisoners who have yet to be convicted of a crime (to be granted conditional release pending conviction).

The Justice Ministry shall also appoint a Transitional Justice Committee in week 1 to weigh and recommend the release of Palestinian and Israeli "security prisoners" who have been convicted of crimes involving violent acts. This can be addressed in several ways. In Northern Ireland, for example, the government gave conditional release to prisoners convicted of violent acts if they were members of groups that had accepted a ceasefire and committed to disarm.[20] This could include supervised release to ensure they do not return to violence of a criminal or political nature. In South Africa, the release of political prisoners took place in a combination of processes from negotiations, unilateral releases meant as goodwill measures, and formal reviews, including by truth and reconciliation commissions.[21] In Chile, political prisoners were addressed primarily through truth and reconciliation processes.[22]

In week 20, the Caretaker Government shall also appoint an independent panel of prosecutors and defense attorneys to review all convictions of civilians (individuals who are not members of the military) in military court. The panel shall, within one year, identify cases where the sources and reliability of the evidence on which the conviction was based would be insufficient or unpersuasive under the procedures and rules of the new civilian justice system. The Justice Ministry shall appoint a special judge to vacate these convictions. In cases where the panel believes there was enough evidence to obtain a conviction, they shall recommend that the State Prosecutor's Office seek a retrial in civilian court. If the prosecutor does not bring new charges within two years of such a recommendation, the Justice Ministry shall release the prisoner unconditionally.

REFUGEES

The right of displaced persons to return to their homes, whether they fled voluntarily or were forced to flee, is a tenet of international customary law.[23] The right of Palestinians to return to the homes from which they fled and were driven in the 1948 and 1967 wars is also anchored in numerous UN Security Council and General Assembly resolutions, most prominently in UNSC Resolution 242 and UNGA Resolution 194.[24] Furthermore, it is one of the so-called core issues that remained unresolved in previous peacemaking attempts and negotiations; Israel would not agree to let any more than a few thousand refugees return, and the Palestinian leadership never had a public mandate to make such large concessions on behalf of refugees.[25]

According to international refugee law, there are three types of resolutions that any refugee should have the option to choose: voluntary repatriation (return), local integration, and resettlement in a third state.[26] Regardless of which of those processes are available to refugees and chosen, refugees require strong economic, social, educational, and other rehabilitative services and support to succeed in starting their new lives. This is even more true when, by virtue of the time passed, refugees' homes, jobs, property, and communities are mostly irrecoverable, as is the case for Palestinian refugees—the lives they left behind simply don't exist. Most Palestinian refugees have never stepped foot in Israel-Palestine.[27]

Palestinian refugees should have the option to choose return, integration, or resettlement. The availability of these options, therefore, will require serious long-term engagement during and after the Transition, but the process will be finalized by the successor(s) to the Caretaker Government, the international community, and the United Nations to ensure that Palestinians are making a meaningful choice. Active engagement from member states to allow Palestinians to integrate locally or resettle elsewhere will also help ensure that the process does not stall out due to changing political winds, violence by spoilers (including among refugees themselves), or other unexpected events.

Avoiding addressing the process and timing for the return of refugees during the Transition will also allow the Caretaker Government to avoid a disorderly inflow of large numbers of refugees during a frail and sensitive moment. While a post-Transition sovereign government or governments will have the authority to determine how and when refugees return, international and civil society organizations with vast experience in resettling and returning refugees in other contexts can assist in the process; this includes organizations that helped resettle and integrate Jews who fled the former USSR and that helped international organizations with experience to create and implement other comprehensive plans of action for refugee return.[28] Furthermore, refugees can make a more informed choice about whether to return depending on the form of government that may emerge after the Transition. These are not steps that the Caretaker Government or the Blueprint can decide—a post-Transition, democratic government or governments should determine a comprehensive resolution to the refugee problem.

The Blueprint does, however, create two pathways for refugee return to begin immediately, although through frameworks that are appropriate for a transitional period and government. The first pathway for immediate return is through a reform of the Entry Law (Appendix B), which will allow for refugees to apply for and obtain permanent residency status on the basis of family unification. This is an idea articulated by Susan Akram and Terry Rempel as part of their larger plan envisioning a temporary protection regime for Palestinian refugees.

> For refugees, family reunification would function similar to "go and see visits" sponsored by the UNHCR and other international agencies in other refugee cases. Returnees would have the opportunity not only to assess the viability of return for themselves, but also to report back to individuals, families, and communities eligible to participate in the broader return option. For Israeli Jews, controlled family reunification would address fears of mass influx and would likewise provide a testing ground for the broader return operation. Israel, moreover, already accepts the principle of family reunification.
>
> Staged return beginning with family reunification would also provide the international community and domestic authorities an opportunity to appraise pilot projects initiated during family reunification, to develop a detailed repatriation operations plan, and to secure international funding for the panoply of returnee needs, in addition to basic food and shelter, to make return sustainable.[29]

The second pathway is through the creation of a mechanism to permit immediate return for Palestinian refugees with a credible claim of imminent risk to their lives. A refugee who receives this status will be entitled to temporary protection status, which will give them all social and civil rights accorded to citizens. Within six months, they will have the option of becoming citizens with full voting rights.

What to Do

BEGIN LIMITED FAMILY REUNIFICATION RETURN

In line with the reformed Entry Law (see Appendix B and Section 3), the Caretaker Government will immediately begin processing permanent residency visa applications under the rubric of family unification. Priority will be given to Palestinian refugees with first-degree relatives currently living in the Territory. A post-Transition government will be responsible for determining the process and qualifications for converting permanent residency into citizenship, as part of a more holistic process involving the right of return and the broader resolution of the Palestinian refugee situation.

IMMEDIATE HUMANITARIAN RETURN OF REFUGEES AT RISK OF DEATH

In week 5, the RRM will permit refugees who make a credible claim of imminent risk to their lives in their current place of residence to return immediately to the Territory as citizens. Refugees will be able to file a claim with the RRM akin to humanitarian parole immigration procedures and obtain a preliminary decision for temporary protection within one month. The process of obtaining full citizenship and voting rights will take no longer than six months.

SUPPORT FOR REFUGEE POPULATIONS

Within the first six months of the Transition, the RRM will offer services and support for Palestinian refugees abroad and internally displaced persons within the Territory, similar to the types of support the Jewish Agency provided to Jews in the former Soviet Union, Ethiopia, and elsewhere—ranging from providing financial support to travel documents and helping facilitate third-country resettlement when requested.

DEVELOP POLICY OPTIONS FOR ADDRESSING REFUGEE RIGHTS
AND RETURN

In addition to the roles described above, starting in year 2, the RRM will develop practical policy options for a satisfactory resolution to the Palestinian refugee problem for consideration by a post-Transition government or governments.

ACKNOWLEDGE RIGHTS OF PALESTINIAN REFUGEES

The Caretaker Government, as part of its mandate to transform Israel-Palestine into a rights-respecting democracy, will publicly acknowledge the state's obligations vis-à-vis Palestinian refugees, including an acknowledgment of the Nakba, accepting historical responsibility for the forcible displacement of hundreds of thousands of Palestinian refugees and for preventing their return.

INDIVIDUAL ACCOUNTABILITY AND RETRIBUTIVE JUSTICE

In year 3, the Transitional Justice Committee will develop a range of policy options for individual accountability for Israeli and Palestinian officials suspected of grave violations of human rights. These could range from truth and reconciliation commissions to creating special tribunals to investigate and prosecute grave crimes committed in the apartheid era. It will be for a post-Transition sovereign government or governments, however, to decide the approach to prosecution, amnesty, truth, and reconciliation, or other pathways for retributive justice and accountability moving forward. "International legal norms affirming that atrocious crimes ought to be punished have provided a powerful antidote to impunity," but that does not mean it is always possible to create accountability on a tight schedule or before other aspects of transitional justice, wrote Diane Orentlicher, former UN independent expert on combating impunity.[30] "While there are of course times when those same norms cannot be enforced, it has seemed preferable to say 'not yet' than to reframe global norms in terms that suggest prosecuting atrocious crimes is nothing more than an option."

The necessity of individual accountability has become even more salient with the crimes committed in Israel's war in Gaza, as well as Hamas's crimes in Israel on October 7, 2023. In addition to immediately pledging to cooperate with the ongoing International Criminal Court investigation into crimes in the OPT, the Caretaker Government shall accede to the Rome Statute of the International Criminal Court. By joining the court as a state party and giving it jurisdiction over crimes committed in the entirety of the Territory—as opposed to only the OPT, as is the case today—the Caretaker Government will increase the chances of domestic accountability by effectively abrogating the exclusive jurisdiction to prosecute atrocious crimes if it, or a future state or states, fail to do so of their own accord.

Elections and the
Culmination of the
Blueprint

SUMMARY

As explained in the introduction, the Blueprint is a plan to end apartheid
and occupation rule in order to create the conditions necessary for the
people of the Territory to decide how they want to configure their state
and government, in whatever number of states the people wish to have.
The Blueprint does not take a position on whether the ideal outcome of
such a decision is to organize permanently under one state, two states, or
more, and whether more than one state is part of a binational, confederation, or other model. At its least aspirational, the Blueprint hopes to
expand the horizon of possibility for viable and just political outcomes.[1]

The Blueprint does, however, recognize the one-state apartheid reality
that is currently in place in Israel-Palestine and seeks to repair and reform
that reality into a democratic one. While the end of the Transition may
appear to effectively create a one-state solution, it is not the endpoint but
the starting point for what emerges after the Transition is complete. Such
an approach has precedent in at least one successful conflict resolution
process in Northern Ireland, which avoided determining the sovereignty
of the territory, prioritizing a process to end the conflict and create demo-

cratic processes for decision-making: "A distinguishing feature about the Northern Ireland 'deal,' as captured by the Good Friday Agreement is that it makes no final accommodation on the contested issue of the jurisdiction's ultimate sovereignty. The Agreement sets out the means to resolve the dispute rather than actually closing the issue."[2] Similarly, the culmination of the Blueprint is a national election that leads to the selection of the first democratically elected parliament and the formation of the first democratic government of the post-Transition era. This new democratic government will then have the choice to stage a referendum on dividing or reconfiguring itself into two or more states, according to policy options developed during and after the Transition.

The Blueprint recommends that the first national-level elections be held no later than three years after the Caretaker Government assumes power. Local municipal and regional council elections will precede the national elections, no later than two years after the start of the Caretaker Government.

At least for the first national elections, the Blueprint recommends an equal number of parliamentary seats for Jewish and Palestinian citizens, in addition to reserved seats for other minority groups. This does not mean that political parties need to be aligned along ethnic, religious, or national identities, either self-defined or imposed from above. What it does mean is an equal number of representatives from each national group such that neither can push through a political agenda without compromise or collaboration across those same ethnic, religious, or national delineations.

The Blueprint offers the following steps:

- The Caretaker Government shall appoint an Elections Authority in month 6.
- By the end of year 1, the Elections Authority shall begin a public education campaign about the planned local and national elections to take place at the end of the Transition.
- By the end of year 2, the Elections Authority shall hold new elections for municipal and other local and regional authorities.
- The Elections Authority will hold national elections for parliament by the end of year 3, which will be the basis of the first post-Transition government.

- At the beginning of year 3, the Governance Committee will formulate policy options for a post-Transition referendum in which the people of the Territory can choose whether to remain as one state or seek an alternative arrangement, including two or more states.
- The first post-Transition government will decide whether and when to hold such a referendum.

DISCUSSION

The Blueprint aims to be a plausible and practical plan for transforming an undemocratic one-state reality into a democratic reality. This is partly to demonstrate that such a transformation is possible and also to identify the order in which such a transformation must take place: first, resolving the problems of apartheid and occupation, and then, only after that, determining the ultimate political formulation for governance. We strongly believe that any just and lasting resolution to this conflict must have democratic legitimacy to have a chance of success.

Thus far we have described the scope and mechanisms necessary for dismantling the structural and legal elements underpinning apartheid and occupation. Those steps must be treated with urgency because they aim to end daily human rights abuses for millions of people quickly but also because a meaningful political process is predicated on a fundamentally more level and more democratic playing field. Once those steps are complete, however, elections must be held. Elections are not the first or most urgent step in a democratic transition, but treating them without urgency would be a mistake. Elections, after all, signify the return of sovereignty to the people of the Territory after the dismantlement of an undemocratic apartheid and occupation regime as well as an unavoidably undemocratic transitional government.

While the end of the Transition culminates in elections for a single government, it is not the endpoint but the starting point for democratic decision-making about governance. The culmination of the Blueprint is a national election for a democratically elected parliament and government that will then have the choice to stage a referendum on dividing or reconfiguring itself into two or more states, according to policy options developed by the Referendum Committee during the Transition, as modified by the new government.

Consociationalism: A Temporary Necessity

One of the biggest challenges of democratic elections as a final stage of the democratic transition will be the risk of bad actors subverting that process to create—or recreate—an oppressive or supremacist majoritarian regime. This is even more concerning when considering that the Blueprint does not attempt to resolve many of the deep-seated power imbalances and injustices prevalent in the Territory—particularly those regarding control over capital, land, natural resources, and the return of refugees.

If a post-Transition government is to succeed in addressing these broader issues, it must have built-in safeguards to assuage fears that it cannot be hijacked by any one group or coalition of groups in ways that harm others or recreate a system of supremacy and domination. To mitigate mistrust, the Blueprint proposes carefully and securely balancing political power, at least until the people are given a democratic choice to determine their political future or futures in a referendum.

The least fraught way of mediating such fears and concerns is through parliamentary consociationalism, which entails mandating certain representational quotas for Palestinian and Jewish citizens, as well as other minority group communities, regardless of demographic changes or actual voter turnout or suppression. Consociationalism is, in its simplest form, a power-sharing arrangement among different groups designed to protect against majoritarianism and to mitigate mistrust.

This is a particularly attractive option considering there is currently near-parity in population size between Jewish and Palestinian residents of the Territory. As of May 9, 2024, the Israeli population—including settlers in the Occupied Palestinian Territory (OPT)—comprised 7.4 million Jews, 2.1 million Arabs, and 564,000 "others."[3] In 2023, the latest year for which data was available, the Palestinian population in the West Bank comprised 3.3 million people and 2.2 million people in the Gaza Strip.[4] Taken together, this means there are roughly 7.6 million Palestinians and 7.4 million Jews living between the Mediterranean Sea and the Jordan

River. However, the Blueprint requires balanced parliamentary quotas regardless of future demographic changes that could make one group a majority in the years leading up to the Transition. Ensuring relative parity in democratic representation in the first election would avoid a skewed outcome, or one that is particularly different from the demographic reality, while allowing Palestinians and Israelis to feel secure in their equal powers in the newly formed government at a sensitive and volatile transitional moment. In other words, the political representation in the first elected government would closely resemble the demographics of the Territory regardless of the electoral outcome. The first—or any—post-Transition government can of course choose to replace consociationalism with a different electoral model.

Political Parties

Consociation does not mean that all Palestinians would have to vote for a Palestinian party or that all Jews would have to vote for a Jewish party; it may well be that Palestinians and Jews who share progressive values are part of a "Socialist" party and those who share conservative or even religious values are part of a "Conservative" party. It does mean that votes are weighted in a way that voter suppression or even voter boycotts do not result in one group controlling the government. The Elections Authority must take meaningful steps, ideally before the first local elections, to encourage the formation of political parties and movements that appeal to and that can cut across ethnic, religious, and national divides. This can take many different forms—regional representation quotas, the formation of parties organized around ideas of economic worldview, organized labor, progressive and conservative values, requiring gender parity among representatives, and more. However, in accordance with the standards set by the Venice Commission, the Blueprint does not ban political parties from forming along religious, ethnic, or national lines.[5]

Democratic Education and Participation

There is no correct model for holding or designing elections; nor is there a single best or most appropriate form of organizing a representative democracy. However, several preparatory steps will increase the success of transitioning to any democratic system.

The Elections Authority must first educate the public about how the election process is intended to work and what they can expect from it. Setting realistic expectations can help mitigate potential spoilers to the process. The more people know the changes that the electoral process and democratic transition are designed to produce, and just as importantly what they will not produce, the less disappointed they are likely to be by the outcomes.

The Caretaker Government and any political parties contending in the first elections should expend great efforts to explain that while elections do mark the end of the transition to a democratic regime, the work of building a democracy, not to mention resolving the conflict and addressing both historical and even some ongoing injustices, are things that future elected governments will need to address. It will be tempting for many people to expect that equalizing, or even attempting to equalize political power, will somehow address economic power imbalances and the control of other resources. That is a dangerous expectation.

Second, the Elections Authority will need to clearly explain the rules defining and delineating legitimacy to participate in the elections for a new democratic parliament, as defined in the Basic Principles. These principles are not a constitution, but until the newly elected democratic government creates a constitution, the Basic Principles shall remain in force even after the Transition is complete. This ensures continuity and stability even if the new government is unable to write or ratify a constitution.

The Blueprint proposes a widely inclusive and clearly defined process for eligibility to stand in elections, with narrow grounds for exclusion. While it may be tempting to broadly exclude persons or parties who have participated in, supported, or been convicted of political violence prior to the Transition, we believe that in the context of nearly a hundred years of protracted conflict, that would be too exclusionary. The Elections Authority will require candidates and parties to commit to the following, which are based on the Venice Commission's "Guidelines on Prohibition and Dissolution of Political Parties":

- commitment to nonviolence;
- declared support for democratic transition and a rejection of apartheid and occupation; and
- a commitment to disarm or integrate any militant groups with which they may be associated.[6]

The Elections Authority can prohibit or dissolve political parties or individual candidates only as permitted by international human rights law, "if it is necessary in a democratic society and if there is concrete evidence that a party is engaged in activities threatening democracy and fundamental freedoms."[7] This could include any party that advocates violence as part of its political program or any party aiming to overthrow the existing order through armed struggle, terrorism, or the organization of any subversive activity. Any disqualification can be appealed to the High Court for the Transition.

The Elections Authority will also need to actively monitor spoilers and potential spoilers during this final and critical step of the Transition. A relatively successful example of such an effort was the Goldstone Commission in South Africa in the lead-up to the country's first democratic elections.[8] The commission spent considerable effort ensuring that elements of the South African security forces did not use violence or other means to disrupt the landmark elections that ended apartheid and heralded a new democratic era. The Elections Authority shall, six months prior to each round of scheduled elections, appoint an independent, representative, and well-resourced Election Monitoring Commission to identify and address any credible threats.

The Day After National Elections

The recent experiences of democracies far more mature than this Transition demonstrate that the days and weeks after elections are no less important or fraught than the period that precedes them. These dangers can take the shape of the January 6 attack on the US Capitol in 2021, attempts to stage a military coup after an election loss like that which took place in Brazil in 2022, or results simply being discarded or rejected as we've seen in countless other countries. There are also far more banal threats to a democratic transition than violence or subversion. Uncertainty, and even more so, deadlock, can render any democracy or democratic elections moot if they don't produce a functioning, democratic government. Accordingly, the Blueprint proposes the following timeline for forming the new, democratic government:

- To ensure that the national elections translate into a functioning democratic system, the new parliament should be sworn in within fifteen days of the Elections Authority certifying the results of the elections.

- The parliament will then have sixty days from that point to form a government. We recommend that the formation of any government require both the support of a simple, numeric majority of the new parliament and also that it receive a majority of both Jewish- and Palestinian-identifying parliamentarians, as defined in the arrangements for consociational electoral structure.

- The Caretaker Government shall remain in place until a democratically elected government is formed, representing the end of the Transition.

While there can and should be no requirement for outside intervention or participation in democratic governance beyond this point, the Caretaker Government's Governance Committee shall prepare a menu of options for ongoing outside assistance after the formation of the new government. The United Nations Department of Peace Operations, in addition to any invited third-country experts, shall commit to seconding technical and political experts, including senior civil servants, to the new government for a period of up to ten years. This is, of course, at the discretion and invitation of the new democratic government although such advisory roles should be well defined in UN resolutions giving such a mission its mandate.

Referendum

Beyond ending apartheid and occupation, the primary goal of the Blueprint is to foster a political reality in which all peoples of the territory can democratically determine their political future as one, two, or more states, with the option of a referendum should they choose to hold one. Mandating a referendum as an externally imposed requirement of the

Blueprint would undermine what should be a sovereign, democratic imperative of defining the future political and geographic configuration of a Territory in one, two, or more states that is currently home to at least two groups who believe it to be their homeland.

Though it does not require it, the Blueprint does encourage the new national government to hold a referendum, rooted in democratic principles that say political decisions of that magnitude must be decided by the people, as well as the belief that such a referendum can enhance the legitimacy of the new state or states that emerge.

At the beginning of year 3, the Governance Committee will formulate policy options for a post-Transition referendum in which the people of the Territory can choose whether to remain as one state or seek an alternative arrangement, including two or more states.

In any such referendum, we strongly recommend that the new government give Palestinian refugees who have not been given citizenship or voting rights in the Transition meaningful pathways to participate in and influence the design of the referendum. Refugees are undeniably primary stakeholders in any attempt to resolve questions of governance and citizenship more broadly and to define their relationship with the state following the Transition.

Acknowledgments

This book was never supposed to be a book. It began as a project of our organization, DAWN, to simply demonstrate that it is indeed possible to develop a plan to dismantle apartheid and occupation and build a rights-respecting state in Israel-Palestine. It was only after a full year of research and reading and writing and speaking with the smartest and broadest range of people we could reach that University of California Law San Francisco professor George Bisharat insisted it should be published as a book and introduced us to our future editor at the University of California Press. We jumped at the opportunity, not only because we relished the chance to reach—and hopefully impact—more people than we ever could with a mere NGO-issued report or position paper, but also because by that point we understood the depth and breadth of work that this proposition deserved.

Our journey of starting to understand the contours of and formulating an approach to the question of how to practically end apartheid and occupation began with a whirlwind circuit of meetings, conversations, and consultations with old friends, professional interlocutors, and new acquaintances in Ramallah, Jerusalem, Tel Aviv, and Haifa, in addition to those who generously accepted our calls on Zoom from Gaza, London, Paris, New York, Cambridge, Barcelona, and many other cities around the world. Among those who patiently helped us work out the early contours and limitations of our endeavor and who were beyond generous with their time, helping us plot our way through this project were: Omar Dajani, Yael Berda, Ubai Aboudi, Smadar Ben Natan, Fady Khoury, Orly Noy,

Ash Bâli, and Nathan Thrall. Among the many others who provided critical feedback and input along the way were, in no particular order: Noura Erekat, Jeff Halper, Awad Abedelfattah, Shawan Jabarin, Dahlia Scheindlin, Munir Nuseibah, Zaha Hassan, Michael Sfard, Amjad Iraqi, Omar Rahman, Daniel Levy, Mouin Rabbani, Hagit Ofran, Omar Barghouti, Noam Sheizaf, Wesam Ahmed, May Pundak, Hassan Jabarin, Hagai El-Ad, Alon Liel, Jamal Benomar, Alma Biblash, Yousef Munayyer, Rania Muhareb, Hugh Lovatt, Diana Buttu, Meron Rapoport, Yousef Jabareen, Mairav Zonszein, Omar Shakir, Haggai Matar, Tahani Mustafa, Shibley Telhami, Michael Lynk, Francesca Albanese, Sahar Aziz, Khaled Elgindy, Tareq Baconi, and Jamil Dakwar. Our apologies to all the many people whose names we invariably forgot to include but whose wisdom, expertise, knowledge, and discussions made it into this book in various ways. (Those listed above did not necessarily review the plan as it is written and none should be presumed to endorse it.) Helping guide us throughout the process were our DAWN colleagues, most of all Adam Shapiro, Raed Jarrar, and our research assistant and intern, Joseph Frankel, as well as John Hursh. Frederick Deknatel was kind enough to loan us his editing prowess as we approached various deadlines. And, of course, thank you to our editors at UC Press, Maura Roessner and Sam Warren, who "got it" from day one and helped us navigate through the haters and doubters. A special thanks for the time and attention of our project manager Julie Van Pelt and copyeditor Leah Caldwell and indexer Thomas Vecchio.

None of this would have been possible without DAWN, the organization that brought us together as authors and paid our salaries from start to finish of this project. We are eternally grateful for the inspiration to imagine a democratic future, not only in Israel-Palestine but across the Middle East, which we and our organization inherited from its founder, Jamal Khashoggi, who was brutally murdered by those desperate to stamp out such dreams—and all those working to realize them. This project would never have come to fruition without the generous support of the Open Society Institute, the Tawakkol Karman Foundation, the Foundation for Systemic Change, ARCA Foundation, and a small number of extremely generous individual donors, including Hassan Elmasry and Rasha Mansouri Elmasry.

From Michael Schaeffer Omer-Man: Thank you to my children, who, as promised, will receive signed copies. Thank you to the entire *+972 Magazine* team and community for helping me grow as a human, a writer, an editor, a thinker, and a dissident over the years. To my mother, a child Holocaust survivor who gave me my moral compass and modeled how to be a decent human in this corrupt and often dark world—none of this happens without you. To my late father, you taught me how to be an intellectual without falling out of—or into—an ivory tower, helped me become the writer I am, and modeled a steadiness that has helped me avoid capsizing in the most turbulent of proverbial seas. To my siblings, you always help me keep things in perspective. And last but not least, to my wife and partner in crime, Emily, thank you for your constant love and support and understanding and encouragement, for always believing in me, for giving me unfettered access to your encyclopedic knowledge of international humanitarian law and the inner trappings of occupation, and most of all for your patience as I disappeared to write and edit at ungodly hours of the night. I dedicate this book to the children of Gaza; I have no words left.

From Sarah Leah Whitson: This book is the product of the people whose ideas, knowledge, experiences, passion, compassion, and inspiration I have been fortunate enough to be exposed to in my work over the last thirty years in pursuit of human rights, freedom, and justice in the Middle East, including Israel-Palestine. I learned a tremendous deal from my colleagues at Human Rights Watch, especially Joe Stork (who sadly passed away before this was published), Eric Goldstein, Sari Bashi, Omar Shakir, William Van Esveld, and Kenneth Roth. For their intellectual sharpness, moral clarity, and decades of friendship, whose thoughts and feelings have formed my own, I owe a great debt to Roger Normand, Dr. Ghassan Abu-Sitta, Prof. Dana Sajdi, and Selma Dabbagh. For modeling courage and fortitude against the odds, I thank my mother, an Armenian refugee from Jerusalem who wound up in Los Angeles but always grounded me in my roots. For his rock-solid love, kindness, and patience, I thank my husband, Josh Zinner. I would be remiss in failing to express my gratitude to my children—Lena, Tobias, and Julian Zinner—for tolerating my demanding work and travel schedule all these years and encouraging and supporting me despite it. I thank my co-author Michael Schaeffer Omer-Man for making our collaboration and endless discussions, editing, and rewriting so seamless, productive, and personally rewarding. This book is dedicated to every mother and father in Israel-Palestine whose face I have seen etched in pain. A vision of hope is the only thing I seek to offer.

APPENDIX A **Guiding Principles for the Transition**

The following are descriptions of the new set of Basic Laws and guiding principles that shall guide the Caretaker Government during the Transition. All laws not revoked shall remain in place. Further descriptions of each step can be found in the relevant sections of the Blueprint.

BASIC LAW: THE TRANSITION

The law gives a mandate to the Caretaker Government to govern the Territory for three years until it is replaced by a democratically elected government, to legislate according to procedures described in Section 1. The law revokes racist and discriminatory laws (including Basic Law: The Jewish Nation-States), ends the military occupation, revokes all emergency regulations, extends existing criminal law to all persons in the Territory, retains current civil and family law in different regions of the Territory, formally dissolves the Palestinian Authority, empowers the special envoy, formally revokes all terrorist designations, authorizes the consolidation of the Palestinian and Israeli population registries, reorganizes and consolidates security forces (Section 7), imposes a temporary freeze on property sales, imposes a temporary freeze on permanent immigration (Section 3), temporarily renames the state to "Israel-Palestine," acknowledges the rights of Palestinian refugees and a responsibility for the Nakba, creates a Refugee and Restitution Ministry and transfers to it all property held by the

Custodian of Absentee Property, authorizes the Justice Ministry to release all administrative detainees and some political prisoners (Section 8), establishes a set of committees and commissions (Appendix E), and defines the temporary consociational system of governance and elections (Section 9). The law shall also instruct the Caretaker Government and the judiciary to treat the Universal Declaration of Human Rights as a secondary source of interpretation and guidance when the law is unclear or when apartheid-era laws are in violation of these principles.[1] The law also makes the legislative changes described in Section 5, including all Basic Laws not explicitly retained or modified in Appendix A of the Guiding Principles.

BASIC LAW: EQUALITY (NEW)

The law establishes full equality for all citizens and individuals within the Territory as a foundational tenet, guaranteeing equal rights and protections under the law. It mandates nondiscrimination on any grounds such as race, gender, religion, nationality, or ethnic origin.

BASIC LAW: FREEDOM OF MOVEMENT (NEW—SEE SECTION 3)

Establishes freedom of movement as a fundamental right, including the right to travel anywhere within the Territory without any categorical restrictions based on ethnic, religious, national identity, or political affiliation. The law permits the operation of internal checkpoints for contraband and weapons screening, but checkpoints may only be operated by civilian police and must be approved and regularly reviewed by the Free Movement Commission, which will exercise strict oversight. The law will guarantee the right of all citizens to enter and exit the country, and it will create temporary visa rules and regulations as described in Section 3.

BASIC LAW: CITIZENSHIP (NEW)

The law defines citizenship and voting rights as essential components of a democratic transition in the Territory. The law mandates the automatic conferment of citizenship to all adults who appear in the updated, consolidated population registry, as defined in Section 6. The law grants irrevocable voting rights to all adult citizens, recognizing their legal and political belonging and providing them with critical protections and privileges. It declares that all citizens are members of the state, and that the state belongs to its citizens. This move is part of a broader effort to dismantle the apartheid and occupation regimes, although it acknowledges that this alone does not resolve all issues of citizenship, especially concerning Palestinian refugees outside the Territory.

BASIC LAW: FREEDOM OF EXPRESSION AND ASSEMBLY

The law guarantees freedom of expression and assembly based on the Organization for Security and Co-operation in Europe's *Guidelines on Freedom of Peaceful Assembly.*[2]

BASIC LAW: PRESUMPTION OF INNOCENCE, RIGHT TO DUE PROCESS

Establishes the presumption of innocence and guarantees rights of due process and habeas corpus in accordance with Article 48 of the EU Charter of Fundamental Rights and the United Nations Basic Principles and Guidelines on Remedies and Procedures on the Right of Anyone Deprived of Their Liberty to Bring Proceedings Before a Court.[3]

BASIC LAW: ABSOLUTE BAN ON TORTURE

Codifies an absolute ban on torture, drawing directly from Article 5 of the Universal Declaration of Human Rights: "No one shall be subjected to torture or to cruel, inhuman or degrading treatment or punishment."[4] Additionally, it shall mandate that the prohibition be included in the new consolidated criminal code.

BASIC LAW: THE STATE ECONOMY (MODIFIED—SEE SECTION 2)

The law outlines the methods for levying taxes and fees and provides rules for handling transactions involving state property.[5] It also sets guidelines for creating the state budget, includes related legislative measures, and covers the production of legal tender, including currency notes and coins. Modifications to extend taxation to all residents of the Territory and to guarantee funding to all municipalities and local government bodies in accordance with Section 2.[6]

BASIC LAW: THE JUDICIARY (MODIFIED — SEE SECTION 4)

The law sets the courts' authority in criminal and disciplinary cases, ensures judicial independence, and mandates transparency in judicial processes.[7] Modified to create a new High Court for the Transition, delineate the geographic and subject-matter jurisdictions of the different court systems in the Territory, consolidate criminal courts, create a unified Courts Authority to organize and supervise courts across the Territory, and enshrine judicial lustration and education programs, in accordance with Section 4.[8]

BASIC LAW: THE STATE COMPTROLLER (RETAINED)

The law defines the powers, responsibilities, and duties of the state comptroller,[9] who also serves as ombudsman.[10]

BASIC LAW: HUMAN DIGNITY AND LIBERTY (RETAINED, MINOR MODIFICATION)

The law establishes that the basic human rights in Israel stem from acknowledging the intrinsic value of individuals, the sanctity of life, and personal freedom.[11] Its aim is to safeguard human dignity and liberty. Human freedom includes the right to enter and exit the country, privacy, intimacy, and protection against searches of private property, body, and possessions, as well as safeguarding the confidentiality of one's communications and documents. Any infringement on human dignity or freedom can only occur as allowed by law.[12] Explicitly defines the Universal Declaration of Human Rights as a primary source of interpretation, alongside the Guiding Principles of the Transition.[13]

Two clauses shall be modified: in section 1, the clause "the principles included in the Declaration of the Establishment of the State of Israel" shall be removed. In section 1(a), the clause "in order to embed the values of the State of Israel as a Jewish and democratic state, in a basic law" shall be removed.

BASIC LAW: FREEDOM OF OCCUPATION (RETAINED)

The law ensures the right of every citizen to engage in any occupation, profession, or trade and is designed to protect economic freedom.

APPENDIX B Laws That Should Be
Immediately Revoked or
Amended

LAWS TO FULLY REVOKE

Trading with the Enemy Act, 1939

Recommendation: Immediately revoke

Explanation: The Trading with the Enemy Act is a piece of legacy legislation from the British Mandate government in 1939, which the Israeli Knesset subsequently legislated and amended several times. The law, as its name suggests, criminalizes trade, commerce, and other interactions between Israeli citizens and citizens or corporations of an "enemy country." At the time of writing, those enemy countries include Iran, Iraq, Syria, and Lebanon, although it is at the discretion of the Israeli finance minister to add countries to that list.

The law, which could at first glance be considered a security measure, has been used over the years to forbid contact between Palestinian citizens of Israel and much of the Arab world, including a significant portion of Palestinian refugees. Over one million Palestinians reside in Lebanon and Syria as refugees. Tens of thousands more lived in Iraq prior to 2003. Prior to Israel's occupation of the West Bank and Gaza Strip in 1967, Israel considered those territories enemy states, and prior to signing the 1994 peace treaty, Israel also considered the Hashemite Kingdom of Jordan, with its millions of Palestinian citizens and residents, an enemy state with which trade and most contacts were forbidden.

Because the only states defined as enemies are Arab and Muslim, and considering that the vast majority of Palestinians are Arab and Muslim, the law primarily affects the latter's ability to maintain cultural, linguistic, and economic ties with their Arab and Muslim brethren. It has restricted Palestinian citizens' ability to maintain cultural, communal, religious, and economic ties that were cut with the imposition of hard borders in 1948 and with Israel's ongoing policy preventing the return of Palestinian refugees. Israeli authorities have used the law to stop the trade of books, to prevent travel to neighboring states, and in other ways that almost exclusively affect its non-Jewish citizens.

Absentee Property Law, 1950

Recommendation: Revoke the legislation, transfer all "absentee property" still under the control of the Custodian of Absentee Property to the new Refugee and Restitution Ministry.

Explanation: Israeli legislators passed the Absentee Property Law in 1950 with the express purpose of taking ownership of property owned by Palestinians who were forced from their homes or otherwise fled during the 1948 war, including internally displaced persons. It is estimated that the Custodian of Absentee Property, established by the law to administer confiscated lands, took possession of some two million dunams of Palestinian-owned land in the years following 1948, which would amount to roughly 10 percent of the entire country. In an interview with journalist Robert Fisk, one former Custodian of Absentee Property estimated that in 1980, 70 percent of privately owned plots of land in Israel may have an "absentee" Palestinian owner.

The Custodian of Absentee Property transferred the vast majority of seized Palestinian property to the Israeli Development Authority and the Jewish National Fund, both of which have explicit mandates to maintain Jewish ownership over that land and to use it for strengthening Jewish settlement on it. Furthermore, Israel designed and amended the law in ways to ensure it did not requisition Jewish-owned "absentee" properties, thus making it inherently discriminatory. Considering the centrality of land control for Israeli apartheid and the success of its settler-colonial project, the Caretaker Government should immediately dismiss and disband the Custodian of Absentee Property and transfer any remaining holdings to a neutral body appointed by the Caretaker Government until such a time as a constitution or transitional justice program decides upon a plan of action for restitution or restoration of property rights. Section 8 of the Blueprint, on restorative justice, prisoners, and refugees, discusses this idea in more detail.

The Law of Return, 1950

Recommendation: Revoke

Explanation: The Law of Return, which gives any Jew from any country the right to immigrate to and become a naturalized citizen of the State of Israel, is perhaps one of Israel's most discriminatory laws, privileging nonnative Jews for immigration while excluding exiled Palestinians native to the Territory. The law gives citizenship rights to Jews with no personal or familial connections to the Territory, but it denies Palestinian refugees, even those born and raised in the territory that became Israel, similar rights and oftentimes even the ability to visit their homeland.

Section 3 of the Blueprint, on restoring freedom of movement, addresses immigration, entry, and exit during the Transition. At the end of or following the Transition period, a permanent immigration system will need to be designed and legislated either in a constitution or by a sovereign, elected parliament.

Citizenship Law, 1952

Recommendation: Revoke

Explanation: The Citizenship Law, like the Law of Return, grants citizenship rights to any Jew who seeks to immigrate to Israel and specifically denies that right to Palestinian refugees. A 2008 amendment allows the government to revoke citizenship on the grounds of "breach of trust or disloyalty." Israel designed and implemented this amendment in a way that targets only Palestinian citizens of Israel. A 2023 amendment permits the revocation of citizenship of an individual convicted and sentenced to prison for terrorist acts and who receives support from the Palestinian Authority, effectively excluding Jewish terrorism convicts and discriminating against Palestinians.

Section 3 of the Blueprint, on restoring freedom of movement, and the New Basic Law: Citizenship address immigration, entry, and exit during the Transition. At the end of or following the Transition, a permanent immigration system will need to be designed and legislated either in a constitution or by a sovereignly elected parliament.

World Zionist Organization–Jewish Agency Law, 1952

Recommendation: Revoke

Explanation: The Jewish Agency Law gives quasi-governmental status to the World Zionist Organization and the Jewish Agency for Israel for the purposes of Jewish settlement, encouraging Jewish immigration, and the absorption of Jewish immigrants and exempting them from taxation. The law is discriminatory because it authorizes activities for the exclusive benefit of the Jewish population and encourages Jewish immigration, both of which help maintain and support the apartheid system by seeking to maintain demographic superiority and control over the land.

Jewish National Fund Law, 1953

Recommendation: Revoke

Explanation: The law authorizes the Jewish National Fund to purchase and develop land for the exclusive benefit of the Jewish people and gives the organization financial benefits in those activities. The organization should be required to re-register as a for-profit or nonprofit corporation under the existing law that applies to all other organizations and corporations.

Jewish Religious Services Law, 1971

Recommendation: Revoke

Explanation: The Jewish Religious Services Law provides funding for Jewish religious services on a local and national level, without providing for equivalent or equal services and funding for religious services for citizens of other religions. While the question of whether there should be state funding and supervision of religious services will need to be decided in a constitution or legislated by an elected, sovereign parliament, a law that explicitly discriminates against Palestinians and non-Jews cannot be allowed to remain on the books. One option for ensuring the continuous provision of services until such a replacement can be codified and enacted is to pass a temporary measure that maintains current levels of funding while guaranteeing equal funding and benefits to religious communal institutions of all religions in the Territory.

Basic Law: Jerusalem, Capital of Israel, 1980

Recommendation: Revoke

Explanation: There are several reasons to revoke the Basic Law: Jerusalem, Capital of Israel. First and foremost, the law is illegal because it amounts to the de jure annexation of occupied territory, a direct violation of the international legal prohibition on the acquisition of territory by force. Furthermore, the law places undue and discriminatory restrictions on the ability of Palestinians in East Jerusalem to govern themselves at a local level.

Temporary Order: Citizenship and Entry to Israel, 2003

Recommendation: Revoke

Explanation: The temporary order amending the Citizenship and Entry Law is commonly referred to as the Family Unification Law, or the Ban of Family Unification Law. This law is explicitly and openly discriminatory against Palestinian citizens of Israel by banning family unification for the spouse or family member of an Israeli citizen who is a resident of the Occupied Palestinian Territory (OPT) or Syria, Lebanon, Iraq, or Iran. Although the law could discriminate against Jewish Israelis in theory if they were to apply for family unification for a spouse from the abovementioned countries and territories, in practice the overwhelming majority of such applications are from Palestinian citizens.

Negev Development Authority Law, 1991

Recommendation: Revoke

Explanation: The Negev Development Authority, created by this legislation, is designed to increase Jewish control over the Negev desert region, including by encouraging and building infrastructure for new settlements and the absorption of Jewish immigrants. While the Caretaker Government may decide to maintain some of the functions of the agency, the agency itself and the legislation authorizing it are too closely associated with its role in maintaining the apartheid regime and therefore should be placed either in a new agency or another more neutral one that is capable of enacting policies for the benefit of all citizens.

Counter-Terrorism Law, 2016

Recommendation: Revoke

Explanation: Among the various attempts to integrate emergency regulations into formal law, the most significant outcome is the 2016 Counter-Terrorism Law. This law introduces new categories of crimes, suspects, and detainees distinct from regular criminal acts when committed with political or nationalistic motives. It grants the defense minister the power to declare any group as a terrorist organization with minimal transparency. The law has been used to criminalize Palestinian human rights organizations, civil society groups, and political parties, imposing harsh prison terms, severe detention conditions, and limiting due process protections. It also allows police to ban gatherings and events preemptively based on subjective judgment. Consequently, the law severely impacts civil rights and targets Palestinians disproportionately, necessitating its complete revocation.

Associations Law (Foreign Funding of NGOs Amendment, 2016)

Recommendation: Revoke

Explanation: The amendment to the Associations Law was introduced and passed with the clear and stated intention to place onerous restrictions on Israeli-registered nonprofit organizations that promote civil and human rights, Palestinian rights specifically, and which oppose Israel's occupation of the Palestinian

territories and its apartheid regime. Furthermore, the public reporting requirements are intended to give the public the impression that these organizations'
work is done at the behest of a foreign power, thus seeking to delegitimize the
public interest of and values behind said work. The law is discriminatory in that
it affects primarily organizations associated with one side of the political map but
also because those organizations tend to work on behalf of Palestinian rights,
which therefore discriminates against Palestinians.

Admissions Committees Law: Amendment to the Cooperative Societies Ordinance

Recommendation: Revoke

Explanation: The 2011 law grants so-called "admissions committees" sweeping discretion to vet applicants for housing and land in hundreds of Jewish
Israeli "community towns" built across vast areas of state land, using arbitrary
and often racist criteria tied to perceived "social suitability" to a town's "social
and cultural fabric."[1] It was enacted to bypass the Supreme Court's ruling in the
Qa'adan case, which barred Jewish towns on state land from excluding Palestinian citizens. A 2023 amendment expanded these committees' reach even
further.

Anti-Boycott Law (2011) and Boycott Entry Law (2017)

Recommendation: Revoke

Explanation: The 2011 Anti-Boycott Law, officially known as the Law for
Prevention of Damage to the State of Israel Through Boycott, establishes a civil
tort for publicly calling for a boycott against individuals or entities due to their
Israeli affiliation, whether based in Israel or settlements. A 2017 amendment to
the Entry into Israel Law permits denying entry to foreigners advocating such
boycotts. Both laws aim to penalize political stances and conscientious economic
actions, reinforcing the occupation and apartheid regimes by deterring and punishing dissent, including activities outside Israel or the OPT.

Tax Deductible Donations for "Settlement": Income Tax Code, Amendment 191, 2012

Recommendation: Revoke

Explanation: The amendment to the tax code makes donations to institutions and organizations that promote Zionist settlement tax deductible, thereby
subsidizing the effort to settle more land by Jews, a key component of the apartheid regime.

Limitations of Civil Liability for Military Acts, Amendment No. 8 to Civil Wrongs Law, 2012

Recommendation: Revoke

Explanation: The law is intended to severely limit the ability of Palestinians to seek damages or other civil remedies against the state for harm, death, and destruction caused by the military. It does so by unreasonably broadening the "act of war" exception to civil liabilities under Israeli law and by wholly indemnifying the state for any military acts in the Gaza Strip retroactive to 2005. It is particularly important to revoke the section of the amendment relating to Gaza in order to leave open the possibility for compensation as part of a future transitional justice process.

SIMPLE AMENDMENTS

Budgets Foundations Law ("Nakba Law" Amendment of 2011)

Recommendation: Remove Amendment No. 40.

Explanation: The amendment to the Budgets Foundations Law, known as the "Nakba Law," aims to prevent and penalize the teaching of Palestinian national narratives and the commemoration of the 1948 displacement of nearly eight hundred thousand Palestinians. This law enforces the Jewish-Israeli national narrative as the only permissible one in state-funded institutions, discriminating against Palestinian citizens. By banning the commemoration of the Nakba, the law further infringes on basic human rights, including free expression and assembly.

State Education Law, 1953

Recommendation: Remove sections 2(a)(1–4, 11, 13). Incorporate into section 2(a) a mandate to teach the values of equality and democracy.

Explanation: While the Caretaker Government will not attempt wholesale reforms of the education system during the Transition, education across the Territory should teach values of democracy and pluralism instead of nationalism and other political ideologies inconsistent with the Guiding Principles and spirit of the Transition.

Broadcast Authority Law, 1953

Recommendation: Remove references to programming relating to Israeli tradition, Judaism, and Zionism and requirements relating to broadcasts on those topics.

Explanation: By mandating the production and broadcast of programming that explicitly advances the national narrative, culture, and language of one group, this section discriminates against other national and religious groups. By promoting Zionism, it supports and advances the values of the apartheid regime and contradicts the values and principles of the Transition.

Interpretation Law, 1981

Recommendation: Remove Article 24.

Explanation: Article 24 makes Hebrew the official version of all legislation, thereby discriminating against the Arabic-speaking population and its ability to access and influence legislative and judicial processes. Add the Universal Declaration of Human Rights and Guiding Principles of the Transition as primary judicial and legislative interpretation sources.

Use of the Hebrew Date Law, 1998

Recommendation: Add "and Islamic" after the word "Hebrew" in the law's title, the title of subsection 2, and in the text of subsection 2. Replace "foreign" (*luazit*) with Gregorian in the title and text of subsection 3. Remove subsection 5.

Explanation: The Use of the Hebrew Date Law requires that all official publications of the state and its agencies include the Hebrew date alongside the Gregorian date, which discriminates against non-Jewish citizens. The suggested amendment requires that the Islamic date be added any place the Hebrew date is required by the law.

Political Parties Law, 1992

Recommendation: Remove "Jewish and" from section 5(1). Remove section 5(2)(a).

Explanation: Section 5(1) of the Political Parties Law prohibits the registration of a political party that rejects the existence of the State of Israel as a Jewish and democratic state. This prohibition discriminates against all political parties that support an inclusive democratic state and is contradictory to the aims and principles of the Transition. Requirements for the registration of political parties and all matters relating to elections will need to be decided and legislated either in a constitution or by a sovereign parliament, but it is important to remove discriminatory standards even in the interim in order to not negatively influence political participation during the Transition period.

Entry into Israel Law, 1952

Recommendation: Suspend all immigration for the duration of the Transition while incorporating the principles below to ensure nondiscrimination and allow for family unification.

Explanation: No person shall be excluded prima facie from eligibility for entry into or movement within the Territory as a tourist during the duration of his/her visa. Despite the suspension of immigration during the Transition, the Caretaker Government will create a family unification process that allows permanent residency—but not citizenship—for first-degree relatives of citizens of the Territory. The Caretaker Government will revoke all individual and categorical entry or exit bans. Suspicion of intention to permanently settle in the Territory shall not be sufficient reason to deny entry to an individual attempting to enter on a short-term or tourist visa. Other criteria in the law shall remain. No group shall receive special privileges regarding entry during the Transition based on ethnic, religious, or national grounds, and the border doctrine shall be driven largely by principles of nondiscrimination. All citizens or residents of the Territory shall have the irrevocable and unconditional right to exit and enter the Territory freely.

APPENDIX C   Timeline for Implementation

Day 1

- The UN General Assembly, with a mandate from the UN Security Council, shall appoint a special envoy to initiate and oversee the Transition (Section 1).

Weeks 1–3

Actions by the Special Envoy (Section 1):

- Begin hiring and assembling a staff to support the envoy during the Transition.
- Organize a Conciliation Conference composed of fifty delegates in Jerusalem.

Weeks 4–8 (Section 1)

Conciliation Conference in Jerusalem (Section 1):

- Debate and ratify the Blueprint.

- Appoint Caretaker Government and cabinet for retained ministries.
- Dissolve the Palestinian Authority—without disbanding most ministries, functions, and security forces.

STAGE TWO: THE TRANSITION

Day 1

Declarations and Fiats by the Caretaker Government:

- End military rule, rescind emergency laws, extend civilian criminal law to Palestinians (Section 2).
- Revoke the cabinet designation of Gaza as "hostile territory" and publicly declare that all "buffer zones" have been rescinded (Section 3).
- End categorical bans on movement (Sections 3 and 7).
- Declare a single national police force, which shall be called the "National Police" (Section 7).
- Revoke racist and discriminatory laws identified in Appendix B (Section 5).
- Ratify the Guiding Principles of the Transition and make the prescribed reforms, revocations, and legislation of new Basic Laws as detailed in Appendix A (Section 2).
- Suspend permanent immigration and implement new visa policies (Sections 3 and 5).
- Extend a single tax system across the Territory (Section 2).
- Forbid the application of the criteria of "eligibility for citizenship/immigration" from all laws and regulations (Section 2).
- Declare a freeze on property sales and transfers of ownership or leases longer than twenty years for the duration of the Transition (Section 5).
- Rename the transitional state as "Israel-Palestine" and suspend the official use of both Israeli and Palestinian national symbols, including the flag, the anthem, and the state seal (Section 5).
- Publicly acknowledge the state's obligations vis-à-vis Palestinian refugees, including an acknowledgment of the Nakba, accepting historical responsibility for the forcible displacement—and preventing the return—of hundreds of thousands of Palestinian refugees (Section 8).

Weeks 1–4

Caretaker Government Actions:

- Reconfigure existing ministries to consolidate some existing ministries and create new ones, including the Refugee and Restitution Ministry (Section 1).
- Establish Special Committees and Commissions (Section 1):
  - Legislative Committee (Section 5)
  - Judicial Appointments Committee (Section 4)
  - Disarmament, Demobilization, and Reintegration Committee (Section 7)
  - Domestic Security Committee (Section 7)
  - Transitional Justice Committee (Section 8)
  - Governance Committee (Section 2)
  - Military Oversight Commission (Section 7)
  - Judicial Oversight Commission (Section 4)
  - Free Movement Commission (Section 3)
- Consolidate the Israeli and Palestinian population registries (Section 2).
- Extend full citizenship to all persons who appear in the new population registry, as well as all persons who were listed in the population registry since June 6, 1967, but whose citizenship or residency the Israeli government revoked for any reason (Sections 1, 2, and 6).
- Policing and Domestic Security (Section 7):
  - Appoint a joint Jewish-Palestinian leadership of the new police force.
  - Define new limited police powers to restrict movement in accordance with the new security doctrine and Guiding Principles.
  - Deploy police at internal checkpoints to replace military and private guards.
  - Rapidly integrate all ranks of Palestinian police into the new National Police.
  - Forbid the military from operating within the Territory.
  - Change the name of the Israel Security Agency (Shin Bet) to the Domestic Intelligence Agency (DIA) and subject it to strict civilian oversight by amending the Shin Bet Law.
- With the approval of the Judiciary Committee, replace the Israeli High Court of Justice with a new High Court for the Transition (Sections 1 and 4).

- Require all members of security forces, starting with commanders and officers, to take an oath of loyalty to the rule of law and the Guiding Principles of the Transition (Section 7).
- Abolish mandatory military conscription and order the military to develop a recruitment process to diversify new enlistees to reflect the population of the Territory (Section 7).
- The new Refugee and Restitution Ministry (Section 8) will take control of all property currently under the control of the Israeli Custodian of Absentee Property and begin developing a menu of policy proposals for restitution and compensation. Permit refugees who make a credible claim of imminent risk to their lives in their current place of residence to return immediately to the Territory as citizens.

Committee Work:

- The Disarmament, Demobilization, and Reintegration (DDR) Committee will begin the disarmament of all irregular forces and several official security institutions (Section 7, Appendix D).
- The DDR Committee shall begin developing a long-term, comprehensive DDR plan together with the UN Department of Peace Operations (Section 7).

Weeks 5–15

Caretaker Government and Executive Actions:

- Release administrative detainees, prisoners convicted of crimes already revoked by the Caretaker Government, and those convicted of patently political, nonviolent crimes, including stone-throwing and all speech crimes (Section 8).
- Starting in week 12, the new Domestic Intelligence Agency will rapidly integrate all Palestinian intelligence agents, appoint a combined Jewish-Palestinian leadership for the duration of the Transition, and commence a two-year continuing education and training program, including language training, for all agents (Section 7).
- The DDR Committee shall develop and publish the criteria that will guide a lustration process for identifying, vetting, and excluding individual members of security forces by week 4 (Section 7).

Committee Work:

- The Judicial Appointments Committee will appoint a new High Court for the Transition (HCT) no later than week 6 to replace the Israeli

High Court of Justice, which is currently a part of the Israeli Supreme Court (Section 4).

- The Judiciary Committee will merge Israel's Courts Administration with the West Bank and Gaza courts administrations (Section 4).
- The Legislative Committee shall commence a comprehensive review and reform racist and discriminatory laws and regulations (Section 5).
- The Refugee and Restitution Ministry and its Transitional Justice Committee shall commence researching and formulating policy options for a comprehensive transitional justice program that a post-Transition government should consider for adoption (Section 8).

Weeks 16–21

- The Justice Ministry shall appoint an independent panel of prosecutors and defense attorneys to review all convictions of civilians (individuals who are not members of the military) in military courts. Within one year, the panel shall identify cases where the sources and reliability of the evidence on which the conviction was based would be insufficient or unpersuasive under the procedures and rules of the new civilian justice system (Section 8).
- The Refugee and Restitution Ministry will begin to offer some services and support for Palestinian refugees abroad and internally displaced persons within the Territory (Section 8).

STAGE THREE

Months 6–12

Caretaker Government and Executive Actions:

- Appoint an Elections Authority in month 6 (Section 9).
- Starting in month 6, the newly merged Courts Administration will publish official translations into Arabic, Hebrew, and English of laws, regulations, and decisions (Section 5).
- Commence a two-year education and training for officers and commanders, regardless of which agency they served in previously, designed to: align standard operating procedures, educate about relevant changes in the law, teach the Internal Security Doctrine (as described below), including a strong emphasis on community policing, and teach both Arabic and Hebrew languages (Section 7).
- The National Police and the DDR Committee shall begin implementing the DDR Committee's recommendations (Section 7).

- The Judicial Oversight Commission shall complete lustration for sitting judges by the end of year 1 (Section 4).
- Starting in month 6, the Judiciary Committee will prepare and implement a continuing education and training program for all judges (Section 4).
- The Foreign Ministry will begin seeking out regional security guarantees, and, if possible, enter into mutual defense treaties to reduce the risk of military confrontation, which the ministry will work to secure in year 1 (Section 7).
- The foreign minister shall begin the process of joining the Non-Proliferation Treaty (NPT) and working with the International Atomic Energy Agency (IAEA) to dismantle the Territory's existing nuclear weapons program and ensure any civilian nuclear program is in compliance with the NPT and IAEA standards and obligations (Section 7).
- The Refugee and Restitution Ministry shall (Section 8):
  - No later than month 6, publish a searchable database of all records of seized, abandoned, and other types of property transfers from Palestinians against their will or under contested circumstances.
  - In month 9, roll out mechanisms for the return of movable property.
  - In month 10, roll out mechanisms for the reclamation of unused immovable property.
  - Beginning in month 6, develop and implement a program for creating connections with and gaining a comprehensive assessment of the needs of different refugee populations and begin providing certain services to them in their current locations.
- By the end of year 1, the Elections Authority shall begin a public education campaign about the planned local and national elections to take place at the end of the Transition (Section 9).

Committee and Commission Work:

- The Governance Committee shall begin to review municipal and local government regulations and ordinances to ensure they do not discriminate or perpetuate apartheid, to be completed by the end of year 2 (Section 2).
- The Land Commission shall start a six-month review of land laws and begin preparing proposals for their reform.
- By the end of year 1, the Free Movement Commission shall start reviewing the necessity of all remaining internal checkpoints and recommending their removal in consultation with the National Police (Section 3).

- Starting in month 6, the Free Movement Commission shall begin developing a plan to dismantle the separation barrier/wall in accordance with the International Court of Justice's 2004 advisory opinion. The commission must finish drafting the plan by the start of year 3 (Section 3).

STAGE FOUR

Years 2 and 3

Caretaker Government and Executive Actions:

- The Caretaker Government must make every effort to end the use of internal checkpoints and supervised crossings by the end of year 3 of the Transition (Section 3).
- The Planning and Development Ministry shall begin dismantling the separation barrier per the plan formulated by the Free Movement Commission (Section 3).

Committee and Commission Work:

- The Legislative Committee shall appoint a subcommittee, the Land Laws Subcommittee, to launch an in-depth review of land laws in the Territory at the start of year 2 of the Transition.
- The Legislative Committee should prioritize reforming by the end of year 3 of the Transition the laws, regulations, and practices that harm or discriminate against individuals and communities targeted by the apartheid regime (Section 5).
- Beginning in year 2, the Refugee and Restitution Ministry shall begin building a menu of policy options for a post-Transition government to consider regarding the fulfillment of refugee rights, including the right of return (Section 8).
- In year 3, the Transitional Justice Committee shall develop a range of policy options for individual accountability for Israeli and Palestinian officials suspected of grave violations of human rights (Section 8).

Elections:

- By the end of year 2, the Elections Authority shall hold new elections for municipal and other local and regional authorities (Section 9).

- By the end of year 3, the Elections Authority shall hold national elections for parliament, which will be the basis of the first post-Transition government (Section 9).
- At the beginning of year 3, the Governance Committee will formulate policy options for a post-Transition referendum in which the people of the Territory can choose whether to remain as one state or seek an alternative arrangement, including two or more states (Section 9).

Mapping Existing Security
Forces

It is important to map out all of the major armed groups and security forces currently active in the Territory to better understand the security environment and what would be needed to consolidate security forces and conduct disarmament, demobilization, and reintegration (DDR).

ISRAELI SECURITY AGENCIES

Israel Defense Forces (IDF): Israel, West Bank, Gaza Strip

The Israeli military has the most diverse set of powers, areas of responsibility, and jurisdictions of any security or law enforcement agency in the Territory. It has principal responsibility for external security. As the military forces of the occupying power, it is the acting sovereign in the Occupied Palestinian Territory (OPT), which gives it not only the principal defense and security responsibility over that territory but also full powers of governance. These powers and responsibilities include legislation, public administration, law enforcement, and judicial roles. The powers extend to all people present in those territories, but for most categories of non-Palestinian persons, they delegate many of those authorities to civilian bodies. It also has sweeping powers within Israel, although most of them are not utilized during peacetime. While the IDF falls under civilian oversight, its soldiers can only be held accountable for their actions under military law.

The IDF is primarily composed of Jewish and male Druze citizens who are subject to compulsory service. Through various arrangements, the Israeli state excludes ultra-Orthodox men and women, Druze women, and Muslim and Christian Arab citizens from compulsory service. A small number of individuals from these excluded groups volunteers for service.

Transition status: Restructured into National Defense Forces

Israel National Police: Israel, West Bank

The Israel Police is a centralized, national police force responsible for law enforcement within the State of Israel. It is a civilian agency under civilian oversight, operating within the civilian legal system, and is largely considered to be a professional police force. While it has responsibility for policing in all areas of Israel, it has notably taken very different and often discriminatory approaches to Jewish versus Palestinian population centers within Israel. The overwhelming majority of officers are Jewish or non-Palestinian. In addition, the IDF has for over half a century delegated certain policing powers to the Israel Police in the majority of the OPT, primarily when it comes to law enforcement against Jewish and Israeli nationals present in the Territory but also for traffic and other types of enforcement vis-à-vis all population groups.

Transition status: Restructured into National Police

Israel Border Police: Israel, West Bank

The Israel Border Police is a gendarmerie force that is under mixed oversight and responsibility. It has been subordinate at different times to different security agencies (the IDF and Israel Police) and continues to hold different jurisdictional roles in varying legal frameworks to this day. At the time of writing, within Israel proper, the Border Police is subordinate to the Israel Police and operates exclusively within a civilian legal framework. In the occupied West Bank, the Border Police is subordinate to the Israeli military and operates under the legal rubric of military law, albeit subjecting Jewish and Israeli citizens to Israeli civilian law. Of note, Israeli authorities have historically used the Border Police almost exclusively to police Palestinian and Arab population groups and centers—in all areas of the Territory—and, in doing so, ensured a far more militarized and adversarial approach to policing those groups.

Transition status: Disbanded

Israel Security Agency (Shin Bet): Israel, West Bank, Gaza Strip

The Israel Security Agency (ISA) (a.k.a., the Shin Bet or "Shabak") is the principal domestic intelligence agency that is also responsible for intelligence in the

OPT. It has broad detention powers but is not a law enforcement agency, so it does not have direct arrest powers. The Shin Bet has three main departments: the Arab Department, responsible for security and counterterrorism across the entire Territory vis-à-vis Arab and Palestinian individuals and groups; the Israel and Foreigners Department, formerly known as the Non-Arab Affairs Department, which is responsible for security, counterterrorism, and counterintelligence vis-à-vis non-Palestinian individuals and groups within the Territory; and the Protective Security Department, which is responsible for securing high-value facilities and infrastructure as well as high-value individuals and officials globally. The ISA is under the exclusive oversight of the Prime Minister's Office, making it a civilian agency but one with little transparency or oversight.

Transition status: Restructured into the Domestic Intelligence Agency

PALESTINIAN SECURITY AGENCIES

National Security Forces: West Bank and Gaza Strip

The National Security Forces (NSF), trained by the United States and other nations, are intended to function as the military for a future Palestinian state.[1] As the successor to the Palestine Liberation Organization's (PLO) Palestinian Liberation Army, the NSF comprises over ten thousand personnel who have primarily received US training in Jordan. The NSF operates in both Gaza and the West Bank, with the West Bank unit under the Palestinian Authority's (PA) command and the Gaza unit under Hamas's control. The liaison branches of the NSF in Ramallah and Gaza coordinate with the Israeli military government on various matters, including updating personal status in the population registry, processing permit and visa requests, and some aspects of security cooperation.

Transition status: Restructured into National Defense Forces

Preventive Security: West Bank

The Preventive Security agency serves as the internal intelligence agency of the PA, mainly focused on preventing threats to Israel from Palestinian armed groups and individuals in the West Bank.[2] While technically part of the PA's Interior Ministry, and reporting to the interior minister, it is widely believed to be under the direct control of the PA president.

Transition status: Merged into the Domestic Intelligence Agency

Presidential Guard: West Bank

The Presidential Guard, a relatively small force based in the West Bank, is primarily responsible for protecting the Palestinian president and handling counterinsurgency and other domestic roles similar to those of riot police and SWAT teams.[3] Reporting directly to the president of the PA, the Presidential Guard receives training from the United States and is the successor to the PLO's Force 17.

Transition status: Disbanded

Izz al-Din al-Qassam Brigades: Gaza Strip

The Izz al-Din al-Qassam Brigades, the military wing of Hamas, are the largest and most powerful armed group in the Gaza Strip.[4] They have fought against Israeli troops in Gaza during the Gaza War and in previous conflicts. The Qassam Brigades have also carried out numerous attacks against Israeli civilians, including rocket attacks, suicide bombings, and the attacks on October 7, 2023. Designated as a terrorist organization in much of the Western world, the Qassam Brigades were estimated to have over thirty thousand members in Gaza before the Gaza War, during which Israel claimed to have killed over ten thousand of their militants, although both of those figures have been disputed.[5]

Transition status: Disbanded

Internal Security Force: Gaza Strip

The Hamas-controlled Internal Security Force (ISF), known as al-Majd, is a domestic intelligence agency based in Gaza operating under Gaza's Interior Ministry.[6] It is tasked with counterintelligence, espionage, and addressing internal dissent against Hamas rule. The ISF comprises the Internal Security Agency and General Intelligence Agency.

Transition status: Disbanded

Palestinian Civil Police: West Bank and Gaza Strip

The Palestinian Civil Police (PCP) is the main civilian policing force in the OPT, having split into two separate entities in the West Bank and Gaza Strip since 2006.[7] In the West Bank, the PCP operates in Area A, which includes major Palestinian urban centers, under PA security responsibilities as per the Oslo Accords. Movements between cities require Israeli military approval. Reporting to the PA's Interior Ministry, the PCP maintains public order, fights crime, and runs PA prisons, with training from a specialized EU mission.

In Gaza, since Hamas took control in 2007, the PCP operates under Hamas's Interior Ministry. Its functions are similar to those in the West Bank, focusing on crime prevention and civil order. The Gaza PCP is staffed by members of various Palestinian militant groups, including Hamas.

Transition status: Restructured into the new National Police

IRREGULAR MILITANT GROUPS

Izz al-Din al-Qassam Brigades

The military wing of Hamas. See above.
   Transition status: Disbanded

Al-Quds Brigades

The al-Quds Brigades are the militant wing of the Palestinian Islamic Jihad (PIJ).[8] They are estimated to have several thousand militants in the Gaza Strip and several hundred in the West Bank, mainly in Jenin and Nablus. Both PIJ and the al-Quds Brigades do not engage in national politics.
   Transition status: Disbanded

Al-Aqsa Martyrs Brigade

The al-Aqsa Martyrs Brigade is considered to be linked to the Fatah political faction, though no official affiliation exists.[9] It consists of smaller militant groups based in various parts of the West Bank, mainly in larger cities. Some members and leaders received amnesty in exchange for disarming, but these agreements eventually fell apart.
   Transition status: Disbanded

Israeli Paramilitary Groups and Militias: Israel, West Bank

There are a number of irregular and state-sponsored militias and paramilitary groups. These include settler militias, "rapid response teams" throughout the Territory, the "Civilian Guard," and certain reserve units of the IDF.
   Transition status: Disbanded

Committees and
Commissions

As outlined in Section 1, the Caretaker Government's initial phase will see the establishment of a number of committees and commissions. These bodies, formed from within the Caretaker Government, are endowed with legislative and executive functions as outlined in the Blueprint. They are crucial for implementing policy and maintaining government operations during the transitional period. Commissions, on the other hand, serve as independent oversight bodies, designed to supervise and provide checks on transitional bodies and state agencies. They draw upon a diverse range of experts, including academics and representatives from civil society groups, to offer balanced and informed oversight and ensure compliance with the Guiding Principles (Appendix A), and to safeguard against attempts by civil servants and others to maintain or reintroduce apartheid-era rules or practices.

Both committees and commissions are mandated to include Palestinian and Jewish members, ensuring inclusive representation. Unique to the commissions is the inclusion of international representatives, either from the special envoy's office or from relevant international agencies and experts, to enhance the credibility and impartiality of the oversight process.

COMMITTEES

- Governance Committee (Section 2)
- Judicial Appointments Committee (Section 4)

- Judiciary Committee (Section 4)
- Legislative Committee (Section 5)
- Disarmament, Demobilization, and Reintegration Committee (Section 7)
- Domestic Security Committee (Section 7)
- Transitional Justice Committee (Section 8)
- Referendum Committee (Section 9)

COMMISSIONS

- Free Movement Commission (Section 3)
- Judicial Oversight Commission (Section 4)
- Military Oversight Commission (Section 7)
- Election Monitoring Commission (Section 9)

Glossary of Terms

Caretaker Government	A temporary government responsible for overseeing the transition process.
Guiding Principles	Principles outlined in the Blueprint to ensure compliance with human rights and democratic principles. These include new and revised Basic Laws.
High Court for the Transition (HCT)	A court appointed to safeguard the Transition process and ensure compliance with the Guiding Principles.
National Police	The integrated civilian police force, composed of the Israel National Police and Palestinian Civil Police, which will be responsible for law enforcement within the Territory.
Occupied Palestinian Territory (OPT)	All of the Palestinian territories that Israel captured and occupied in June 1967 (the West Bank including East Jerusalem, and the Gaza Strip), which today comprise the State of Palestine.
Oslo process	The "Oslo process" is used to include not only the Oslo Accords but also the Clinton parameters, the Bush Road Map, the Olmert plan, and others that follow the same contours and reflect mostly the same approach.

The Territory

All of the area between the Mediterranean Sea and the Jordan River, including Israel, the West Bank including East Jerusalem, and the Gaza Strip.

The Transition

The transition period starting from the onset of the Caretaker Government's mandate and ending with the formation of a democratically elected government three years later.

Notes

INTRODUCTION AND FAQS

Epigraph: Tareq Baconi, "The Two-State Solution Is an Unjust, Impossible Fantasy," *New York Times*, April 1, 2024, https://www.nytimes.com/2024/04/01/opinion/two-state-solution-israel-palestine.html.

1. Baconi, "The Two-State Solution Is an Unjust, Impossible Fantasy"; "In the Wake of the War in Gaza, Is the Two-State Solution Still Viable?," *Foreign Affairs*, February 21, 2024, https://www.foreignaffairs.com/ask-the-experts/israel-palestine-two-state-solution-still-viable.

2. International Court of Justice, Legal Consequences Arising from the Policies and Practices of Israel in the Occupied Palestinian Territory, Including East Jerusalem, Advisory Opinion, July 19, 2024, https://www.icj-cij.org/sites/default/files/case-related/186/186-20240719-adv-01-00-en.pdf.

3. Agence France Presse, "New Tally Puts Oct 7 Attack Death Toll in Israel at 1,189," May 28, 2024, https://www.barrons.com/news/new-tally-puts-oct-7-attack-death-toll-in-israel-at-1-189-3e038de6.

4. Micah Goodman and Eylon Levy, *Catch-67: The Left, the Right, and the Legacy of the Six-Day War* (Yale University Press, 2018).

5. The Arab Peace Initiative, also known as the Saudi peace initiative, is a ten-sentence proposal offering normalization of Arab state ties with Israel in exchange for Israeli withdrawal from the Occupied Palestinian Territory (OPT). Gawdat Bahgat, "The Arab Peace Initiative: An Assessment," *Middle*

East Policy 16, no. 1 (March 2009): 33–39, https://doi.org/10.1111/j.1475-4967 .2009.00377.x.

6. P. R. Kumaraswamy, *Historical Dictionary of the Arab-Israeli Conflict* (Rowman & Littlefield, 2015).

7. Eric Cortellessa, "Two States Is Israel's Only Hope, Says Former Prime Minister," *Time*, November 6, 2023, https://time.com/6332127/israel-palestine-war-ehud-barak/.

8. Michael Barnett, Nathan Brown, Marc Lynch, and Shibley Telhami, "Israel's One-State Reality," *Foreign Affairs*, April 14, 2023, https://www .foreignaffairs.com/middle-east/israel-palestine-one-state-solution.

9. International Court of Justice, Legal Consequences Arising from the Policies and Practices of Israel in the Occupied Palestinian Territory, Including East Jerusalem, Advisory Opinion, July 19, 2024.

10. Noura Erakat and John Reynolds, "Understanding Apartheid," *Jewish Currents*, November 1, 2022, https://jewishcurrents.org/understanding-apartheid.

CHAPTER 1. INTERNATIONAL LAW FRAMEWORK

1. International Court of Justice, Legal Consequences Arising from the Policies and Practices of Israel in the Occupied Palestinian Territory, Including East Jerusalem, Advisory Opinion, July 19, 2024, https://www.icj-cij.org/sites /default/files/case-related/186/186-20240719-adv-01-00-en.pdf.

2. League of Nations, The Covenant of the League of Nations, 1919, Article 22, https://avalon.law.yale.edu/20th_century/leagcov.asp#art22. The text of the covenant does not explicitly reference Palestine but refers to it indirectly as one of the territories of the former Ottoman Empire over which it established mandates, including the British Mandate over Palestine: "Certain communities formerly belonging to the Turkish Empire have reached a stage of development where their existence as independent nations can be provisionally recognized subject to the rendering of administrative advice and assistance by a Mandatory until such time as they are able to stand alone. The wishes of these communities must be a principal consideration in the selection of the Mandatory."

3. UN General Assembly, Resolution 181 (II), Future Government of Palestine, A/RES/181(II), November 29, 1947, https://undocs.org/A/RES /181(II).

4. In addition to its occupation of Palestinian territories in 1967, Israel occupied Lebanese territory (the Shebaa Farms) and Syrian territory (the Golan Heights). It illegally annexed the Shebaa Farms and the Golan Heights in 1981. Asher Kaufman, "The Israel-Hezbollah Conflict and the Shebaa Farms," *Kroc Institute for International Peace Studies Policy Brief*, no. 13 (November 2006), https://kroc.nd.edu/assets/227136/israel_hezbollah.pdf.

5. International Committee of the Red Cross (ICRC), Geneva Convention Relative to the Protection of Civilian Persons in Time of War (Fourth Geneva Convention), August 12, 1949, https://ihl-databases.icrc.org/ihl/INTRO/380; ICRC, Customary IHL Database, https://ihl-databases.icrc.org/customary-ihl/eng /docs/home; ICRC, Convention (IV) Respecting the Laws and Customs of War on Land and Its Annex: Regulations Concerning the Laws and Customs of War on Land, The Hague, adopted October 18, 1907, entered into force January 26, 1910, https://ihl-databases.icrc.org/en/ihl-treaties/hague-conv-iv-1907.

6. International Court of Justice, Israeli Wall Advisory Proceedings, https:// www.icj-cij.org/sites/default/files/case-related/131/131-20040709-ADV-01-00-EN.pdf; ICRC, Geneva Convention Relative to the Protection of Civilian Persons in Time of War (Fourth Geneva Convention).

7. See John Dugard, UN Secretary-General, Question of the Violation of Human Rights in the Occupied Arab Territories, Including Palestine, Report of the Special Rapporteur of the Commission on Human Rights on the Situation of Human Rights in the Palestinian Territories Occupied by Israel Since 1967, A/57/366, August 29, 2002, ii 21.

8. We refer to the occupation starting in 1967 because of the global consensus, both legally and politically, that the laws of armed conflict apply to the territories Israel occupied in 1967, and our discussion of occupation refers to military occupation as described in international humanitarian law.

9. Rome Statute of the International Criminal Court, July 17, 1998, Article 7(1)(h), https://www.icc-cpi.int/resource-library/documents/rs-eng.pdf.

10. Orna Ben-Naftali, Aeyal Gross, and Keren Michaeli, "Illegal Occupation: Framing the Occupied Palestinian Territory," *Berkeley Journal of International Law* 23, no. 3 (2005): 586, https://lawcat.berkeley.edu/record/1119804/files /fulltext.pdf.

11. See Ardi Imseis, "Negotiating the Illegal: On the United Nations and the Illegal Occupation of Palestine, 1967–2020," *European Journal of International Law* 31, no. 3 (December 15, 2020): 1055–85, https://doi.org/10.1093/ejil/chaa055; Aeyal Gross, *The Writing on the Wall: Rethinking the International Law of Occupation* (Cambridge University Press, 2017), https://doi.org/10.1017/9781316536308; United Nations, Report of the Special Rapporteur on the Situation of Human Rights in the Palestinian Territories Occupied Since 1967, UN Doc. A/72/43106, October 23, 2017, https://www.unwatch.org/wp-content/uploads/2009/12/Lynk -Report-Oct-2017-A_72_43106.pdf; Yaël Ronen, "Illegal Occupation and Its Consequences," *Israel Law Review* 41 (2008): 201–45; Ben-Naftali, Gross, and Michaeli, "Illegal Occupation: Framing the Occupied Palestinian Territory."

12. Human Rights Watch, *Born Without Civil Rights: Israel's Use of Draconian Military Orders to Repress*, December 17, 2019, https://www.hrw.org /report/2019/12/17/born-without-civil-rights/israels-use-draconian-military-orders-repress.

13. Ibid., 1.

14. Ibid.

15. UN General Assembly, Report of the Special Rapporteur on the Situation of Human Rights in the Palestinian Territories Occupied Since 1967, A/77/356, September 20, 2022, https://undocs.org/A/77/356.

16. Ibid.

17. The related crime against humanity of persecution, as defined under the Rome Statute and customary international law, consists of widespread and systematic deprivation of fundamental rights of a racial, ethnic, or other group with discriminatory intent.

18. UN General Assembly, International Convention on the Suppression and Punishment of the Crime of Apartheid, November 30, 1973, https://treaties.un.org/Pages/ViewDetails.aspx?src=IND&mtdsg_no=IV-7&chapter=4&clang=_en.

19. The reference to a racial group is understood today to address not only treatment on the basis of genetic traits but also treatment on the basis of descent and national or ethnic origin, as defined in the International Convention on the Elimination of all Forms of Racial Discrimination.

20. The ICCPR is the International Covenant on Civil and Political Rights. The ICESCR is the International Covenant on Economic, Social and Cultural Rights. The CERD is the Committee on the Elimination of Racial Discrimination.

21. Human Rights Watch, "Abusive Israeli Policies Constitute Crimes of Apartheid, Persecution," April 27, 2021, p. 1, https://www.hrw.org/news/2021/04/27/abusive-israeli-policies-constitute-crimes-apartheid-persecution.

22. UN General Assembly, Report of the Special Rapporteur on the Situation of Human Rights in the Palestinian Territories Occupied Since 1967, A/77/356, September 20, 2022.

23. Sulejman Ahmedi, "The Distinctive Legal Features of Crimes Against Humanity," *European Journal of Interdisciplinary Studies* 2, no. 2 (April 30, 2016): 124–28, https://doi.org/10.26417/ejis.v2i2.p124-128.

24. International Court of Justice, Legal Consequences Arising from the Policies and Practices of Israel in the Occupied Palestinian Territory, Including East Jerusalem, Advisory Opinion, July 19, 2024.

25. Ardi Imseis, *The United Nations and the Question of Palestine: Rule by Law and the Structure of International Legal Subalternity* (Cambridge University Press, 2023).

26. International Court of Justice, Order Regarding the Application of the Convention on the Prevention and Punishment of the Crime of Genocide in the Gaza Strip, January 26, 2024, https://www.icj-cij.org/sites/default/files/case-related/192/192-20240126-ord-01-00-en.pdf; South Africa, "Application for Provisional Measures," ICC-01/09-02/11-702, International Criminal Court,

filed June 12, 2020; DAWN, "Expert Panel Concludes Israel Committing Geno-cide Against Palestinians in Gaza," January 9, 2024, https://dawnmena.org/expert-panel-concludes-israel-committing-genocide-against-palestinians-in-gaza; Human Rights Network, "Genocide in Gaza: Analysis of International Law and Its Application to Israel's Military Actions Since October 7, 2023," May 15, 2024, https://www.humanrightsnetwork.org/genocide-in-gaza.

27. DAWN, "Expert Panel Concludes Israel Committing Genocide Against Palestinians in Gaza." Also see Amnesty International, *"You Feel Like You Are Subhuman": Israel's Genocide Against Palestinians in Gaza*, December 2024, https://www.amnesty.org/en/documents/mde15/8668/2024/en/.

28. Imseis, *The United Nations and the Question of Palestine.*

29. Ibid.

30. UN General Assembly, Report of the Special Rapporteur on the Situation of Human Rights in the Palestinian Territories Occupied Since 1967, A/77/356, September 20, 2022.

31. Jonathan Kuttab, "The International Criminal Court's Failure to Hold Israel Accountable," Arab Center, Washington, DC, September 12, 2023, https://arabcenterdc.org/resource/the-international-criminal-courts-failure-to-hold-israel-accountable.

32. UN General Assembly, Report of the Special Rapporteur on the Situation of Human Rights in the Palestinian Territories Occupied Since 1967, A/77/356, September 20, 2022.

33. Aisling Byrne, "Building a Police State in Palestine," *Foreign Policy* (blog), January 18, 2011, https://foreignpolicy.com/2011/01/18/building-a-police-state-in-palestine.

CHAPTER 2. WHEN WILL THE BLUEPRINT
BE RELEVANT?

Epigraph: Langston Hughes, "I Look at the World," *Poetry*, January 2009. Copy-right © 2009. Reprinted by permission of Harold Ober Associates and Interna-tional Literary Properties LLC.

1. Micah Goodman and Eylon Levy, *Catch-67: The Left, the Right, and the Legacy of the Six-Day War* (Yale University Press, 2018); I. Mateo Cohen, "The Right-Wing 'One-State Solution': Narrative, Proposals, and the Future of the Conflict," *Israel Studies* 27, no. 1 (December 2021): 132–55, https://doi.org/10.2979/israelstudies.27.1.06.

2. Tovah Lazaroff, "Palestinians Will Have 'an Entity,' Not a State, Says Gantz," *Jerusalem Post*, February 20, 2022, https://www.jpost.com/middle-east/article-697070.

3. Asaf Calderon, "What's So Scary About a State of All Its Citizens?," *+972 Magazine*, March 13, 2019, https://www.972mag.com/whats-scary-israel-state-citizens.

4. For example, as Yuval Noah Harari wrote in a 2014 *Washington Post* op-ed, "both Theodor Herzl and Ben-Gurion supported a plan for Jewish national autonomy under the suzerainty of the Ottoman Empire." There have also been versions of Zionism, like the Cultural Zionism of Ahad Ha'am, which were not necessarily predicated on the existence of a Jewish nation-state but more on the emergence of a Hebrew culture.

5. Michael Schaeffer Omer-Man, "Why Israel's Opposition Won't Talk About the Real Goal of Judicial Overhaul," *+972 Magazine*, February 21, 2023, https://www.972mag.com/judiciary-annexation-levin-zionism.

6. Ksenia Svetlova, "More Israelis, Palestinians Support the 'One-State' Solution," *Al-Monitor*, February 13, 2020, https://www.al-monitor.com/originals/2020/02/israel-palestinians-west-bank-two-state-solution-one-state.html.

7. Hadeel al-Shalchi, "The Palestinian Authority Is Promising Change. Many Palestinians Say It's Not Enough," NPR, February 28, 2024, https://www.npr.org/2024/02/28/1234242951/palestinian-authority-resignation-gaza-west-bank.

8. Noa Landau and Jack Khoury, "'Two-State Solution Is Over,' Top Palestinian Diplomat Says After Trump's Jerusalem Speech," *Haaretz*, December 7, 2017, https://www.haaretz.com/middle-east-news/palestinians/2017-12-07/ty-article/.premium/two-state-solution-is-over-top-palestinian-diplomat-says/0000017f-f77c-d5bd-a17f-f77e16910000.

9. Leila Farsakh, "The Question of Palestinian Statehood and the Future of Decolonization," *Middle East Report*, no. 302 (Spring 2022): 1, https://merip.org/2022/05/the-question-of-palestinian-statehood-and-the-future-of-decolonization.

10. Yusif Shehada, "Does Foreign Aid Accelerate Corruption? The Case of the Palestinian National Authority," *Journal of Holy Land and Palestine Studies* 14, no. 2 (2015): 165–87.

11. Josef Federman, "Israel Revokes Palestinian FM's Travel Permit over UN Move," AP News, January 8, 2023, https://apnews.com/article/politics-israel-government-91ba538476380a16aad4e2cbdae2e235.

12. Noura Erakat, *Justice for Some: Law and the Question of Palestine* (Stanford University Press, 2019).

13. Patrick Wintour, "Hamas Presents New Charter Accepting a Palestine Based on 1967 Borders," *The Guardian*, May 1, 2017, https://www.theguardian.com/world/2017/may/01/hamas-new-charter-palestine-israel-1967-borders.

14. Abby Sewell, "Hamas Official Says Group Would Lay Down Its Arms If an Independent Palestinian State Is Established," AP News, April 25, 2024, https://apnews.com/article/hamas-khalil-alhayya-qatar-ceasefire-1967-borders-4912532b11a9cec29464eab234045438.

15. Hillel Cohen, *Good Arabs: The Israeli Security Agencies and the Israeli Arabs, 1948–1967* (University of California Press, 2011).

16. Ibid.

17. Mark Mazzetti and Ronen Bergman, "'Buying Quiet': Inside the Israeli Plan That Propped Up Hamas," *New York Times*, December 10, 2023, https://www.nytimes.com/2023/12/10/world/middleeast/israel-qatar-money-prop-up-hamas.html.

18. Udi Dekel, Arik Barbing, and Attila Somfalvi, "So What Yes? New Thinking on the Palestinian Conception—Episode 2: Does Another Palestinian Leadership Exist?," *Hebrew, Podcastrategi: The Institute for National Security Studies (INSS)*, May 9, 2024, https://soundcloud.com/inss2006/2a-6.

19. Adi Kolplewitz, "Palestinian Support for a One-State Solution at Highest Since Last Year," *Jerusalem Post*, April 8, 2022, https://www.jpost.com/opinion/article-703629; Palestinian Center for Policy and Research, "Press Release: Public Opinion Poll No (91)," March 20, 2024, https://www.pcpsr.org/en/node/969.

20. I. William Zartman, "Mediation: Ripeness and Its Challenges in the Middle East," *International Negotiation* 20, no. 3 (October 26, 2015): 479–93, https://doi.org/10.1163/15718069-12341317.

21. Nathan Thrall, *The Only Language They Understand: Forcing Compromise in Israel and Palestine* (Metropolitan Books, Henry Holt and Company, 2017).

22. Zartman, "Mediation: Ripeness and Its Challenges in the Middle East."

23. Vladimir Ze'ev Jabotisnky, "The Iron Wall," in the Jewish Virtual Library, first published November 4, 1923, https://www.jewishvirtuallibrary.org/quot-the-iron-wall-quot.

24. Ibid.

25. The UN General Assembly has also asked the ICJ to determine "the legal consequences that arise for all States and the United Nations" if it rules the occupation is illegal.

26. Nik Martin and Burak Ünveren, "Israel Sanctions: Who Has Imposed Curbs over Gaza War?," *DW.com*, May 3, 2024, https://www.dw.com/en/israel-sanctions-who-has-imposed-curbs-over-gaza-war/a-68792324.

27. Agence France Presse, "Turkey Presses UN for Arms Embargo on Israel in Joint Letter," November 3, 2024, https://www.barrons.com/news/turkey-presses-un-for-arms-embargo-on-israel-in-joint-letter-6f9f6a63.

28. DAWN, "International Criminal Court: Investigate Biden, Blinken and Austin for Aiding and Abetting Israeli Crimes in Gaza," February 24, 2025, https://dawnmena.org/international-criminal-court-investigate-biden-blinken-and-austin-for-aiding-and-abetting-israeli-crimes-in-gaza/.

29. Aamer Madhani, Tia Goldenberg, and Zeke Miller, "Trump Won't Rule Out Deploying US Troops to Support Rebuilding Gaza, Sees 'Long-Term' US Ownership," AP News, February 4, 2025, https://apnews.com/article/trump-netanyahu-washington-ceasefire-1c8deec4dd46177e08e07d669d595ed3.

30. Philip I. Levy, "Sanctions on South Africa: What Did They Do?," *American Economic Review* 89, no. 2 (May 1, 1999): 415–20, https://doi.org/10.1257/aer.89.2.415.

31. Research shows that, while economic crises correlate with certain types of regime change, regime change is not necessarily democratic or liberalizing. There are nevertheless ways that economic crises can contribute to changing political coalitions and power structures.

32. Vilde Lunnan Djuve and Carl Henrik Knutsen, "Economic Crisis and Regime Transitions from Within," *Journal of Peace Research* 61, no. 3 (May 2024): 446–61.

33. Min Tang, Narisong Huhe, and Qiang Zhou, "Contingent Democratization: When Do Economic Crises Matter?," *British Journal of Political Science* 47, no. 1 (January 2017): 71–90, https://doi.org/10.1017/S0007123415000095.

34. Emily Rose, "Israeli Startups Act to Relocate over Judicial Shakeup, Survey Finds," Reuters, July 23, 2023, https://www.reuters.com/world/middle-east/israeli-startups-act-relocate-over-judicial-shakeup-survey-finds-2023-07-23; Lee Yaron, "The October 7 Effect: The Israelis Leaving Israel, and the Diaspora Jews Replacing Them," *Haaretz*, September 6, 2024, https://www.haaretz.com/israel-news/2024-09-06/ty-article-magazine/.premium/the-october-7-effect-the-israelis-leaving-israel-and-the-diaspora-jews-replacing-them/00000191-b6b7-d13c-a39b-bebff9830000; Adrian Filut, "Economic Concerns Mount as Israel Faces Drop in Foreign Investments and Services Export," *Calcalist*, March 18, 2024, https://www.calcalistech.com/ctechnews/article/ldor8dzx5.

35. Reuters, "Moody's Cuts Israel's Rating, Warns of Drop to 'Junk,'" September 27, 2024, https://www.reuters.com/world/middle-east/moodys-cuts-israels-rating-warns-drop-junk-2024-09-27.

CHAPTER 3. THE DAY AFTER THE BLUEPRINT

Epigraph: Mahmoud Darwish, "A Soldier Dreams of White Tulips," in *Unfortunately, It Was Paradise* (University of California Press, 2013).

1. Omar M. Dajani, "Shadow or Shade: The Roles of International Law in Palestinian-Israeli Peace Talks," *Yale Journal of International Law* 32, no. 61 (2007): 62–124.

2. Michael Schaeffer Omer-Man, "Israelis Don't Get to Hold a Referendum on Palestine," *+972 Magazine*, July 6, 2016, https://www.972mag.com/israelis-dont-get-to-hold-a-referendum-on-palestine.

3. Fionnuala Ní Aoláin and Colm Campbell, "The Paradox of Transition in Conflicted Democracies," *Human Rights Quarterly* 27, no. 1 (February 2005): 172–213, https://doi.org/10.1353/hrq.2005.0001.

4. Dahlia Scheindlin, "Not Two States, Not One State: A New Way Out of Disaster for Israelis and Palestinians," *Haaretz*, November 30, 2023, https://www.haaretz.com/israel-news/2023-11-30/ty-article/.premium/not-two-states-not-one-state-a-new-way-out-of-disaster-for-israelis-and-palestinians/0000018c-1fc0-d21c-abae-7ffc7f960000.

5. A Land for All, "Two States: One Homeland," https://www.alandforall.org/english-program; Hiba Husseini and Yossi Beilin, *The Holy Land Confederation as a Facilitator for the Two-State Solution* (2022), https://content.ecf.org.il/files/Holy%20Land%20Confederation%20-%20English_compressed.pdf.

6. Bizuneh Yimenu, review of *Federalism and Decentralization in the Contemporary Middle East and North Africa*, edited by Aslı Ü. Bâli and Omar M. Dajani, *Publius* 54, no. 1 (2023): e5–e11, https://doi.org/10.1093/publius/pjad033.

CHAPTER 4. THE CHALLENGE OF SECURITY, VIOLENCE, AND INSTABILITY

1. James P. Pfiffner, "US Blunders in Iraq: De-Baathification and Disbanding the Army," *Intelligence and National Security* 25, no. 1 (February 2010): 76–85, https://doi.org/10.1080/02684521003588120.

2. The professionalism, size, and strength of the White South African security forces made external involvement less necessary, though lessons from failed integration in Rwanda and relatively successful efforts in Zimbabwe and Namibia point to the utility of an external peacekeeping force to act as a stabilizing force. Stephen F. Burgess, "Fashioning Integrated Security Forces After Conflict," *African Security* 1, no. 2 (2008): 69–91, https://www.jstor.org/stable/48598782.

3. Ibid.

4. Gavin Cawthra, "Security Governance in South Africa," *African Security Review* 14, no. 3 (January 2005): 95–105, https://doi.org/10.1080/10246029.2005.9627376.

5. Civilian Secretariat for Police Service, "2016 White Paper on Policing," *South African Government Gazette*, September 1, 2017, https://www.gov.za/sites/default/files/gcis_document/201709/41082gon914.pdf; South African Government, "Intelligence White Paper," https://www.gov.za/documents/intelligence-white-paper; International Human Rights Law Institute, ed., *The Chicago Principles on Post-Conflict Justice* (2008).

6. Abraham F. Lowenthal and Sergio Bitar, *From Authoritarian Rule Toward Democratic Governance: Learning from Political Leaders* (International IDEA, 2015).

7. Diane F. Orentlicher, "'Settling Accounts' Revisited: Reconciling Global Norms with Local Agency," *International Journal of Transitional Justice* 1, no. 1 (March 1, 2007): 10–22, https://doi.org/10.1093/ijtj/ijm010.

8. Ibid.

9. Peter Beaumont, Quique Kierszenbaum, and Sufian Taha, "'This Is More Than a Reaction to Rockets': Communal Violence Spreads in Israel," *The Guardian*, May 13, 2021, https://www.theguardian.com/world/2021/may/13/this-is-more-than-a-reaction-to-rockets-communal-violence-spreads-in-israel.

10. Oren Ziv, "How Israeli Police Are Colluding with Settlers Against Palestinian Citizens," *+972 Magazine*, May 13, 2021, https://www.972mag.com/israel-police-settlers-lyd.

11. *Times of Israel*, "Police Unprepared to Deal with Multi-Front Outbreak of Violence, Chief Warns," June 6, 2023, https://www.timesofisrael.com/police-unprepared-to-deal-with-multi-front-outbreak-of-violence-chief-warns.

12. Ibid.

13. Shane Bauer, "The Israeli Settlers Attacking Their Palestinian Neighbors," *New Yorker*, February 26, 2024, https://www.newyorker.com/magazine/2024/03/04/israel-west-bank-settlers-attacks-palestinians.

14. Loveday Morris, "An Angry Mob at an Israeli University Stirs Fears of Jewish-Arab Violence," *Washington Post*, October 30, 2023, https://www.washingtonpost.com/world/2023/10/30/israel-gaza-jews-palestinians-netanya.

15. Lorenzo Tondo and Quique Kierszenbaum, "Israeli Soldiers and Police Tipping Off Groups That Attack Gaza Aid Trucks," *The Guardian*, May 21, 2024, https://www.theguardian.com/world/article/2024/may/21/israeli-soldiers-and-police-tipping-off-groups-that-attack-gaza-aid-trucks.

16. Gerald Dapaah Gyamfi, "Exploring the Roles of Police Leaders in Countries in Transition," *International Journal of Risk and Contingency Management* 9, no. 4 (October 2020): 1–17, https://doi.org/10.4018/IJRCM.2020100101.

17. Ibid.

18. International Federation for Human Rights (FIDH) and Public Committee Against Torture in Israel (PCATI), "War Crimes in the Interrogation Chamber: The Israeli Systematic Policy of Torture, Inhuman and Degrading Treatment, Unlawful Deportation, and Denial of Fair Trial of Palestinian Detainees," Communication to the Office of the Prosecutor of the International Criminal Court Under Article 15 of the Rome Statute, June 2022, https://stoptorture.org.il/wp-content/uploads/2022/06/FIDH-PCATI_Art.-15-communication-June-2022.pdf; "B2. Al-Haq, 'Torturing Each Other: The Widespread Practices of Arbitrary Detention and Torture in the Palestinian Territory,' Ramallah, July 2008 (Excerpts)," *Journal of Palestine Studies* 38, no. 1 (October 1, 2008): 166–69, https://doi.org/10.1525/jps.2008.38.1.166.

19. Vilde Lunnan Djuve and Carl Henrik Knutsen, "Economic Crisis and Regime Transitions from Within," *Journal of Peace Research* 61, no. 3 (May 2024): 446–61.

20. Amit Reddy, "Do Democratic Transitions Produce Better Human Development Outcomes? Empirical Evidence from 40 Years of Regime Changes"

(master's thesis, Georgetown University, 2012), https://www.proquest.com/dissertations-theses/do-democratic-transitions-produce-better-human/docview/1010625224/se-2.

21. European Commission for Democracy Through Law (Venice Commission), "Guidelines on Prohibition and Dissolution of Political Parties and Analogous Measures," September 29, 2004, https://www.venice.coe.int/webforms/documents/default.aspx?pdffile=CDL-INF(2000)001-e; International Human Rights Law Institute, *The Chicago Principles on Post-Conflict Justice.*

SECTION 1. ESTABLISH A CARETAKER GOVERNMENT

1. United Nations missions such as UNTAC in Cambodia, UNTAET in East Timor, UNMIL in Liberia, UNAMSIL in Sierra Leone, and UNMISS in South Sudan were mandated by UN Security Council resolutions. As in many of those missions, the UN Department of Peace Operations should be responsible for recruiting and setting up auxiliary staffing and logistics for the international elements of the mission.

2. Mandy Turner, "Creating 'Partners for Peace': The Palestinian Authority and the International Statebuilding Agenda," *Journal of Intervention and Statebuilding* 5, no. 1 (March 2011): 1–21, https://doi.org/10.1080/17502977.2011.541777.

3. Robert Barron, "Palestinian Politics Timeline: Since the 2006 Election," US Institute of Peace, https://www.usip.org/palestinian-politics-timeline-2006-election.

4. Sharon Weinblum, "Disqualifying Political Parties and 'Defending Democracy' in Israel," *Constellations* 22, no. 2 (2015): 314–25, https://doi.org/10.1111/1467-8675.12161; Israeli Ministry of Defense: National Bureau for Counter Terror Financing, "Designations Lists (DATA)," https://nbctf.mod.gov.il:443/en/Minister%20Sanctions/Designation/Pages/downloads.aspx.

5. Philip Pettit, "Popular Sovereignty and Constitutional Democracy," *University of Toronto Law Journal* 72, no. 3 (June 1, 2022): 251–86, https://doi.org/10.3138/utlj-2021-0048.

6. Abraham F. Lowenthal and Sergio Bitar, *From Authoritarian Rule Toward Democratic Governance: Learning from Political Leaders* (International IDEA, 2015).

7. UN General Assembly, Report of the Special Rapporteur [Francesca Albanese] on the Situation of Human Rights in the Palestinian Territories Occupied Since 1967, A/77/356, September 20, 2022, https://undocs.org/A/77/356.

8. Fionnuala Ní Aoláin and Colm Campbell, "The Paradox of Transition in Conflicted Democracies," *Human Rights Quarterly* 27, no. 1 (February 2005): 172–213, https://doi.org/10.1353/hrq.2005.0001.

9. Lowenthal and Bitar, *From Authoritarian Rule Toward Democratic Governance.*

10. Ibid.

11. Lisa O'Carroll, "How Did the Good Friday Agreement Come About and Why Is It So Significant?," *The Guardian*, April 7, 2023, https://www.theguardian.com/world/2023/apr/07/how-did-the-good-friday-agreement-come-about-and-why-is-it-so-significant; Ní Aoláin and Campbell, "The Paradox of Transition in Conflicted Democracies."

12. Raffaella A. Del Sarto and Menachem Klein, "Oslo: Three Decades Later," *Israel Studies Review* 38, no. 2 (June 1, 2023): 1–11, https://doi.org/10.3167/isr.2023.380202.

13. O'Carroll, "How Did the Good Friday Agreement Come About and Why Is It So Significant?"

14. Ibid.

15. Jarat Chopra and Tanja Hohe, "Participatory Intervention," *Global Governance: A Review of Multilateralism and International Organizations* 10, no. 3 (August 3, 2004): 289–305, https://doi.org/10.1163/19426720-01003004; Todd A. Eisenstadt and Tofigh Maboudi, "Being There Is Half the Battle: Group Inclusion, Constitution-Writing, and Democracy," *Comparative Political Studies* 52, no. 13–14 (November 2019): 2135–70, https://doi.org/10.1177/0010414019830739.

16. Ní Aoláin and Campbell, "The Paradox of Transition in Conflicted Democracies."

17. Yehezkel Landau, *Healing the Holy Land: Interreligious Peacebuilding in Israel/Palestine* (US Institute of Peace, 2003), https://lccn.loc.gov/2003373618.

18. Ronen Bergman, *Rise and Kill First: The Secret History of Israel's Targeted Assassinations*, translated by Ronnie Hope (Random House, 2018).

19. Yaron Ezrahi, "You Don't Make Peace with Friends. You . . . ," *Chicago Tribune*, September 15, 1993, https://www.chicagotribune.com/news/ct-xpm-1993-09-15-9309150118-story.html.

20. Tal Schneider, "For Years, Netanyahu Propped Up Hamas. Now It's Blown Up in Our Faces," *Times of Israel*, October 8, 2023, https://www.timesofisrael.com/for-years-netanyahu-propped-up-hamas-now-its-blown-up-in-our-faces.

21. Daniel Bar-Tal, "From Intractable Conflict Through Conflict Resolution to Reconciliation: Psychological Analysis," *Political Psychology* 21, no. 2 (June 2000): 351–65, https://doi.org/10.1111/0162-895X.00192.

22. Eisenstadt and Maboudi, "Being There Is Half the Battle."

23. Richard J. Goldstone, "The South African Bill of Rights," *Texas International Law Journal* 32, no. 3 (1997): 451–69.

24. Aslı Bâli, professor of law at Yale Law School, unpublished interview consulting on the design of the Blueprint, July 17, 2023.

25. Steven Levitsky and Lucan Way, "The Myth of Democratic Recession," *Journal of Democracy* 26, no. 1 (January 2015): 45–58, https://doi.org/10.1353/jod.2015.0007.

SECTION 2. END MILITARY RULE AND REVOKE
EMERGENCY LAWS

1. Human Rights Watch, *Separate and Unequal*, December 19, 2010, https://www.hrw.org/report/2010/12/19/separate-and-unequal/israels-discriminatory-treatment-palestinians-occupied.

2. Amnesty International, *Israel's Apartheid Against Palestinians: Cruel System of Domination and Crime Against Humanity*, February 1, 2022, https://www.amnesty.org/en/documents/mde15/5141/2022/en.

3. Mohammed Ibrahim Al Mashni, Yusramizza Binti Md Isa, and Nor Azlina Binti Mohd Noor Yusuff, "Historical Evolution of the Palestinian Legal and Judicial System 1516 to Present," *Journal of Positive School Psychology* 6, no. 5 (2022): 2692–705.

4. V. Azarov, "From Discretion to Necessity: Third State Responsibility for Israel's Control of Stay and Entry into Palestinian Territory," *Journal of Human Rights Practice* 6, no. 2 (July 1, 2014): 327–55, https://doi.org/10.1093/jhuman/huu014.

5. Ibid.

6. Richard Falk and Virginia Q. Tilley, "Israeli Practices Towards the Palestinian People and the Question of Apartheid," *Palestine and the Israeli Occupation* 1, no. 1 (Spring 2017): 1–65.

7. Hillel Cohen, *Good Arabs: The Israeli Security Agencies and the Israeli Arabs, 1948–1967* (University of California Press, 2011).

8. Amnesty International, *Israel's Apartheid Against Palestinians*.

9. Ibid.

10. Ibid.

11. Association for Civil Rights in Israel, "One Rule, Two Legal Systems," October 2014, https://law.acri.org.il/en/wp-content/uploads/2015/02/Two-Systems-of-Law-English-FINAL.pdf.

12. Emily Schaeffer Omer-Man, "Separate and Unequal: Israel's Dual Criminal Justice System in the West Bank," *Palestine-Israel Journal* 21, no. 3 (2016), https://pij.org/articles/1682/separate-and-unequal-israels-dual-criminal-justice-system-in-the-west-bank.

13. Association for Civil Rights in Israel, "One Rule, Two Legal Systems."

14. Luigi Daniele, "Enforcing Illegality: Israel's Military Justice in the West Bank," *Questions of International Law*, no. 44 (2017): 21–40.

15. Yael Berda, *Living Emergency: Israel's Permit Regime in the Occupied West Bank* (Stanford University Press, 2018).

16. Ibid.

17. Israel's ban on family unification for Palestinians is discussed in greater detail in Section 5. It is an emergency regulation that, under the guise of security, excludes Israeli citizens from the process of seeking residency and citizenship for their noncitizen spouse if that spouse is a national of an "enemy state," which notably includes the Palestinian territories. Because Palestinian citizens of Israel represent nearly the only citizens who are blocked from accessing family unification under this ban, the law is discriminatory in its disparate impact against them.

18. Addameer: Prisoner Support and Human Rights Association, "Statistics," April 4, 2024, https://www.addameer.org/statistics; HaMoked: Center for the Defence of the Individual, "Statistics on 'Security Inmates,'" April 2024, https://hamoked.org/prisoners-charts.php.

19. Abeer Baker and Anat Matar, eds., *Threat: Palestinian Political Prisoners in Israel* (Pluto Press, 2011), https://doi.org/10.2307/j.ctt183p121.

20. Ibid.

21. Adalah: The Legal Center for Arab Minority Rights in Israel, "Israel's 2016 Counter-Terrorism Law and 1945 Emergency Regulations Regarding the Outlawing of Six Palestinian Human Rights and Civil Society Groups," November 23, 2021, https://www.adalah.org/uploads/uploads/Adalah_Expert_Opinion_Palestinian6_Nov2021.pdf.

22. Association for Civil Rights in Israel, "One Rule, Two Legal Systems."

23. Addameer, "Introduction to Israeli Military Orders," July 2017, https://www.addameer.org/israeli_military_judicial_system/military_orders.

24. Asher Arian, David Nachmias, and Ruth Amir, "Transition of Government Power," in *Executive Governance in Israel*, by Asher Arian, David Nachmias, and Ruth Amir, 126–46 (Palgrave Macmillan UK, 2002), https://doi.org/10.1057/9781403990150_7.

25. Jarat Chopra and Tanja Hohe, "Participatory Intervention," *Global Governance: A Review of Multilateralism and International Organizations* 10, no. 3 (August 3, 2004): 289–305, https://doi.org/10.1163/19426720-01003004.

26. Yael Berda, "Managing 'Dangerous Populations': How Colonial Emergency Laws Shape Citizenship," *Security Dialogue* 51, no. 6 (December 2020): 557–78, https://doi.org/10.1177/0967010620901908.

27. Ibid.

28. Azarov, "From Discretion to Necessity."

SECTION 3. RESTORE FREEDOM OF MOVEMENT

1. Daniel Monterescu, "The Ghettoization of Israel's 'Mixed Cities,'" *+972 Magazine*, December 5, 2015, https://www.972mag.com/the-ghettoization-of-israels-mixed-cities.

2. Hillel Cohen, *Good Arabs: The Israeli Security Agencies and the Israeli Arabs, 1948–1967* (University of California Press, 2011).

3. Ibid.

4. Omar Shakir, *A Threshold Crossed: Israeli Authorities and the Crimes of Apartheid and Persecution*, Human Rights Watch, April 27, 2021, https://www .hrw.org/report/2021/04/27/threshold-crossed/israeli-authorities-and-crimes-apartheid-and-persecution.

5. Cohen, *Good Arabs*.

6. V. Azarov, "From Discretion to Necessity: Third State Responsibility for Israel's Control of Stay and Entry into Palestinian Territory," *Journal of Human Rights Practice* 6, no. 2 (July 1, 2014): 327–55, https://doi.org/10.1093/jhuman /huu014.

7. Yael Berda, *Living Emergency: Israel's Permit Regime in the Occupied West Bank* (Stanford University Press, 2018).

8. Ibid.

9. Carey James, "Mere Words: The Enemy Entity Designation of the Gaza Strip," *Hastings International Comparative Law Review* 32, no. 2 (2009): 643–67, https://repository.uclawsf.edu/hastings_international_comparative_law_ review/vol32/iss2/8.

10. Simon Perry, Robert Apel, Graeme R. Newman, and Ronald V. Clarke, "The Situational Prevention of Terrorism: An Evaluation of the Israeli West Bank Barrier," *Journal of Quantitative Criminology* 33, no. 4 (December 2017): 727–51, https://doi.org/10.1007/s10940-016-9309-6; Matthew Longo, Daphna Canetti, and Nancy Hite-Rubin, "A Checkpoint Effect? Evidence from a Natural Experiment on Travel Restrictions in the West Bank," *American Journal of Political Science* 58, no. 4 (2014): 1006–23, https://doi.org/10.1111/ajps.12109.

11. Human Rights Watch, *Born Without Civil Rights: Israel's Use of Draconian Military Orders to Repress*, December 17, 2019, https://www.hrw.org /report/2019/12/17/born-without-civil-rights/israels-use-draconian-military-orders-repress.

12. Hagar Kotef and Merav Amir, "Between Imaginary Lines: Violence and Its Justifications at the Military Checkpoints in Occupied Palestine," in *Movement and the Ordering of Freedom*, by Hagar Kotef, 27–51 (Duke University Press, 2015), https://doi.org/10.1215/9780822375753-002.

13. Michael Dumper, "Policing Divided Cities: Stabilization and Law Enforcement in Palestinian East Jerusalem," *International Affairs* 89, no. 5 (September 2013): 1247–64, https://doi.org/10.1111/1468-2346.12070.

14. International Court of Justice, Advisory Opinion Concerning Legal Consequences of the Construction of a Wall in the Occupied Palestinian Territory, July 9, 2004, https://www.refworld.org/jurisprudence/caselaw/icj/2004/en/35595.

15. Ibid.

16. Yael Berda, *Colonial Bureaucracy and Contemporary Citizenship* (Cambridge University Press, 2022), https://doi.org/10.1017/9781009053495.

17. Azarov, "From Discretion to Necessity."

18. Ibid.

SECTION 4. THE COURTS

1. Israeli Ministry of Foreign Affairs, "The Judiciary: The Court System," https://embassies.gov.il/MFA/AboutIsrael/state/Democracy/Pages/The%20Judiciary-%20The%20Court%20System.aspx.

2. European Council on Foreign Affairs (ECFR), "Mapping Palestinian Politics: Judicial System," March 20, 2018, https://ecfr.eu/special/mapping_palestinian_politics/justice_system.

3. Fionnuala Ní Aoláin and Colm Campbell, "The Paradox of Transition in Conflicted Democracies," *Human Rights Quarterly* 27, no. 1 (February 2005): 172–213, https://doi.org/10.1353/hrq.2005.0001.

4. In the current system, Israel's Supreme Court justices also sit as justices in the High Court of Justice, where they hear administrative and constitutional appeals as a court of first and final instance. Appellate courts are addressed in the main text.

5. The Dayton Constitution for Bosnia and Herzegovina prescribed a Constitutional Court with nine justices, including "three international judges to be selected and appointed by the President of the European Court of Human Rights." Joseph Marko, "Bosnia-Herzegovina: The Role of the Judiciary in a Divided Society," *Constitutional Review* 5, no. 2 (November 18, 2019): 194, https://doi.org/10.31078/consrev521.

6. Amnesty International, "Tunisia: New Draft Constitution Undermines Independence of Judiciary and Weakens Human Rights Safeguards," July 5, 2022, https://www.amnesty.org/en/latest/news/2022/07/tunisia-new-draft-constitution-undermines-independence-of-judiciary-and-weakens-human-rights-safeguards.

7. Nimer Sultany, "Activism and Legitimation in Israel's Jurisprudence of Occupation," *Social and Legal Studies* 23, no. 3 (September 2014): 315–39, https://doi.org/10.1177/0964663914521449.

8. Ibid.

9. Lior Kodner, Elyakim Rubinstein, and Avi Himi, "Netanyahu Is Destroying Israel and He Is Doing It With His Eyes Open," *Haaretz, This Week* (podcast), December 13, 2022, https://www.haaretz.co.il/digital/podcast/weekly/2022-12-13/ty-article-podcast/00000185-0a6e-d43f-afc7-bbeeb1cd0000.

10. Ruti G. Teitel, *Transitional Justice* (Oxford University Press, 2002).

11. For the purposes of Palestinian representation, "regions of the Territory" shall be understood to include: the Gaza Strip, the northern West Bank, the southern West Bank, Jerusalem (including Ramallah and Bethlehem), the Center (Lyd, Jaffa, etc.), the Central Plains (Tulkarm, Tira, Kfar Kassem, Qalansuwa, etc.), the Galilee, and the Naqab.

12. For the purposes of Israeli (Jewish) representation, "regions of the Territory" shall be understood to include: Jerusalem (including Modi'in, Ma'aleh Adumim, Beitar Ilit), the Center (Tel Aviv, Lod, Herzliya, Kfar Saba, Rishon Lezion, Rehovot, etc.), the Coastal Plains (Kfar Saba, Netanya, Hadera, the Sharon, etc.), the Galilee, the southern coastal region (Ashdod, Ashkelon, Gaza-area settlements), and the Negev.

SECTION 5. REVOKE RACIST, DISCRIMINATORY LAWS

1. Amnesty International, *Israel's Apartheid Against Palestinians: Cruel System of Domination and Crime Against Humanity*, February 1, 2022, https://www.amnesty.org/en/documents/mde15/5141/2022/en.

2. Rania Muhareb, Elizabeth Rghebi, Pierce Clancy, Joseph Schechla, Nada Awad, and Maha Abdallah, *Israeli Apartheid: Tool of Zionist Settler Colonialism*, Al Haq, November 29, 2022, https://www.alhaq.org/publications/20940.html.

3. Yael Berda, *Colonial Bureaucracy and Contemporary Citizenship* (Cambridge University Press, 2022), https://doi.org/10.1017/9781009053495.

4. Yael Berda, *Living Emergency: Israel's Permit Regime in the Occupied West Bank* (Stanford University Press, 2018).

5. Ibid.

6. John Reynolds, "'Intent to Regularise': The Israeli Supreme Court and the Normalisation of Emergency," *Adalah Review* 104 (2013), https://www.adalah.org/en/content/view/8127.

7. Adalah: The Legal Center for Arab Minority Rights in Israel, "Israel's 2016 Counter-Terrorism Law and 1945 Emergency Regulations Regarding the Outlawing of Six Palestinian Human Rights and Civil Society Groups," November 23, 2021, https://www.adalah.org/uploads/uploads/Adalah_Expert_Opinion_Palestinian6_Nov2021.pdf.

8. Adalah, "Discriminatory Laws in Israel," https://www.adalah.org/en/law/index.

9. Henriette Chacar, "Israel's Knesset Passes Law Barring Palestinian Spouses," Reuters, March 10, 2022, https://www.reuters.com/world/middle-east/israels-knesset-passes-law-barring-palestinian-spouses-2022-03-10.

10. Berda, *Colonial Bureaucracy and Contemporary Citizenship.*

11. Omar Shakir, *A Threshold Crossed: Israeli Authorities and the Crimes of Apartheid and Persecution,* Human Rights Watch, April 27, 2021, https://www.hrw.org/report/2021/04/27/threshold-crossed/israeli-authorities-and-crimes-apartheid-and-persecution.

12. Geremy Forman and Alexandre (Sandy) Kedar, "From Arab Land to 'Israel Lands': The Legal Dispossession of the Palestinians Displaced by Israel in the Wake of 1948," *Environment and Planning D: Society and Space* 22, no. 6 (December 2004): 809–30, https://doi.org/10.1068/d402.

13. Elhanan Miller, "Abbas Toughens Law Against Palestinians Selling Land to Jews," *Times of Israel,* October 21, 2014, http://www.timesofisrael.com/abbas-toughens-law-against-palestinians-selling-land-to-jews.

14. Adalah, "Flag and Emblem Law," https://www.adalah.org/en/law/view/540.

15. South African Law Reform Commission, *Report on Activities of the South African Law Reform Commission 2022/2023,* 2023, https://www.justice.gov.za/salrc/anr/2022-2023-anr-salrc.pdf.

16. Forman and Kedar, "From Arab Land to 'Israel Lands.'"

17. Miller, "Abbas Toughens Law Against Palestinians Selling Land to Jews."

18. Fourth Geneva Convention, see Article 49, sixth paragraph, cited in Vol. 2, Chap. 38, Section 334, https://ihl-databases.icrc.org/ihl/INTRO/380; Rome Statute of the International Criminal Court, July 17, 1998, 2187 U.N.T.S. 90, Art. 8(2)(b)(viii).

19. International Committee of the Red Cross (ICRC), "Rule 130. Transfer of Own Civilian Population into Occupied Territory," Customary IHL Database, https://ihl-databases.icrc.org/en/customary-ihl/v1/rule130#Fn_9AD70858_00003.

20. International Court of Justice, Legal Consequences Arising from the Policies and Practices of Israel in the Occupied Palestinian Territory, Including East Jerusalem, Advisory Opinion, July 19, 2024.

21. International Court of Justice, "Request for Advisory Opinion Transmitted to the Court Pursuant to General Assembly Resolution 77/247 of 30 December 2022: Legal Consequences Arising from the Policies and Practices of Israel in the Occupied Palestinian Territory, Including East Jerusalem," https://www.icj-cij.org/sites/default/files/case-related/186/186-20230117-REQ-01-00-EN.pdf.

22. Israel Democracy Institute, "Nation-State Law Explainer," November 2023, https://en.idi.org.il/articles/24241.

23. Anti-Defamation League, "South African Flag (Apartheid Era)," https://www.adl.org/resources/hate-symbol/south-african-flag-apartheid-era.

24. Serena Merrino, "Currency and Settler Colonialism: The Palestinian Case," *Review of International Political Economy* 28, no. 6 (November 2, 2021): 1729–50, https://doi.org/10.1080/09692290.2020.1803951.

SECTION 6. CITIZENSHIP AND VOTING RIGHTS

1. Oren Yiftachel, "'Ethnocracy' and Its Discontents: Minorities, Protests, and the Israeli Polity," *Critical Inquiry* 26, no. 4 (2000): 725–56.

2. Association for Civil Rights in Israel, "One Rule, Two Legal Systems: Israel's Regime of Laws in the West Bank," October 2014, https://law.acri.org.il/en/wp-content/uploads/2015/02/Two-Systems-of-Law-English-FINAL.pdf.

3. Amnesty International, *Israel's Apartheid Against Palestinians: Cruel System of Domination and Crime Against Humanity,* February 1, 2022, https://www.amnesty.org/en/documents/mde15/5141/2022/en.

4. Ibid.

5. Leora Bilsky, "'Speaking Through the Mask': Israeli Arabs and the Changing Faces of Israeli Citizenship," *Middle East Law and Governance* 1, no. 2 (2009): 166–209, https://consensus.app/papers/speaking-mask-israeli-arabs-changing-faces-israeli-bilsky/78ae958a4b0f52f3bbe52c376f7d2520.

6. Sohail Hossain Hassanein, "Crime, Politics and Police in the Palestinian's Society in Israel," *Social Identities* 22, no. 4 (July 3, 2016): 376–96, https://doi.org/10.1080/13504630.2015.1106312.

7. Danielle C. Jefferis, "Institutionalizing Statelessness: The Revocation of Residency Rights of Palestinians in East Jerusalem," *International Journal of Refugee Law* 24, no. 2 (May 1, 2012): 202–30, https://doi.org/10.1093/ijrl/ees026.

8. Ibid.

9. B'Tselem, "Statistics on Revocation of Residency in East Jerusalem," April 19, 2023, http://www.btselem.org/jerusalem/revocation_statistics.

10. Nir Hasson, "Just 5 Percent of E. Jerusalem Palestinians Have Received Israeli Citizenship since 1967," *Haaretz*, May 29, 2022, https://www.haaretz.com/israel-news/2022-05-29/ty-article/why-so-few-palestinians-from-jerusalem-have-israeli-citizenship/00000181-0c46-d090-abe1-ed7fefc20000.

11. "Local Outline Plan Jerusalem 2000," English translation of Hebrew original, 2018, https://www.alhaq.org/cached_uploads/download/alhaq_files/en/wp-content/uploads/2018/03/LocalOutlinePlanJerusalem2000.pdf.

12. Amnesty International, *Israel's Apartheid Against Palestinians.*

13. Ibid.

14. Omar Shakir, *A Threshold Crossed: Israeli Authorities and the Crimes of Apartheid and Persecution*, Human Rights Watch, April 27, 2021, https://www.hrw.org/report/2021/04/27/threshold-crossed/israeli-authorities-and-crimes-apartheid-and-persecution.

15. Michael Schaeffer Omer-Man, "Who Gets to Vote in Israel's Version of Democracy," *+972 Magazine*, January 3, 2019, https://www.972mag.com/gets-vote-israels-democracy-2019.

16. Shakir, *A Threshold Crossed*.

17. Abeer Baker and Anat Matar, eds., *Threat: Palestinian Political Prisoners in Israel* (Pluto Press, 2011), https://doi.org/10.2307/j.ctt183p121.

18. *Al Jazeera*, "Timeline: Hamas-Fatah Conflict," May 4, 2011, https://www.aljazeera.com/news/2011/5/4/timeline-hamas-fatah-conflict.

19. Ibid.

20. International Committee of the Red Cross (ICRC), "Occupation and International Humanitarian Law: Questions and Answers," November 3, 2022, https://www.icrc.org/en/document/ihl-occupying-power-responsibilities-occupied-palestinian-territories.

21. RFI, "UN Rapporteur Says Israel's War in Gaza Is 'Emptying the Land Completely,'" November 1, 2024, https://www.rfi.fr/en/podcasts/international-report/20241101-un-rapporteur-says-israel-s-war-in-gaza-is-emptying-the-land-completely.

22. Gisha, "Gaza Up Close: Visualizing the Impact of the Closure on the Gaza Strip," June 28, 2023, https://features.gisha.org/gaza-up-close.

23. Karim A. A. Khan KC, "Statement of ICC Prosecutor Karim A. A. Khan KC: Applications for Arrest Warrants in the Situation in the State of Palestine," International Criminal Court, May 20, 2024, https://www.icc-cpi.int/news/statement-icc-prosecutor-karim-aa-khan-kc-applications-arrest-warrants-situation-state.

24. Wafaa Shurafa and Bassem Mroue, "Netanyahu Seeks Open-Ended Control over Security and Civilian Affairs in Gaza in New Postwar Plan," AP News, February 23, 2024, https://apnews.com/article/israel-hamas-war-news-02-23-2024-a5da6005cfa6734225af35ca460a75fb.

25. Fionnuala Ní Aoláin and Colm Campbell, "The Paradox of Transition in Conflicted Democracies," *Human Rights Quarterly* 27, no. 1 (February 2005): 172–213, https://doi.org/10.1353/hrq.2005.0001.

26. Yael Berda, *Colonial Bureaucracy and Contemporary Citizenship* (Cambridge University Press, 2022), https://doi.org/10.1017/9781009053495.

27. Bill Van Esveld, "'Forget About Him, He's Not Here': Israel's Control of Palestinian Residency in the West Bank and Gaza," Human Rights Watch, February 5, 2012, https://www.hrw.org/report/2012/02/05/forget-about-him-hes-not-here/israels-control-palestinian-residency-west-bank-and.

SECTION 7. SECURITY FORCES AND DISARMAMENT

1. Adolfo Arranz, Jonathan Saul, Stephen Farrell, Simon Scarr, and Clare Trainor, "Inside the Tunnels of Gaza," Reuters, December 31, 2023, https://www.reuters.com/graphics/ISRAEL-PALESTINIANS/GAZA-TUNNELS/gkvldmzorvb.

2. Rasha Khatib, Martin McKee, and Salim Yusuf, "Counting the Dead in Gaza: Difficult but Essential," *The Lancet* 404, no. 10449 (July 20, 2024): 237–38, https://doi.org/10.1016/S0140-6736(24)01169-3.

3. State of Palestine, Ministry of Health, "Daily Report on the Effects of the Israeli Aggression in Palestine: From October 7th until May 21, 2024," May 21, 2024; Edith M. Lederer, "The Unprecedented Destruction of Housing in Gaza Hasn't Been Seen Since World War II, the UN Says," AP News, May 2, 2024, https://apnews.com/article/un-report-gaza-destruction-housing-economy-recovery-4f61dcca7db3fd5eb3da5c6a25001e12; Raja Abdulrahim, Helmuth Rosales, Bilal Shbair, Anjali Singhvi, Erika Solomon, Iyad Abuheweila, Abu Bakr Bashir, et al., "Gaza in Ruins After a Year of War," *New York Times*, October 7, 2024, https://www.nytimes.com/interactive/2024/10/07/world/middleeast/israel-gaza-destruction-hamas-war.html; Inter-Agency Standing Committee (IASC), "Statement by Principals of the Inter-Agency Standing Committee: Stop the Assault on Palestinians in Gaza and on Those Trying to Help Them," November 1, 2024, https://interagencystandingcommittee.org/inter-agency-standing-committee/statement-principals-inter-agency-standing-committee-stop-assault-palestinians-gaza-and-those-trying.

4. Daniel Bar-Tal, ed., *Shared Beliefs in a Society: Social Psychological Analysis* (Sage Publications, 2000).

5. Omar Shakir, *A Threshold Crossed: Israeli Authorities and the Crimes of Apartheid and Persecution*, Human Rights Watch, April 27, 2021, https://www.hrw.org/report/2021/04/27/threshold-crossed/israeli-authorities-and-crimes-apartheid-and-persecution.

6. Yael Berda, *Colonial Bureaucracy and Contemporary Citizenship* (Cambridge University Press, 2022), https://doi.org/10.1017/9781009053495.

7. Ze'ev Drory, "Society Strength as a Base for Military Power: The State of Israel During the Early 1950s," *Israel Affairs* 12, no. 3 (2006): 412–29, https://doi.org/10.1080/13537120600744669.

8. Interview with a senior officer in the Palestinian National Security Forces, June 15, 2023.

9. International Human Rights Law Institute, ed., *The Chicago Principles on Post-Conflict Justice* (2008).

10. Civilian Secretariat for Police Service, "2016 White Paper on Policing," *South African Government Gazette*, September 1, 2017, https://www.gov.za/sites/default/files/gcis_document/201709/41082gon914.pdf.

11. Centre for Human Rights, University of Pretoria, "Overview of Global and Regional Human Rights Standards on the Police Use of Force," May 20, 2020, https://www.chr.up.ac.za/images/centrenews/2020/Global_and_Regional_Rules_on_Police_Use_of_Force_20_May_2020.pdf.

12. International Human Rights Law Institute, *The Chicago Principles on Post-Conflict Justice.*

13. United Nations, *2.10: The UN Approach to DDR*, February 2021, https://www.unddr.org/wp-content/uploads/2021/02/IDDRS-2.10-The-UN-Approach-To-DDR.pdf.

14. Ibid.

15. Ibid.

16. UN Peacebuilding Support Office, "DDR and Peacebuilding: Thematic Review of DDR Contributions to Peacebuilding and the Role of the Peacebuilding Fund," https://www.un.org/peacebuilding/sites/www.un.org.peacebuilding/files/documents/ddr_pbf_thematic_review.pdf.

17. International Human Rights Law Institute, *The Chicago Principles on Post-Conflict Justice.*

18. US Department of State, "Prosecuting Serious Crimes and Human Rights Violations," https://2009-2017.state.gov/j/gcj/transitional/257569.htm.

19. Anne F. Bayefsky, "Office of the United Nations High Commissioner for Human Rights," in *The UN Human Rights Treaty System in the 21st Century*, ed. Anne Bayefsky, 451–58 (Brill | Nijhoff, 2000), https://doi.org/10.1163/9789004502758_044.

20. Ibid.

21. Ibid.

22. Bar-Tal, *Shared Beliefs in a Society.*

23. James Dobbins et al., "East Timor," in *Overcoming Obstacles to Peace: Local Factors in Nation-Building*, 125–50 (RAND Corporation, 2013), http://www.jstor.org/stable/10.7249/j.ctt3fgzrv.14.

24. Stephen F. Burgess, "Fashioning Integrated Security Forces After Conflict," *African Security* 1, no. 2 (2008): 69–91, https://www.jstor.org/stable/48598782.

SECTION 8. RESTORATIVE JUSTICE, PRISONERS, AND REFUGEES

1. International Human Rights Law Institute, ed., *The Chicago Principles on Post-Conflict Justice* (2008).

2. OHCHR, "A/76/180: Promotion of Truth, Justice, Reparation and Guarantees of Non-Recurrence—Note by the Secretary-General," https://www.ohchr

.org/en/documents/thematic-reports/a76180-promotion-truth-justice-reparation-and-guarantees-non-recurrence.

3. Dustin N. Sharp, "Addressing Dilemmas of the Global and the Local in Transitional Justice," *SSRN Electronic Journal* (2013), https://doi.org/10.2139/ssrn.2288853.

4. Ibid.; International Court of Justice, Legal Consequences Arising from the Policies and Practices of Israel in the Occupied Palestinian Territory, Including East Jerusalem, Advisory Opinion, July 19, 2024.

5. International Human Rights Law Institute, *The Chicago Principles on Post-Conflict Justice.*

6. Colleen Murphy, *The Conceptual Foundations of Transitional Justice* (Cambridge University Press, 2017), https://doi.org/10.1017/9781316084229.

7. Nadim Khoury, "6. Transitional Justice in Palestine/Israel: Whose Justice? Which Transition?," in *Rethinking Statehood in Palestine*, by Leila H. Farsakh, 153–72 (University of California Press, 2021), https://doi.org/10.1515/9780520385634-010.

8. Murphy, *The Conceptual Foundations of Transitional Justice.*

9. Khoury, "6. Transitional Justice in Palestine/Israel."

10. United Nations, "A/HRC/54/24: International Legal Standards Underpinning the Pillars of Transitional Justice—Report of the Special Rapporteur on the Promotion of Truth, Justice, Reparation and Guarantees of Non-Recurrence, Fabián Salvioli," July 10, 2023, https://www.ohchr.org/en/documents/thematic-reports/ahrc5424-international-legal-standards-underpinning-pillars-transitional.

11. The Conference on Jewish Material Claims Against Germany, Inc., "Ethical Guidelines and Practices Including Conflict of Interest Policy," June 28, 2022, https://www.claimscon.org/wp-content/uploads/2022/07/Ethical-Guidelines-COI-Policy-and-Disclosure-Forms_adopted-6-28-22.pdf.

12. Abeer Baker and Anat Matar, eds., *Threat: Palestinian Political Prisoners in Israel* (Pluto Press, 2011), https://doi.org/10.2307/j.ctt183p121.

13. OHCHR, "Special Rapporteur Says Israel's Unlawful Carceral Practices in the Occupied Palestinian Territory Are Tantamount to International Crimes and Have Turned It into an Open-Air Prison," https://www.ohchr.org/en/news/2023/07/special-rapporteur-says-israels-unlawful-carceral-practices-occupied-palestinian.

14. HaMoked: Center for the Defence of the Individual, "Statistics on 'Security Inmates,'" https://hamoked.org/prisoners-charts.php.

15. UN Human Rights Council, "Report of the Special Rapporteur on the Situation of Human Rights in the Palestinian Territories Occupied Since 1967," A/HRC/53/59, https://www.ohchr.org/en/documents/country-reports/ahrc5359-report-special-rapporteur-situation-human-rights-palestinian.

16. Hagar Shezaf and Maya Horodniceanu, "Israel's Other Justice System Has Rules of Its Own," *Haaretz*, April 25, 2022, https://www.haaretz.com/israel-news/2022-04-25/ty-article-magazine/.highlight/israels-other-justice-system-has-rules-of-its-own/00000180-6566-d824-ad9e-e7664fa10000.

17. Addameer: Prisoner Support and Human Rights Association, "The Impact of Israel's New Ultranationalist Government on the Palestinian Prisoners' Movement," January 31, 2023, https://www.addameer.org/sites/default/files/publications/The%20Impact%20of%20Israel%E2%80%99s%20New%20Ultranationalist%20Government%20on%20the%20Palestinian%20Prisoners%E2%80%99%20Movement%2031.1.23.pdf; and *Escalating Oppression: Israel's Systematic Violations Intensify in Palestine Post-October 7, 2023*, January 23, 2024, https://www.addameer.org/sites/default/files/publications/Full%20Report%20on%20the%20situation%20after%20October%207th.pdf.

18. UN Human Rights Council, "Report of the Special Rapporteur on the Situation of Human Rights in the Palestinian Territories Occupied Since 1967."

19. Baker and Matar, *Threat: Palestinian Political Prisoners in Israel*.

20. C. D. Dwyer, "Risk, Politics and the 'Scientification' of Political Judgement: Prisoner Release and Conflict Transformation in Northern Ireland," *British Journal of Criminology* 47, no. 5 (April 24, 2007): 779–97, https://doi.org/10.1093/bjc/azm025.

21. Elrena Van der Spuy, "The National Peace Accord and Police Reform in South Africa: The Role of the Police Board as an Interim Policy Mechanism, 1992–1994," *Journal of Contemporary History* 33, no. 1 (2008): 37–58.

22. Manuel Cárdenas, Darío Páez, Bernard Rimé, and Maitane Arnoso, "How Transitional Justice Processes and Official Apologies Influence Reconciliation: The Case of the Chilean 'Truth and Reconciliation' and 'Political Imprisonment and Torture' Commissions," *Journal of Community and Applied Social Psychology* 25, no. 6 (November 2015): 515–30, https://doi.org/10.1002/casp.2231.

23. International Committee of the Red Cross (ICRC), "Rule 132. Participation in Public Affairs," https://ihl-databases.icrc.org/en/customary-ihl/v1/rule132.

24. UN Security Council, Resolution 242, "The Situation in the Middle East," S/RES/242, November 22, 1967; UN General Assembly, Resolution 194 (III), "Palestine: Progress Report of the United Nations Mediator," A/RES/194, December 11, 1948.

25. ReliefWeb, "The Core Issues of the Israeli-Palestinian Conflict," November 23, 2007, https://reliefweb.int/report/israel/core-issues-israeli-palestinian-conflict.

26. UNHCR US, "Handbook on Procedures and Criteria for Determining Refugee Status under the 1951 Convention and the 1967 Protocol Relating to the Status of Refugees," https://www.unhcr.org/us/media/handbook-procedures-and-criteria-determining-refugee-status-under-1951-convention-and-1967.

27. Rex Brynen and Roula El-Rifai, *Palestinian Refugees: Challenges of Repatriation and Development* (I. B. Tauris, 2007).

28. Alexander Betts, "Comprehensive Plans of Action: Insights from CIREFCA and the Indochinese CPA," Working Paper no. 120, UNHCR, Evaluation and Policy Analysis Unit, January 2006, https://www.unhcr.org/sites/default/files/legacy-pdf/43eb6a152.pdf.

29. Susan M. Akram and Terry Rempel, "Temporary Protection as an Instrument for Implementing the Right of Return for Palestinian Refugees," *Boston University International Law Journal* 22 (2004): 1.

30. Diane F. Orentlicher, "'Settling Accounts' Revisited: Reconciling Global Norms with Local Agency," *International Journal of Transitional Justice* 1, no. 1 (March 1, 2007): 10–22, https://doi.org/10.1093/ijtj/ijm010.

SECTION 9. ELECTIONS AND THE CULMINATION OF THE BLUEPRINT

1. Fionnuala Ní Aoláin and Colm Campbell, "The Paradox of Transition in Conflicted Democracies," *Human Rights Quarterly* 27, no. 1 (February 2005): 172–213, https://doi.org/10.1353/hrq.2005.0001.

2. Ibid.

3. Israel Central Bureau of Statistics, "Statistics: Israel's Independence Day 2024," May 9, 2024, https://www.cbs.gov.il/he/mediarelease/doclib/2024/141/11_24_141e.pdf.

4. Palestinian Central Bureau of Statistics, "Indicators," https://www.pcbs.gov.ps/site/lang__en/881/default.aspx#Census.

5. European Commission for Democracy Through Law (Venice Commission), "Guidelines on Prohibition and Dissolution of Political Parties and Analogous Measures," September 29, 2004, https://www.venice.coe.int/webforms/documents/default.aspx?pdffile=CDL-INF(2000)001-e.

6. Ibid.

7. Ibid.

8. "South Africa: Human Rights Developments," in *Human Rights Watch World Report 1994*, https://www.hrw.org/reports/1994/WR94/Africa-07.htm.

APPENDIX A. GUIDING PRINCIPLES FOR THE TRANSITION

1. United Nations, Universal Declaration of Human Rights, December 10, 1948, https://www.un.org/en/about-us/universal-declaration-of-human-rights.

2. Organization for Security and Co-operation in Europe (OSCE), *Guidelines on Freedom of Peaceful Assembly*, 2nd ed. (OSCE Office for Democratic Institutions and Human Rights, 2010), https://www.osce.org/files/f/documents/4/0/73405.pdf.

3. European Union Agency for Fundamental Rights, "Article 48: Presumption of Innocence and Right of Defence," in EU Charter of Fundamental Rights, Official Journal of the European Union, C 303/17-14.12.2007, https://fra.europa.eu/en/eu-charter/article/48-presumption-innocence-and-right-defence; UN Human Rights Council, "Report of the Working Group on Arbitrary Detention: United Nations Basic Principles and Guidelines on Remedies and Procedures on the Right of Anyone Deprived of Their Liberty to Bring Proceedings Before a Court," A/HRC/30/37, July 6, 2015, https://www.refworld.org/reference/themreport/unhrc/2015/en/106782.

4. United Nations, Universal Declaration of Human Rights, Article 5, https://www.un.org/en/about-us/universal-declaration-of-human-rights.

5. The Knesset, Basic Law: State Economy, https://main.knesset.gov.il/EN/activity/documents/BasicLawsPDF/BasicLawStateEconomy.pdf.

6. The Knesset, Basic Laws of the State of Israel, https://main.knesset.gov.il:443/EN/activity/Pages/BasicLaws.aspx.

7. The Knesset, Basic Law: The Judiciary, https://main.knesset.gov.il/EN/activity/documents/BasicLawsPDF/BasicLawTheJudiciary.pdf.

8. The Knesset, Basic Laws of the State of Israel.

9. The Knesset, Basic Law: State Comptroller, https://main.knesset.gov.il/EN/activity/documents/BasicLawsPDF/BasicLawStateComptroller.pdf.

10. The Knesset, Basic Laws of the State of Israel.

11. The Knesset, Basic Law: Human Dignity and Liberty, https://main.knesset.gov.il/EN/activity/documents/BasicLawsPDF/BasicLawLiberty.pdf.

12. The Knesset, Basic Laws of the State of Israel.

13. United Nations, Universal Declaration of Human Rights, Article 5.

APPENDIX B. LAWS THAT SHOULD BE IMMEDIATELY REVOKED OR AMENDED

1. Adalah: The Legal Center for Arab Minority Rights in Israel, "Admissions Committees Law (2023)," https://www.adalah.org/en/law/view/494#:~:text=In%202023%2C%20the%20Israeli%20Knesset%20to%20operate%20an%20admissions%20committee.

APPENDIX D. MAPPING EXISTING SECURITY FORCES

1. Hugh Lovatt and Saleh Hijazi, "Mapping Palestinian Politics: Security Forces," European Council on Foreign Relations (ECFR), April 19, 2018, https://ecfr.eu/special/mapping_palestinian_politics.

2. Ibid.

3. Ibid.

4. Ibid.

5. Merlyn Thomas, Jake Horton, and Benedict Garman, "Israel Gaza: Checking Israel's Claim to Have Killed 10,000 Hamas Fighters," BBC, February 29, 2024, https://www.bbc.com/news/world-middle-east-68387864.

6. Lovatt and Hijazi, "Mapping Palestinian Politics: Security Forces."

7. Ibid.

8. Ibid.

9. Ibid.

Bibliography

Abdulrahim, Raja, Helmuth Rosales, Bilal Shbair, Anjali Singhvi, Erika Solomon, Iyad Abuheweila, Abu Bakr Bashir, et al. "Gaza in Ruins After a Year of War." *New York Times*, October 7, 2024. https://www.nytimes.com /interactive/2024/10/07/world/middleeast/israel-gaza-destruction-hamas -war.html.

Abunimah, Ali. *One Country: A Bold Proposal to End the Israeli-Palestinian Impasse.* Henry Holt & Company, 2006.

ACLU. *Promotion and Protection of All Human Rights, Civil, Political, Economic, Social and Cultural Rights, Including the Right to Development.* 2016. https://doi.org/10.1163/2210-7975_HRD-9970-2016149.

Adalah: The Legal Center for Arab Minority Rights in Israel. "Admissions Committees Law (2023)." https://www.adalah.org/en/law/view/494#:~: text=In%202023%2C%20the%20Israeli%20Knesset%20to%20operate% 20an%20admissions%20committee.

———. "Discriminatory Laws in Israel." https://www.adalah.org/en/law/index.

———. "Flag and Emblem Law." https://www.adalah.org/en/law/view/540.

———. "Israel's 2016 Counter-Terrorism Law and 1945 Emergency Regulations Regarding the Outlawing of Six Palestinian Human Rights and Civil Society Groups." November 23, 2021. https://www.adalah.org/uploads/uploads /Adalah_Expert_Opinion_Palestinian6_Nov2021.pdf.

Addameer: Prisoner Support and Human Rights Association. *Escalating Oppression: Israel's Systematic Violations Intensify in Palestine*

Post-October 7, 2023. January 23, 2024. https://www.addameer.org/sites
/default/files/publications/Full%20Report%20on%20the%20situation%20
after%20October%207th.pdf.

———. "The Impact of Israel's New Ultranationalist Government on the
Palestinian Prisoners' Movement." January 31, 2023. https://www
.addameer.org/sites/default/files/publications/The%20Impact%20of%20
Israel%E2%80%99s%20New%20Ultranationalist%20Government%
20on%20the%20Palestinian%20Prisoners%E2%80%99%20Movement%
2031.1.23.pdf.

———. "Introduction to Israeli Military Orders." July 2017. https://www
.addameer.org/israeli_military_judicial_system/military_orders.

———. "Statistics." April 4, 2024. https://www.addameer.org/statistics.

Addameer: Prisoner Support and Human Rights Association, Al Mezan Center
for Human Rights, and Al-Haq, Law in the Service of Man. "Israel's Policies
to Maintain and Entrench Its Settler-Colonial Apartheid Regime: Violent
Suppression of Demonstrations and Ensuing Wilful Killing and Injuries,
Arbitrary Detention, Torture, and Smear and Delegitimisation Campaigns
Against Human Rights Defenders and Organisations." Joint Submission to
the UN Independent International Commission of Inquiry on the Occupied
Palestinian Territory, including East Jerusalem, and Israel, February 2,
2023. https://www.addameer.org/news/4980.

Agence France Presse. "New Tally Puts Oct 7 Attack Death Toll in Israel at
1,189." May 28, 2024. https://www.barrons.com/news/new-tally-puts-
oct-7-attack-death-toll-in-israel-at-1-189-3e038de6.

———. "Turkey Presses UN for Arms Embargo on Israel in Joint Letter."
November 3, 2024. https://www.barrons.com/news/turkey-presses-un-
for-arms-embargo-on-israel-in-joint-letter-6f9f6a63.

Ahmedi, Sulejman. "The Distinctive Legal Features of Crimes Against Humanity." *European Journal of Interdisciplinary Studies* 2, no. 2 (April 30, 2016):
124–28. https://doi.org/10.26417/ejis.v2i2.p124-128.

Akram, Susan M., ed. *"No Security Without Law": Prospects for Implementing a
Rights-Based Approach in Palestinian-Israeli Security Negotiations, in
International Law and the Israeli-Palestinian Conflict: A Rights-Based
Approach to Middle East Peace.* Routledge, 2011.

Akram, Susan M., and Terry Rempel. "Temporary Protection as an Instrument
for Implementing the Right of Return for Palestinian Refugees." *Boston
University International Law Journal* 22 (2004).

A Land for All. "Two States: One Homeland." https://www.alandforall.org
/english-program.

Albanese, Francesca. "Situation of Human Rights in the Palestinian Territories
Occupied Since 1967." UN General Assembly, September 21, 2022. https://
www.un.org/unispal/wp-content/uploads/2022/10/A.77.356_210922.pdf.

Al Jazeera. "Timeline: Hamas-Fatah Conflict." May 4, 2011. https://www
.aljazeera.com/news/2011/5/4/timeline-hamas-fatah-conflict.

Al Mashni, Mohammed Ibrahim, Yusramizza Binti Md Isa Yusuff, and Nor
Azlina Binti Mohd Noor. "Historical Evolution of the Palestinian Legal and
Judicial System 1516 to Present." *Journal of Positive School Psychology* 6,
no. 5 (2022): 2692–705.

Al-Shalchi, Hadeel. "The Palestinian Authority Is Promising Change. Many
Palestinians Say It's Not Enough." NPR, February 28, 2024. https://www
.npr.org/2024/02/28/1234242951/palestinian-authority-resignation-gaza-
west-bank.

Ambos, Kai. "The Legal Framework of Transitional Justice: A Systematic Study
with a Special Focus on the Role of the ICC." In *Building a Future on Peace
and Justice*, edited by Kai Ambos, Judith Large, and Marieke Wierda,
19–103. Springer Berlin Heidelberg, 2009. https://doi.org/10.1007/978-3-540-
85754-9_4.

Amnesty International. *Israel's Apartheid Against Palestinians: Cruel System
of Domination and Crime Against Humanity.* February 1, 2022. https://
www.amnesty.org/en/documents/mde15/5141/2022/en.

———. "Tunisia: New Draft Constitution Undermines Independence of Judiciary
and Weakens Human Rights Safeguards." July 5, 2022. https://www.amnesty
.org/en/latest/news/2022/07/tunisia-new-draft-constitution-undermines-
independence-of-judiciary-and-weakens-human-rights-safeguards.

———. *"You Feel Like You Are Subhuman": Israel's Genocide Against Palestinians in Gaza.* December 2024. https://www.amnesty.org/en/documents
/mde15/8668/2024/en/.

Anthony, C., Daniel Egel, Charles Ries, Craig Bond, Andrew Liepman, Jeffrey
Martini, Steven Simon, et al. *The Costs of the Israeli-Palestinian Conflict.*
RAND Corporation, 2015. https://doi.org/10.7249/RR740-1.

Anti-Defamation League (ADL). "South African Flag (Apartheid Era)." https://
www.adl.org/resources/hate-symbol/south-african-flag-apartheid-era.

Arian, Asher, David Nachmias, and Ruth Amir. "Transition of Government
Power." In *Executive Governance in Israel*, by Asher Arian, David Nachmias,
and Ruth Amir, 126–46. Palgrave Macmillan UK, 2002. https://doi.org/10
.1057/9781403990150_7.

Arielli, Nir, Jacob Stoil, and Mary Elizabeth Walters. "The Case for Sending a
Multinational Force to Gaza." November 2023. https://mitvim.org.il/wp-
content/uploads/2023/11/English20-20The20Case20for20Sending20a20
Multi-National20Force20to20Gaz.pdf.

Arranz, Adolfo, Jonathan Saul, Stephen Farrell, Simon Scarr, and Clare Trainor.
"Inside the Tunnels of Gaza." Reuters, December 31, 2023. https://www
.reuters.com/graphics/ISRAEL-PALESTINIANS/GAZA-TUNNELS
/gkvldmzorvb/.

Association for Civil Rights in Israel. "One Rule, Two Legal Systems: Israel's Regime of Laws in the West Bank." October 2014. https://law.acri.org.il/en/wp-content/uploads/2015/02/Two-Systems-of-Law-English-FINAL.pdf.

Avalon Project. "A Decade of American Foreign Policy 1941–1949: United States Position on the Palestine Problem; Statement by Ambassador Warren R. Austin, United States Representative in the Security Council, March 19, 1948." https://avalon.law.yale.edu/20th_century/decad166.asp.

Azarov, V. "From Discretion to Necessity: Third State Responsibility for Israel's Control of Stay and Entry into Palestinian Territory." *Journal of Human Rights Practice* 6, no. 2 (July 1, 2014): 327–55. https://doi.org/10.1093/jhuman/huu014.

Baconi, Tareq. "Opinion: The Two-State Solution Is an Unjust, Impossible Fantasy." *New York Times*, April 1, 2024. https://www.nytimes.com/2024/04/01/opinion/two-state-solution-israel-palestine.html.

Bahgat, Gawdat. "The Arab Peace Initiative: An Assessment." *Middle East Policy* 16, no. 1 (March 2009): 33–39. https://doi.org/10.1111/j.1475-4967.2009.00377.x.

Baker, Abeer, and Anat Matar, eds. *Threat: Palestinian Political Prisoners in Israel*. Pluto Press, 2011. https://doi.org/10.2307/j.ctt183p121.

Bâli, Aslı Ü. "International Law and Rights-Based Remedies in the Israel-Palestine Conflict: Settlements." *Hastings International and Comparative Law Review* 28, no. 3 (Spring 2005): 387–404. https://repository.uclawsf.edu/cgi/viewcontent.cgi?article=1642&context=hastings_international_comparative_law_review.

Bâli, Aslı Ü., and Omar M. Dajani, eds. *Federalism and Decentralization in the Contemporary Middle East and North Africa*. Cambridge University Press, 2023. https://doi.org/10.1017/9781108923682.

Barghouti, Omar. "Organizing for Self-Determination, Ethical De-Zionization and Resisting Apartheid." *Contemporary Arab Affairs* 2, no. 4 (October 1, 2009): 576–86. https://doi.org/10.1080/17550910903237145.

Barnett, Michael, Nathan Brown, Marc Lynch, and Shibley Telhami. "Israel's One-State Reality." *Foreign Affairs*, April 14, 2023. https://www.foreignaffairs.com/middle-east/israel-palestine-one-state-solution.

———, eds. *The One State Reality: What Is Israel/Palestine?* Cornell University Press, 2023.

Barron, Robert. "Palestinian Politics Timeline: Since the 2006 Election." US Institute of Peace. https://www.usip.org/palestinian-politics-timeline-2006-election.

Bar-Tal, Daniel. "From Intractable Conflict Through Conflict Resolution to Reconciliation: Psychological Analysis." *Political Psychology* 21, no. 2 (June 2000): 351–65. https://doi.org/10.1111/0162-895X.00192.

BIBLIOGRAPHY   231

———, ed. *Shared Beliefs in a Society: Social Psychological Analysis*. Sage Publications, 2000.

Bashi, Sari, and Kenneth Mann. *Disengaged Occupiers: The Legal Status of Gaza*. Gisha, 2007.

Bashir, Bashir, and Will Kymlicka. "Introduction: Struggles for Inclusion and Reconciliation in Modern Democracies." In *The Politics of Reconciliation in Multicultural Societies*, edited by Bashir Bashir and Will Kymlicka, 1–24. Oxford University Press, 2008.

Bassan-Nygate, Lotem. "The Micro-Foundations of Naming and Shaming." University of Wisconsin–Madison. Working Paper, 2021.

Bauer, Shane. "The Israeli Settlers Attacking Their Palestinian Neighbors." *New Yorker*, February 26, 2024. https://www.newyorker.com/magazine/2024/03/04/israel-west-bank-settlers-attacks-palestinians.

Bayefsky, Anne F. "Office of the United Nations High Commissioner for Human Rights." In *The UN Human Rights Treaty System in the 21st Century*, edited by Anne Bayefsky, 451–58. Brill | Nijhoff, 2000. https://doi.org/10.1163/9789004502758_044.

Beaumont, Peter, Quique Kierszenbaum, and Sufian Taha."'This Is More Than a Reaction to Rockets': Communal Violence Spreads in Israel." *The Guardian*, May 13, 2021. https://www.theguardian.com/world/2021/may/13/this-is-more-than-a-reaction-to-rockets-communal-violence-spreads-in-israel.

Belgian Constitution (English Translation). *Belgian Official Gazette*, March 30, 2021.

Ben-Naftali, Orna, Aeyal Gross, and Keren Michaeli. "Illegal Occupation: Framing the Occupied Palestinian Territory." *Berkeley Journal of International Law* 23, no. 2 (2005): 551–614. https://lawcat.berkeley.edu/record/1119804/files/fulltext.pdf.

Benomar, Jamal. Blueprint interview. Video call, August 23, 2023.

Berda, Yael. *Colonial Bureaucracy and Contemporary Citizenship*. Cambridge University Press, 2022. https://doi.org/10.1017/9781009053495.

———. *Living Emergency: Israel's Permit Regime in the Occupied West Bank*. Stanford University Press, 2018.

———. "Managing 'Dangerous Populations': How Colonial Emergency Laws Shape Citizenship." *Security Dialogue* 51, no. 6 (December 2020): 557–78. https://doi.org/10.1177/0967010620901908.

Bergman, Ronen. *Rise and Kill First: The Secret History of Israel's Targeted Assassinations*. Translated by Ronnie Hope. Random House, 2018.

Betts, Alexander. "Comprehensive Plans of Action: Insights from CIREFCA and the Indochinese CPA." Working Paper no. 120. UNHCR, Evaluation and Policy Analysis Unit, January 2006. https://www.unhcr.org/sites/default/files/legacy-pdf/43eb6a152.pdf.

Bilsky, Leora. "'Speaking Through the Mask': Israeli Arabs and the Changing Faces of Israeli Citizenship." *Middle East Law and Governance* 1, no. 2 (2009): 166–209.

Bisharat, George E. "Maximizing Rights: The One State Solution to the Palestinian-Israeli Conflict." *Global Jurist* 8, no. 2 (January 12, 2008). https://doi.org/10.2202/1934-2640.1266.

Blair, Dennis C. "Military Support for Democracy." *PRISM* 3, no. 3 (June 2012): 3–16. https://www.jstor.org/stable/26469742.

Bland, Byron. "Searching for Mandela: Finding a Way Beyond the Israeli-Palestinian Impasse." *Dynamics of Asymmetric Conflict* 7, no. 2–3 (September 2, 2014): 183–97. https://doi.org/10.1080/17467586.2014.968795.

Bogaards, Matthijs. "Consociationalism and the State." *Nationalism and Ethnic Politics* 30, no. 1 (January 2, 2024): 46–64. https://doi.org/10.1080/13537113.2023.2208395.

Booth, William, and Ruth Eglash. "Netanyahu Thinks a 'State-Minus' Is Enough for the Palestinians." *Washington Post*, May 24, 2023. https://www.washingtonpost.com/world/middle_east/israeli-leader-thinks-a-state-minus-is-enough-for-the-palestinians/2017/01/26/658fa5a6-e3cf-11e6-879b-356663383f1b_story.html.

Botelho, Catarina Santos. "European Constitutional Courts and Transitions to Democracy." *American Journal of Comparative Law* 69, no. 4 (December 31, 2021): 885–89. https://doi.org/10.1093/ajcl/avab021.

Brahm, Eric. "Conflict Stages." Beyond Intractability, July 6, 2016. https://www.beyondintractability.org/essay/conflict_stages.

Breaking the Silence. "Military Rule: Testimonies of Soldiers from the Civil Administration, Gaza DCL and COGAT 2011–2021." 2022. https://www.breakingthesilence.org.il/inside/wp-content/uploads/2022/07/Military_rule_testimony_booklet.pdf.

Bronee, Sten A. "The History of the Comprehensive Plan of Action." *International Journal of Refugee Law* 5, no. 4 (1993): 534–43.

Brynen, Rex, and Roula El-Rifai. *Palestinian Refugees: Challenges of Repatriation and Development.* I. B. Tauris, 2007.

B'Tselem. "Statistics on Revocation of Residency in East Jerusalem." April 19, 2023. http://www.btselem.org/jerusalem/revocation_statistics.

———. "This Is Apartheid: A Regime of Jewish Supremacy from the Jordan River to the Mediterranean Sea." January 12, 2021. https://www.btselem.org/publications/fulltext/202101_this_is_apartheid.

"B2. Al-Haq, 'Torturing Each Other: The Widespread Practices of Arbitrary Detention and Torture in the Palestinian Territory,' Ramallah, July 2008 (Excerpts)." *Journal of Palestine Studies* 38, no. 1 (October 1, 2008): 166–69. https://doi.org/10.1525/jps.2008.38.1.166.

Buntman, F., and T.-Y. Huang. "The Role of Political Imprisonment in Developing and Enhancing Political Leadership: A Comparative Study of South
Africa's and Taiwan's Democratization." *Journal of Asian and African
Studies* 35, no. 1 (January 1, 2000): 43–66. https://doi.org/10.1177
/002190960003500104.

Burgess, Stephen F. "Fashioning Integrated Security Forces After Conflict."
African Security 1, no. 2 (December 3, 2008): 69–91. https://doi.org/10.1080
/19362200802479772.

Byrne, Aisling. "Building a Police State in Palestine." *Foreign Policy* (blog),
January 18, 2011. https://foreignpolicy.com/2011/01/18/building-a-police-
state-in-palestine.

Calderon, Asaf. "What's So Scary About a State of All Its Citizens?" *+972
Magazine*, March 13, 2019. https://www.972mag.com/whats-scary-israel-
state-citizens.

Cannizzaro, Enzo. "The Strange Story of the 'Conditional' Admission of the
State of Palestine to the United Nations." *EJIL: Talk!* (blog), June 11, 2024.
https://www.ejiltalk.org/the-strange-story-of-the-conditional-admission-
of-the-state-of-palestine-to-the-united-nations.

Cantekin, Aytekin. "Ripeness and Readiness Theories in International Conflict
Resolution." *Journal of Mediation and Applied Conflict Analysis* 3, no. 2
(February 14, 2017): 414–28. https://doi.org/10.33232/jmaca.3.2.7917.

Cárdenas, Manuel, Darío Páez, Bernard Rimé, and Maitane Arnoso. "How
Transitional Justice Processes and Official Apologies Influence Reconcilia-
tion: The Case of the Chilean 'Truth and Reconciliation' and 'Political
Imprisonment and Torture' Commissions." *Journal of Community and
Applied Social Psychology* 25, no. 6 (November 2015): 515–30. https://doi
.org/10.1002/casp.2231.

Cardozo Israeli Supreme Court Project. "About the Supreme Court of Israel."
https://versa.cardozo.yu.edu/about-supreme-court-israel.

Carvajalino, Jinú, and Maja Davidović. "Escaping or Reinforcing Hierarchies?
Norm Relations in Transitional Justice." *International Studies Review* 25,
no. 3 (June 23, 2023). https://doi.org/10.1093/isr/viad022.

Cawthra, Gavin. "Security Governance in South Africa." *African Security
Review* 14, no. 3 (January 2005): 95–105. https://doi.org/10.1080/10246029
.2005.9627376.

Centre for Human Rights, University of Pretoria. "Overview of Global and
Regional Human Rights Standards on the Police Use of Force." May 20,
2020. https://www.chr.up.ac.za/images/centrenews/2020/Global_and_
Regional_Rules_on_Police_Use_of_Force_20_May_2020.pdf.

Chacar, Henriette. "Israel's Knesset Passes Law Barring Palestinian Spouses."
Reuters, March 10, 2022. https://www.reuters.com/world/middle-east
/israels-knesset-passes-law-barring-palestinian-spouses-2022-03-10.

"Chapter 13: Chronology of Apartheid Legislation 1." In *Truth and Reconciliation Commission of South Africa Report*. Truth and Reconciliation Commission of South Africa, 1998. https://www.justice.gov.za/trc/report/finalreport/Volume%201.pdf.

Chopra, Jarat, and Tanja Hohe. "Participatory Intervention." *Global Governance: A Review of Multilateralism and International Organizations* 10, no. 3 (August 3, 2004): 289–305. https://doi.org/10.1163/19426720-01003004.

Civilian Secretariat for Police Service. "2016 White Paper on Policing." *South African Government Gazette*, September 1, 2017. https://www.gov.za/sites/default/files/gcis_document/201709/41082gon914.pdf.

Cohen, Hillel. *Good Arabs: The Israeli Security Agencies and the Israeli Arabs, 1948–1967*. University of California Press, 2011.

Cohen, I. Mateo. "The Right-Wing 'One-State Solution': Narrative, Proposals, and the Future of the Conflict." *Israel Studies* 27, no. 1 (December 2021): 132–55. https://doi.org/10.2979/israelstudies.27.1.06.

The Conference on Jewish Material Claims Against Germany, Inc. "Ethical Guidelines and Practices Including Conflict of Interest Policy." June 28, 2022. https://www.claimscon.org/wp-content/uploads/2022/07/Ethical-Guidelines-COI-Policy-and-Disclosure-Forms_adopted-6-28-22.pdf.

Constitution of Bosnia and Herzegovina 1995 (Rev. 2009). 2009. https://www.constituteproject.org/constitution/Bosnia_Herzegovina_2009.

Constitution of the Republic of Kosovo (with Amendments I–XXVI). 2008. Republic of Kosovo, Assembly. https://www.constituteproject.org/constitution/Kosovo_2016.

Cook, Jonathan. "Video: Netanyahu Brags He Deceived US to Destroy Oslo Accords." *Electronic Intifada*, July 20, 2010. https://electronicintifada.net/content/video-netanyahu-brags-he-deceived-us-destroy-oslo-accords/8934.

Cordell, Karl, and Stefan Wolff, eds. *The Routledge Handbook of Ethnic Conflict*. 2nd ed. Routledge Handbooks. Routledge, Taylor & Francis Group, 2016.

Cortellessa, Eric. "Two States Is Israel's Only Hope, Says Former Prime Minister." *Time*, November 6, 2023. https://time.com/6332127/israel-palestine-war-ehud-barak.

Dahbour, Omar. "Self-Determination and Power-Sharing in Israel/Palestine." *Ethnopolitics* 15, no. 4 (August 7, 2016): 393–407. https://doi.org/10.1080/17449057.2016.1212516.

Dajani, Omar. "Shadow or Shade? The Roles of International Law in Palestinian-Israeli Peace Talks." *Yale Journal of International Law* 32, no. 61 (2007): 62–123.

Daniele, Luigi. "Enforcing Illegality: Israel's Military Justice in the West Bank." *Questions of International Law*, no. 44 (2017): 21–40.

———. "Incidentality of the Civilian Harm in International Humanitarian Law and Its *Contra Legem* Antonyms in Recent Discourses on the Laws of War." *Journal of Conflict and Security Law* 29, no. 1 (April 27, 2024): 21–54. https://doi.org/10.1093/jcsl/krae004.

Daniels, Peter. "National Security Strategy Development: South Africa Case Study." Africa Center for Strategic Studies, March 2019. https://africacenter.org/wp-content/uploads/2019/04/2019-04-NSSD-Case-Study-South-Africa-Defense-Policy-Review.pdf.

DAWN. "Expert Panel Concludes Israel Committing Genocide Against Palestinians in Gaza." January 9, 2024. https://dawnmena.org/expert-panel-concludes-israel-committing-genocide-against-palestinians-in-gaza.

Dekel, Udi, Arik Barbing, and Attila Somfalvi. "So What Yes? New Thinking on the Palestinian Conception—Episode 2: Does Another Palestinian Leadership Exist?" *Hebrew. Podcastrategi: The Institute for National Security Studies (INSS)*, May 9, 2024. https://soundcloud.com/inss2006/2a-6.

Djerejian, Edward P., Samih al-Abid, Gilad Sher, Khalil Shikaki, Marwan Muasher, Nathan J. Brown, Tariq Dana, and Dahlia Scheindlin. "Two States or One? Reappraising the Israeli-Palestinian Impasse." Carnegie Endowment for International Peace, September 20, 2018. https://carnegieendowment.org/research/2018/09/two-states-or-one-reappraising-the-israeli-palestinian-impasse?lang=en.

Djuve, Vilde Lunnan, and Carl Henrik Knutsen. "Economic Crisis and Regime Transitions from Within." *Journal of Peace Research* 61, no. 3 (May 2024): 446–61.

Dobbins, James, et al. "East Timor." In *Overcoming Obstacles to Peace: Local Factors in Nation-Building*, 125–50. RAND Corporation, 2013. http://www.jstor.org/stable/10.7249/j.ctt3fgzrv.14.

Dorsch, Michael T., and Paul Maarek. "Economic Downturns, Inequality, and Democratic Improvements." *European Journal of Political Economy* 62 (March 2020). https://doi.org/10.1016/j.ejpoleco.2020.101856.

Drory, Ze'ev. "Society Strength as a Base for Military Power: The State of Israel During the Early 1950s." *Israel Affairs* 12, no. 3 (July 2006): 412–29. https://doi.org/10.1080/13537120600744669.

Dugard, John. UN Secretary-General. Question of the Violation of Human Rights in the Occupied Arab Territories, Including Palestine, Report of the Special Rapporteur of the Commission on Human Rights on the Situation of Human Rights in the Palestinian Territories Occupied by Israel Since 1967. A/57/366, August 29, 2002, ii 21.

Dumper, Michael. "Policing Divided Cities: Stabilization and Law Enforcement in Palestinian East Jerusalem." *International Affairs* 89, no. 5 (September 2013): 1247–64. https://doi.org/10.1111/1468-2346.12070.

Duthie, Roger. "Transitional Justice and Displacement." *International Journal of Transitional Justice* 5, no. 2 (July 1, 2011): 241–61. https://doi.org/10.1093/ijtj/ijr009.

Dwyer, Clare D. "Risk, Politics and the 'Scientification' of Political Judgement: Prisoner Release and Conflict Transformation in Northern Ireland." *British Journal of Criminology* 47, no. 5 (April 24, 2007): 779–97. https://doi.org/10.1093/bjc/azm025.

Efron, Shira, and Ghaith al-Omari. "How Pentagon Bureaucracy Could Undermine West Bank Security." The Washington Institute for Near East Policy. June 16, 2022. https://www.washingtoninstitute.org/policy-analysis/how-pentagon-bureaucracy-could-undermine-west-bank-security.

Efron, Shira, and Ilan Goldenberg. "United States Policy Toward the Gaza Strip." RAND. February 13, 2018. https://www.rand.org/content/dam/rand/pubs/external_publications/EP60000/EP67493/EP-67493.pdf.

Efron, Shira, and Evan Gottesman. "In Search of a Viable Option." Israel Policy Forum, n.d. https://israelpolicyforum.org/in-search-of-a-viable-option/.

Egel, Daniel, C. Ross Anthony, Shira Efron, Rita Karam, Mary E. Vaiana, and Charles P. Ries. *Alternatives in the Israeli-Palestinian Conflict*. Research Report, RR-A725-1. RAND Corporation, 2021.

Eghbariah, Rabea. "Toward Nakba as a Legal Concept." *Columbia Law Review* 124, no. 4 (May 2024).

Eisenstadt, Todd A., and Tofigh Maboudi. "Being There Is Half the Battle: Group Inclusion, Constitution-Writing, and Democracy." *Comparative Political Studies* 52, no. 13–14 (November 2019): 2135–70. https://doi.org/10.1177/0010414019830739.

El-Ad, Hagai. "Palestinians Perpetually Participating." *Tikkun* 32, no. 2 (April 1, 2017): 38. https://doi.org/10.1215/08879982-3858259.

El Kurd, Dana. "Introduction: Delayed Statehood; Palestine Before and After the Oslo Accords." In *Polarized and Demobilized: Legacies of Authoritarianism in Palestine*. Oxford University Press, 2020. https://doi.org/10.1093/oso/9780190095864.003.0001.

Erakat, Noura. "Beyond Sterile Negotiations: Looking for a Leadership with a Strategy." *Jadaliyya* (blog). https://www.jadaliyya.com/Details/25223.

———. *Justice for Some: Law and the Question of Palestine*. Stanford University Press, 2019.

Erakat, Noura, and John Reynolds. "Understanding Apartheid." *Jewish Currents*, November 1, 2022. https://jewishcurrents.org/understanding-apartheid.

Esveld, Bill Van. "'Forget About Him, He's Not Here': Israel's Control of Palestinian Residency in the West Bank and Gaza." Human Rights Watch, February 5, 2012. https://www.hrw.org/report/2012/02/05/forget-about-him-hes-not-here/israels-control-palestinian-residency-west-bank-and.

European Commission for Democracy Through Law (Venice Commission). "Guidelines on Prohibition and Dissolution of Political Parties and Analogous Measures." September 29, 2004. https://www.venice.coe.int/webforms /documents/default.aspx?pdffile=CDL-INF(2000)001-e.

European Council on Foreign Affairs (ECFR). "Mapping Palestinian Politics: Judicial System." March 20, 2018. https://ecfr.eu/special/mapping_ palestinian_politics/justice_system.

European Union Agency for Fundamental Rights. "Article 48: Presumption of Innocence and Right of Defence." In EU Charter of Fundamental Rights, Official Journal of the European Union, C 303/17-14.12.2007. https://fra .europa.eu/en/eu-charter/article/48-presumption-innocence-and-right-defence.

Ezrahi, Yaron. "You Don't Make Peace with Friends. You . . . ." *Chicago Tribune*, September 15, 1993. https://www.chicagotribune.com/news/ct-xpm-1993 -09-15-9309150118-story.html.

Facing History & Ourselves. "South Africa: Transition to Democracy." July 31, 2018. https://www.facinghistory.org/resource-library/transition-democracy.

Falk, Richard, and Virginia Q. Tilley. "Israeli Practices Towards the Palestinian People and the Question of Apartheid." *Palestine and the Israeli Occupation* 1, no. 1 (Spring 2017): 1–65.

Farsakh, Leila. "A Common State in Israel-Palestine: Historical Origins and Lingering Challenges." *Ethnopolitics* 15, no. 4 (August 7, 2016): 380–92. https://doi.org/10.1080/17449057.2016.1210348.

———. "The Question of Palestinian Statehood and the Future of Decolonization." *Middle East Report*, no. 302 (Spring 2022): 1. https://merip.org/2022/05/the-question-of-palestinian-statehood-and-the-future-of-decolonization.

———. *Rethinking Statehood in Palestine: Self-Determination and Decolonization Beyond Partition*. New Directions in Palestinian Studies. University of California Press, 2021.

Federman, Josef. "Israel Revokes Palestinian FM's Travel Permit over UN Move." AP News, January 8, 2023. https://apnews.com/article/politics-israel-government-91ba538476380a16aad4e2cbdae2e235.

Filatov, Victor. "Transitional Justice Model Implementation's Mechanisms' Characteristics." *Cuestiones Políticas* 41, no. 78 (August 28, 2023): 16–24. https://doi.org/10.46398/cuestpol.4178.00.

Filut, Adrian. "Economic Concerns Mount as Israel Faces Drop in Foreign Investments and Services Export." *Calcalist*, March 18, 2024. https://www .calcalistech.com/ctechnews/article/ldor8dzx5.

Forman, Geremy, and Alexandre (Sandy) Kedar. "From Arab Land to 'Israel Lands': The Legal Dispossession of the Palestinians Displaced by Israel in the Wake of 1948." *Environment and Planning D: Society and Space* 22, no. 6 (December 2004): 809–30. https://doi.org/10.1068/d402.

Francis, Sahar. "Israel's Military Justice System as an Annexationist Tool." In *Prolonged Occupation and International Law*, edited by Nada Kiswanson and Susan Power, 159–75. Brill | Nijhoff, 2023. https://doi.org/10.1163 /9789004503939_009.

Freedman, Eliyahu. "Analysis: Why Does Israel's Ben-Gvir Want a 'National Guard'?" *Al Jazeera*, April 3, 2023. https://www.aljazeera.com/news/2023 /4/3/analysis-why-does-israels-ben-gvir-want-a-national-guard.

Gabiam, Nell. "Negotiating Rights: Palestinian Refugees and the Protection Gap." *Anthropological Quarterly* 79, no. 4 (September 2006): 717–30. https://doi.org/10.1353/anq.2006.0049.

Geddes, Barbara, Joseph Wright, and Erica Frantz. "Autocratic Breakdown and Regime Transitions: A New Data Set." *Perspectives on Politics* 12, no. 2 (June 2014): 313–31. https://doi.org/10.1017/S1537592714000851.

Gisha. "Gaza Up Close." June 28, 2023. https://features.gisha.org/gaza-up-close.

Goldstone, Richard. "Interim Report on Criminal Political Violence by Elements Within the South African Police, the Kwazulu Police, and the Inkatha Freedom Party." Goldstone Commission on the Prevention of Political Violence and Intimidation, March 18, 1994.

———. "The South African Bill of Rights." *Texas International Law Journal* 32, no. 2 (1997): 451–69.

Goldstone Commission on the Prevention of Political Violence and Intimidation. "Final Report of the Multi-National Panel Regarding the Curbing of Public Violence and Intimidation During the Forthcoming Election." August 11, 1993. https://searchworks.stanford.edu/view/2740653.

Goodman, Micah, and Eylon Levy. *Catch-67: The Left, the Right, and the Legacy of the Six-Day War*. Yale University Press, 2018.

Graham-Harrison, Emma, and Toby Helm. "Netanyahu Defies Biden, Insisting There's 'No Space' for Palestinian State." *The Observer*, January 20, 2024. https://www.theguardian.com/world/2024/jan/20/netanyahu-defies-biden-insisting-theres-no-space-for-palestinian-state.

Gross, Aeyal. *The Writing on the Wall: Rethinking the International Law of Occupation*. Cambridge University Press, 2017. https://doi.org/10.1017 /9781316536308.

Grossman, Guy, Devorah Manekin, and Yotam Margalit. "How Sanctions Affect Public Opinion in Target Countries: Experimental Evidence From Israel." *Comparative Political Studies* 51, no. 14 (December 2018): 1823–57. https:// doi.org/10.1177/0010414018774370.

Gyamfi, Gerald Dapaah. "Exploring the Roles of Police Leaders in Countries in Transition." *International Journal of Risk and Contingency Management* 9, no. 4 (October 2020): 1–17. https://doi.org/10.4018 /IJRCM.2020100101.

Haggard, Stephan, and Robert Kaufman. "The Political Economy of Democratic Transitions." In *Transitions to Democracy*, edited by Lisa Anderson, 72–96. Columbia University Press, 1999. https://www.jstor.org/stable/10.7312 /ande11590.6.

Halper, Jeff. *Decolonizing Israel, Liberating Palestine: Zionism, Settler Colonialism, and the Case for One Democratic State*. Pluto Press, 2021.

HaMoked: Center for the Defence of the Individual. "Statistics on 'Security Inmates.'" April 2024. https://hamoked.org/prisoners-charts.php.

Harari, Yuval Noah. "Opinion: Will Zionism Survive the War?" *Washington Post*, May 13, 2024. https://www.washingtonpost.com/opinions/2024 /05/13/israel-independence-day-zionism-future/.

Hassanein, Sohail Hossain. "Crime, Politics and Police in the Palestinian's Society in Israel." *Social Identities* 22, no. 4 (July 3, 2016): 376–96. https:// doi.org/10.1080/13504630.2015.1106312.

Hasson, Nir. "Just 5 Percent of E. Jerusalem Palestinians Have Received Israeli Citizenship Since 1967." *Haaretz*, May 29, 2022. https://www.haaretz.com /israel-news/2022-05-29/ty-article/why-so-few-palestinians-from-jerusalem-have-israeli-citizenship/00000181-0c46-d090-abe1-ed7fefc20000.

Hoffman, Jon. "Rethinking Security and Stability in the Middle East." PRISME: Pathways to Renewed and Inclusive Security in the Middle East. Published as part of the SALAM Project. Winter 2023. https:// prismeinitiative.org/blog/rethinking-security-stability-middle-east-jon-hoffman/.

Horn, Nico. "The Forerunners of the Namibian Constitution." In *Constitutional Democracy in Namibia: A Critical Analysis After Two Decades*, edited by Anton Bösl, Nico Horn, and André du Pisani, 63–82. Macmillan Education Namibia, 2010.

Horowitz, Donald L. *Constitutional Processes and Democratic Commitment*. Yale University Press, 2021. https://doi.org/10.2307/j.ctv1s5nzk6.

Human Rights Network. "Genocide in Gaza: Analysis of International Law and Its Application to Israel's Military Actions Since October 7, 2023." May 15, 2024. https://www.humanrightsnetwork.org/genocide-in-gaza.

Human Rights Watch. "Abusive Israeli Policies Constitute Crimes of Apartheid, Persecution." April 27, 2021. https://www.hrw.org/news/2021/04/27 /abusive-israeli-policies-constitute-crimes-apartheid-persecution.

———. *Born Without Civil Rights: Israel's Use of Draconian Military Orders to Repress*. December 17, 2019. https://www.hrw.org/report/2019/12/17 /born-without-civil-rights/israels-use-draconian-military-orders-repress.

———. *Separate and Unequal*. December 19, 2010. https://www.hrw.org /report/2010/12/19/separate-and-unequal/israels-discriminatory-treatment-palestinians-occupied.

Husseini, Hiba, and Yossi Beilin. *The Holy Land Confederation as a Facilitator for the Two-State Solution.* 2022. https://content.ecf.org.il/files/Holy%20Land%20Confederation%20-%20English_compressed.pdf.

———. "An Israeli-Palestinian Confederation Is the Best Path to Peace." *Foreign Policy* (blog), May 23, 2022. https://foreignpolicy.com/2022/05/23/israeli-palestinian-confederation-peace.

Ibrahim 'Abd al-Hamid Sajdiya v. Minister of Defense HCJ 253/88 (Israeli High Court of Justice August 14, 1988).

Imseis, Ardi. "Negotiating the Illegal: On the United Nations and the Illegal Occupation of Palestine, 1967–2020." *European Journal of International Law* 31, no. 3 (December 15, 2020): 1055–85. https://doi.org/10.1093/ejil/chaa055.

———, ed. "Report of the Committee on the Admission of New Members Concerning the Application of Palestine for Admission to Membership in the United Nations." *Palestine Yearbook of International Law Online* 17, no. 1 (2014): 209–13. https://doi.org/10.1163/22116141-01701017.

———. *The United Nations and the Question of Palestine: Rule by Law and the Structure of International Legal Subalternity.* Cambridge University Press, 2023.

Institute for National Security Studies (INSS). "Undermining the Status Quo in the West Bank: Implications of Government Moves from the Perspective of Central Command." https://www.inss.org.il/publication/central-command.

Inter-Agency Standing Committee (IASC). "Statement by Principals of the Inter-Agency Standing Committee: Stop the Assault on Palestinians in Gaza and on Those Trying to Help Them." November 1, 2024. https://interagencystandingcommittee.org/inter-agency-standing-committee/statement-principals-inter-agency-standing-committee-stop-assault-palestinians-gaza-and-those-trying.

International Committee of the Red Cross (ICRC). Convention (IV) Respecting the Laws and Customs of War on Land and Its Annex: Regulations Concerning the Laws and Customs of War on Land. The Hague. Adopted October 18, 1907, entered into force January 26, 1910. https://ihl-databases.icrc.org/en/ihl-treaties/hague-conv-iv-1907.

———. Fourth Geneva Convention Relative to the Protection of Civilian Persons in Time of War (Fourth Geneva Convention). August 12, 1949. https://ihl-databases.icrc.org/ihl/INTRO/380.

———. "IHL on the Occupying Power's Responsibilities in the Occupied Palestinian Territory." March 28, 2023. https://www.icrc.org/en/document/ihl-occupying-power-responsibilities-occupied-palestinian-territories.

———. International Humanitarian Law Databases. https://ihl-databases.icrc.org/en.

———. "Occupation and International Humanitarian Law: Questions and Answers." November 3, 2022. https://www.icrc.org/en/document/ihl-occupying-power-responsibilities-occupied-palestinian-territories.

———. "Rule 130. Transfer of Own Civilian Population into Occupied Territory." https://ihl-databases.icrc.org/en/customary-ihl/v1/rule130#Fn_9AD70858_00003.

———. "Rule 132. Participation in Public Affairs." https://ihl-databases.icrc.org/en/customary-ihl/v1/rule132.

International Court of Justice (ICJ). "The General Assembly of the United Nations Requests an Advisory Opinion from the Court in Its Resolution A/RES/77/247 on Israeli Practices Affecting the Human Rights of the Palestinian People in the O." January 20, 2023. https://www.icj-cij.org/node/106313.

———. Israeli Wall Advisory Proceedings. https://www.icj-cij.org/sites/default/files/case-related/131/131-20040709-ADV-01-00-EN.pdf.

———. Legal Consequences Arising from the Policies and Practices of Israel in the Occupied Palestinian Territory, Including East Jerusalem. Advisory Opinion. July 19, 2024. https://www.icj-cij.org/sites/default/files/case-related/186/186-20240719-adv-01-00-en.pdf.

———. Order Regarding the Application of the Convention on the Prevention and Punishment of the Crime of Genocide in the Gaza Strip. January 26, 2024. https://www.icj-cij.org/sites/default/files/case-related/192/192-20240126-ord-01-00-en.pdf.

———. "Request for Advisory Opinion Transmitted to the Court Pursuant to General Assembly Resolution 77/247 of 30 December 2022: Legal Consequences Arising from the Policies and Practices of Israel in the Occupied Palestinian Territory, Including East Jerusalem." https://www.icj-cij.org/sites/default/files/case-related/186/186-20230117-REQ-01-00-EN.pdf.

International Federation for Human Rights (FIDH). "Palestinian Detainees in Israel: Inhuman Conditions of Detention." February 17, 2003. https://www.fidh.org/IMG/pdf/ps365a.pdf.

International Federation for Human Rights (FIDH) and Public Committee Against Torture in Israel (PCATI). "War Crimes in the Interrogation Chamber: The Israeli Systematic Policy of Torture, Inhuman and Degrading Treatment, Unlawful Deportation, and Denial of Fair Trial of Palestinian Detainees." Communication to the Office of the Prosecutor of the International Criminal Court Under Article 15 of the Rome Statute. June 2022. https://stoptorture.org.il/wp-content/uploads/2022/06/FIDH-PCATI_Art.-15-communication-June-2022.pdf.

International Human Rights Law Institute, ed. *The Chicago Principles on Post-Conflict Justice*. 2008.

"In the Wake of the War in Gaza, Is the Two-State Solution Still Viable?" *Foreign Affairs*, February 21, 2024. https://www.foreignaffairs.com/ask-the-experts/israel-palestine-two-state-solution-still-viable.

Israel Central Bureau of Statistics. "Gaps Between Jews and Arabs, 2020–2021 Selected Data from the Society in Israel Report No. 14." June 19, 2023. https://www.cbs.gov.il/en/mediarelease/Pages/2023/Gaps-Between-Jews-and-Arabs-2020-2021-,-Selected-Data-from-the-Society-in-Israel-Report-No-14.aspx.

———. "Statistics: Israel's Independence Day 2024." May 9, 2024. https://www.cbs.gov.il/he/mediarelease/doclib/2024/141/11_24_141e.pdf.

Israel Democracy Institute. "Nation-State Law Explainer." November 2023. https://en.idi.org.il/articles/24241.

Israeli Judicial Authority. "The Israeli Judicial Authority." https://www.gov.il/en/departments/the_judicial_authority/govil-landing-page.

Israeli Ministry of Defense: National Bureau for Counter Terror Financing. "Designations Lists (DATA)." https://nbctf.mod.gov.il:443/en/Minister%20Sanctions/Designation/Pages/downloads.aspx.

Israeli Ministry of Foreign Affairs. "The Judiciary: The Court System." https://embassies.gov.il/MFA/AboutIsrael/state/Democracy/Pages/The%20Judiciary-%20The%20Court%20System.aspx.

Israel Ministry of Justice. "The Legal Framework for the Use of Administrative Detention as a Means of Combating Terrorism." Foreign Relations and International Organizations Department, March 2003.

Jabareen, Dr. Yousef T. "An Equal Constitution for All? On a Constitution and Collective Rights for Arab Citizens in Israel." May 2007. Mossawa Center: The Advocacy Center for Arab Citizens in Israel.

Jabotisnky, Vladimir Ze'ev. "The Iron Wall." Jewish Virtual Library, November 4, 1923. https://www.jewishvirtuallibrary.org/quot-the-iron-wall-quot.

James, Carey. "Mere Words: The Enemy Entity Designation of the Gaza Strip." *Hastings International Comparative Law Review* 32, no. 2 (2009): 643–67. https://repository.uclawsf.edu/hastings_international_comparative_law_review/vol32/iss2/8.

Jefferis, Danielle C. "Institutionalizing Statelessness: The Revocation of Residency Rights of Palestinians in East Jerusalem." *International Journal of Refugee Law* 24, no. 2 (May 1, 2012): 202–30. https://doi.org/10.1093/ijrl/ees026.

Julio, Claudia Fuentes, and Paula Drumond, eds. *Human Rights and Conflict Resolution: Bridging the Theoretical and Practical Divide.* Routledge, 2017. https://doi.org/10.4324/9781315409375.

Karmi, Ghada. "The One-State Solution: An Alternative Vision for Israeli-Palestinian Peace." *Journal of Palestine Studies* 40, no. 2 (January 1, 2011): 62–76. https://doi.org/10.1525/jps.2011.XL.2.62.

Kaufman, Asher. "The Israel-Hezbollah Conflict and the Shebaa Farms." *Kroc Institute for International Peace Studies Policy Brief*, no. 13 (November 2006). https://kroc.nd.edu/assets/227136/israel_hezbollah.pdf.

Kelman, Herbert C. "A One-Country/Two-State Solution to the Israeli-Palestinian Conflict." *Middle East Policy*, no. 1 (2011): 27–41.

Khan, Karim A. A., KC. "Statement of ICC Prosecutor Karim A. A. Khan KC: Applications for Arrest Warrants in the Situation in the State of Palestine." International Criminal Court, May 20, 2024. https://www.icc-cpi.int/news /statement-icc-prosecutor-karim-aa-khan-kc-applications-arrest-warrants -situation-state.

Khatib, Rasha, Martin McKee, and Salim Yusuf. "Counting the Dead in Gaza: Difficult but Essential." *The Lancet* 404, no. 10449 (July 20, 2024): 237–38. https://doi.org/10.1016/S0140-6736(24)01169-3.

Khoury, Nadim. "6. Transitional Justice in Palestine/Israel: Whose Justice? Which Transition?" In *Rethinking Statehood in Palestine*, by Leila H. Farsakh, 153–72. University of California Press, 2021. https://doi.org/10.1515 /9780520385634-010.

The Knesset. Basic Laws of the State of Israel. https://main.knesset.gov.il:443 /EN/activity/Pages/BasicLaws.aspx.

Knight, Virginia Curtin. "Namibia's Transition to Independence." *Current History* 88, no. 538 (May 1989): 225–28, 239–41.

Kodner, Lior, Elyakim Rubinstein, and Avi Himi. "Netanyahu Is Destroying Israel and He Is Doing It with His Eyes Open." *Haaretz, This Week* (podcast), December 13, 2022. https://www.haaretz.co.il/digital/podcast/weekly/2022-12-13/ty-article-podcast/00000185-0a6e-d43f-afc7-bbeeb1cd0000.

Kolplewitz, Adi. "Palestinian Support for a One-State Solution at Highest Since Last Year." *Jerusalem Post*, April 8, 2022. https://www.jpost.com/opinion /article-703629.

Konno, Noboru, Ikujiro Nonaka, and Jay Ogilvy. "Scenario Planning: The Basics." *World Futures* 70, no. 1 (January 2, 2014): 28–43. https://doi.org /10.1080/02604027.2014.875720.

Konrad, Edo. "How Israeli Police Are Colluding with Settlers Against Palestinian Citizens." *+972 Magazine*, May 13, 2021. https://www.972mag.com /israel-police-settlers-lyd.

Kotef, Hagar, and Merav Amir. "Between Imaginary Lines: Violence and Its Justifications at the Military Checkpoints in Occupied Palestine." In *Movement and the Ordering of Freedom*, by Hagar Kotef, 27–51. Duke University Press, 2015. https://doi.org/10.1215/9780822375753 -002.

Kumaraswamy, P. R. *Historical Dictionary of the Arab-Israeli Conflict.* Rowman & Littlefield, 2015.

Kuperman, Alan J. "Muscular Mediation and Ripeness Theory." *Ethnopolitics* 21, no. 2 (March 15, 2022): 163–77. https://doi.org/10.1080/17449057.2022 .2004777.

Kuttab, Jonathan. *Beyond the Two-State Solution*. Nonviolence International, 2020.

———. "The International Criminal Court's Failure to Hold Israel Accountable." Arab Center, Washington, DC, September 12, 2023. https://arabcenterdc .org/resource/the-international-criminal-courts-failure-to-hold-israel- accountable.

Landau, Noa, and Jack Khoury. "'Two-State Solution Is Over,' Top Palestinian Diplomat Says After Trump's Jerusalem Speech." *Haaretz*, December 7, 2017. https://www.haaretz.com/middle-east-news/palestinians/2017-12-07 /ty-article/.premium/two-state-solution-is-over-top-palestinian-diplomat- says/0000017f-f77c-d5bd-a17f-f77e16910000.

Landau, Yehezkel. *Healing the Holy Land: Interreligious Peacebuilding in Israel /Palestine*. US Institute of Peace, 2003. https://lccn.loc.gov/2003373618.

Lazaroff, Tovah. "Palestinians Will Have 'an Entity,' Not a State, Says Gantz." *Jerusalem Post*, February 20, 2022. https://www.jpost.com/middle-east /article-697070.

Lederer, Edith M. "UN Assembly Approves Resolution Granting Palestine New Rights and Reviving Its UN Membership Bid." AP News, May 10, 2024. https://apnews.com/article/un-resolution-palestinians-membership- rights-us-assembly-875560e897f27d6600090420f36404e4.

———. "The Unprecedented Destruction of Housing in Gaza Hasn't Been Seen Since World War II, the UN Says." AP News, May 2, 2024. https://apnews .com/article/un-report-gaza-destruction-housing-economy-recovery- 4f61dcca7db3fd5eb3da5c6a25001e12.

Levitsky, Steven, and Lucan Way. "The Myth of Democratic Recession." *Journal of Democracy* 26, no. 1 (January 2015): 45–58. https://doi.org/10.1353 /jod.2015.0007.

Levy, Brian, Alan Hirsch, Vinothan Naidoo, and Musa Nxele. "South Africa: When Strong Institutions and Massive Inequalities Collide." Carnegie Endowment for International Peace, March 2021.

Levy, Philip I. "Sanctions on South Africa: What Did They Do?" *American Economic Review* 89, no. 2 (May 1, 1999): 415–20. https://doi.org/10 .1257/aer.89.2.415.

Lijphart, Arend. "Constitutional Design for Divided Societies." *Journal of Democracy* 15, no. 2 (2004): 96–109. https://doi.org/10.1353/jod .2004.0029.

"Local Outline Plan Jerusalem 2000." English translation of Hebrew original, 2018. https://www.alhaq.org/cached_uploads/download/alhaq_files/en /wp-content/uploads/2018/03/LocalOutlinePlanJerusalem2000.pdf.

Longo, Matthew, Daphna Canetti, and Nancy Hite-Rubin. "A Checkpoint Effect? Evidence from a Natural Experiment on Travel Restrictions in the West Bank." *American Journal of Political Science* 58, no. 4 (2014): 1006–23. https://doi.org/10.1111/ajps.12109.

Lovatt, Hugh, and Saleh Hijazi. "Mapping Palestinian Politics: Security Forces." European Council on Foreign Relations, April 19, 2018. https://ecfr.eu /special/mapping_palestinian_politics.

Lowenthal, Abraham F., and Sergio Bitar. *From Authoritarian Rule Toward Democratic Governance: Learning from Political Leaders.* International IDEA, 2015.

Lubell, Maayan. "Netanyahu Says No Palestinian State as Long as He's Prime Minister." Reuters, March 16, 2015. https://www.reuters.com/article /idUSKBN0MC1I7.

Madhani, Aamer, Tia Goldenberg, and Zeke Miller. "Trump Won't Rule Out Deploying US Troops to Support Rebuilding Gaza, Sees 'Long-Term' US Ownership." AP News, February 4, 2025. https://apnews.com/article/trump-netanyahu-washington-ceasefire-1c8deec4dd46177e08e07d669d595ed3.

Maiese, Michelle. "Destructive Escalation." Beyond Intractability, 2003. https:// www.beyondintractability.org/essay/escalation.

Mainwaring, Scott. "The Transition to Democracy in Brazil." *Journal of Interamerican Studies and World Affairs* 28, no. 1 (1986): 149–80. https:// doi.org/10.2307/165739.

Mansfield, Anna Morawiec. "Ethnic but Equal: The Quest for a New Democratic Order in Bosnia and Herzegovina." *Columbia Law Review* 103, no. 8 (December 2003): 2052. https://doi.org/10.2307/3593383.

Marko, Joseph. "Bosnia-Herzegovina: The Role of the Judiciary in a Divided Society." *Constitutional Review* 5, no. 2 (November 18, 2019): 194. https:// doi.org/10.31078/consrev521.

Martín, Héctor Centeno, Eric Wiebelhaus-Brahm, Ana Belén Nieto-Librero, and Dylan Wright. "Explaining the Timeliness of Implementation of Truth Commission Recommendations." *Journal of Peace Research* 59, no. 5 (September 2022): 710–26. https://doi.org/10.1177 /00223433211057011.

Martin, Nik, and Burak Ünveren. "Israel Sanctions: Who Has Imposed Curbs over Gaza War?" *DW.com*, May 3, 2024. https://www.dw.com /en/israel-sanctions-who-has-imposed-curbs-over-gaza-war/a-68792324.

Mazzetti, Mark, and Ronen Bergman. "'Buying Quiet': Inside the Israeli Plan That Propped Up Hamas." *New York Times*, December 10, 2023. https:// www.nytimes.com/2023/12/10/world/middleeast/israel-qatar-money-prop-up-hamas.html.

Medzini, Arnon. "Life on the Border: The Impact of the Separation Barrier on the Residents of the Barta'a Enclave Demilitarized Zone." *Journal of*

Borderlands Studies 31, no. 4 (October 2016): 401–25. https://doi.org/10.10
80/08865655.2016.1188667.

Meridor, Dan, and Ron Eldadi. "Israel's National Security Doctrine: The Report
of the Committee on the Formulation of the National Security Doctrine
(Meridor Committee), Ten Years Later." Institute for National Security
Studies (INSS), February 2019. https://www.inss.org.il/wp-content
/uploads/2019/02/Memo187_11.pdf.

Merrino, Serena. "Currency and Settler Colonialism: The Palestinian Case."
Review of International Political Economy 28, no. 6 (November 2, 2021):
1729–50. https://doi.org/10.1080/09692290.2020.1803951.

Milhem, Feras, and Jamil Salem. "Building the Rule of Law in Palestine: Rule of
Law Without Freedom." In *International Law and the Israeli-Palestinian
Conflict: A Rights-Based Approach to Middle East Peace*. Routledge, 2010.
https://ssrn.com/abstract=1584564.

Miller, Elhanan. "Abbas Toughens Law Against Palestinians Selling Land to
Jews." *Times of Israel*, October 21, 2014. http://www.timesofisrael.com
/abbas-toughens-law-against-palestinians-selling-land-to-jews.

Monterescu, Daniel. "The Ghettoization of Israel's 'Mixed Cities.'" *+972 Magazine*,
December 5, 2015. https://www.972mag.com/the-ghettoization-of-israels-
mixed-cities.

Morris, Loveday. "An Angry Mob at an Israeli University Stirs Fears of
Jewish-Arab Violence." *Washington Post*, October 30, 2023. https://www
.washingtonpost.com/world/2023/10/30/israel-gaza-jews-palestinians-
netanya.

Muhareb, Rania, Elizabeth Rghebi, Pierce Clancy, Joseph Schechla, Nada
Awad, and Maha Abdallah. "Israeli Apartheid: Tool of Zionist Settler
Colonialism." Al Haq, November 29, 2022. https://www.alhaq.org
/publications/20940.html.

Murphy, Colleen. *The Conceptual Foundations of Transitional Justice*. Cambridge University Press, 2017. https://doi.org/10.1017/9781316084229.

National Committee for the Heads of the Arab Local Authorities in Israel. "The
Future Vision of the Palestinian Arabs in Israel." 2006. http://www.adalah
.org/newsletter/eng/dec06/tasawor-mostaqbali.pdf.

Ní Aoláin, Fionnuala, and Colm Campbell. "The Paradox of Transition in
Conflicted Democracies." *Human Rights Quarterly* 27, no. 1 (February
2005): 172–213. https://doi.org/10.1353/hrq.2005.0001.

Nystuen, Gro. *Achieving Peace or Protecting Human Rights? Conflicts Between
Norms Regarding Ethnic Discrimination in the Dayton Peace Agreement*.
Brill | Nijhoff, 2005. https://doi.org/10.1163/9789047408291.

O'Carroll, Lisa. "How Did the Good Friday Agreement Come About and Why Is It
So Significant?" *The Guardian*, April 7, 2023. https://www.theguardian.com

/world/2023/apr/07/how-did-the-good-friday-agreement-come-about-and-why-is-it-so-significant.

Oechslin, Manuel. "Targeting Autocrats: Economic Sanctions and Regime Change." *European Journal of Political Economy* 36 (December 2014): 24–40. https://doi.org/10.1016/j.ejpoleco.2014.07.003.

OHCHR. "A/HRC/48/60: Accountability: Prosecuting and Punishing Gross Violations of Human Rights and Serious Violations of International Humanitarian Law in the Context of Transitional Justice Processes—Report of the Special Rapporteur on the Promotion of Truth, Justice, Reparation and Guarantees of Non-Recurrence." July 9, 2021. https://www.ohchr.org/en/documents/thematic-reports/ahrc4860-accountability-prosecuting-and-punishing-gross-violations-human.

———. "A/HRC/51/34: Role and Responsibilities of Non-State Actors in Transitional Justice Processes—Report of the Special Rapporteur on the Promotion of Truth, Justice, Reparation and Guarantees of Non-Recurrence, Fabián Salvioli." July 12, 2022. https://www.ohchr.org/en/documents/thematic-reports/ahrc5134-role-and-responsibilities-non-state-actors-transitional-justice.

———. "A/HRC/54/24: International Legal Standards Underpinning the Pillars of Transitional Justice—Report of the Special Rapporteur on the Promotion of Truth, Justice, Reparation and Guarantees of Non-Recurrence, Fabián Salvioli." July 10, 2023. https://www.ohchr.org/en/documents/thematic-reports/ahrc5424-international-legal-standards-underpinning-pillars-transitional.

———. "A/76/180: Promotion of Truth, Justice, Reparation and Guarantees of Non-Recurrence—Note by the Secretary-General." July 19, 2021. https://www.ohchr.org/en/documents/thematic-reports/a76180-promotion-truth-justice-reparation-and-guarantees-non-recurrence.

———. "A/78/181: Report of the Special Rapporteur on the Promotion of Truth, Justice, Reparation and Guarantees of Non-Recurrence, Fabián Salvioli—Financing of Reparation for Victims of Serious Violations of Human Rights and Humanitarian Law." July 14, 2023. https://www.ohchr.org/en/documents/thematic-reports/a78181-report-special-rapporteur-promotion-truth-justice-reparation-and.

———. "Special Rapporteur Says Israel's Unlawful Carceral Practices in the Occupied Palestinian Territory Are Tantamount to International Crimes and Have Turned It into an Open-Air Prison." July 10, 2023. https://www.ohchr.org/en/news/2023/07/special-rapporteur-says-israels-unlawful-carceral-practices-occupied-palestinian.

O'kane, Eamonn. "When Can Conflicts Be Resolved? A Critique of Ripeness." *Civil Wars* 8, no. 3–4 (September 2006): 268–84. https://doi.org/10.1080/13698240601060710.

Omer-Man, Emily Schaeffer. "Separate and Unequal: Israel's Dual Criminal Justice System in the West Bank." *Palestine-Israel Journal* 21, no. 3 (2016). https://pij.org/articles/1682/separate-and-unequal-israels-dual-criminal-justice-system-in-the-west-bank.

Omer-Man, Michael Schaeffer. "Israelis Don't Get to Hold a Referendum on Palestine." *+972 Magazine*, July 6, 2016. https://www.972mag.com/israelis-dont-get-to-hold-a-referendum-on-palestine.

———. "Who Gets to Vote in Israel's Version of Democracy." *+972 Magazine*, January 3, 2019. https://www.972mag.com/gets-vote-israels-democracy-2019.

———. "Why Israel's Opposition Won't Talk About the Real Goal of Judicial Overhaul." *+972 Magazine*, February 21, 2023. https://www.972mag.com/judiciary-annexation-levin-zionism.

Orentlicher, Diane F. "'Settling Accounts' Revisited: Reconciling Global Norms with Local Agency." *International Journal of Transitional Justice* 1, no. 1 (March 1, 2007): 10–22. https://doi.org/10.1093/ijtj/ijm010.

———. "Settling Accounts: The Duty to Prosecute Human Rights Violations of a Prior Regime." *Yale Law Journal* 100, no. 8 (June 1991): 2537. https://doi.org/10.2307/796903.

Orentlicher, Diane F., and UN Independent Expert to Update the Set of Principles for the Protection and Promotion of Human Rights Through Action to Combat Impunity. "Impunity: Report of the Independent Expert to Update the Set of Principles to Combat Impunity, Diane Orentlicher: Addendum." February 8, 2005. https://digitallibrary.un.org/record/541829.

Organisation for Economic Co-Operation and Development (OECD). *Evaluating Peacebuilding Activities in Settings of Conflict and Fragility: Improving Learning for Results.* DAC Guidelines and Reference Series. 2012. https://doi.org/10.1787/9789264106802-en.

Organization for Security and Co-operation in Europe (OSCE). *Guidelines on Freedom of Peaceful Assembly*, 2nd ed. OSCE Office for Democratic Institutions and Human Rights, 2010. https://www.osce.org/files/f/documents/4/0/73405.pdf.

Organization of American States. "Plan of Action: To Strengthen Democracy, Create Prosperity and Realize Human Potential." https://www.oas.org/dil/Plan_of_Action_Quebec.pdf.

Palestinian Center for Policy and Research. "Press Release: Public Opinion Poll No (91)." March 20, 2024. https://www.pcpsr.org/en/node/969.

Palestinian Central Bureau of Statistics. "Indicators." https://www.pcbs.gov.ps/site/lang__en/881/default.aspx#Census.

Perry, Simon, Robert Apel, Graeme R. Newman, and Ronald V. Clarke. "The Situational Prevention of Terrorism: An Evaluation of the Israeli West Bank

Barrier." *Journal of Quantitative Criminology* 33, no. 4 (December 2017): 727–51. https://doi.org/10.1007/s10940-016-9309-6.

Pettit, Philip. "Popular Sovereignty and Constitutional Democracy." *University of Toronto Law Journal* 72, no. 3 (June 1, 2022): 251–86. https://doi.org/10 .3138/utlj-2021-0048.

Pfiffner, James P. "US Blunders in Iraq: De-Baathification and Disbanding the Army." *Intelligence and National Security* 25, no. 1 (February 2010): 76–85. https://doi.org/10.1080/02684521003588120.

Piqani, Darinka. "A Tale of Three Constitutional Courts in Democratic Transitions." *European Constitutional Law Review* 17, no. 1 (March 2021): 163–76. https://doi.org/10.1017/S1574019621000109.

Posner, Eric A., and Adrian Vermeule. "Transitional Justice as Ordinary Justice." *Harvard Law Review* 117, no. 3 (January 2004): 761. https://doi .org/10.2307/4093461.

Purkey, Anna Lise. "A Dignified Approach: Legal Empowerment and Justice for Human Rights Violations in Protracted Refugee Situations." *Journal of Refugee Studies* 27, no. 2 (June 1, 2014): 260–81. https://doi.org/10.1093 /jrs/fet031.

Rasgon, Adam, and Ronen Bergman. "Secret Hamas Files Show How It Spied on Everyday Palestinians." *New York Times*, May 13, 2024. https://www .nytimes.com/2024/05/13/world/europe/secret-hamas-files-palestinians .html.

Reddy, Amit. "Do Democratic Transitions Produce Better Human Development Outcomes? Empirical Evidence from 40 Years of Regime Changes." Master's thesis, Georgetown University, 2012. https://www.proquest.com/disserta- tions-theses/do-democratic-transitions-produce-better-human/docview /1010625224/se-2.

ReliefWeb. "The Core Issues of the Israeli-Palestinian Conflict." November 23, 2007. https://reliefweb.int/report/israel/core-issues-israeli-palestinian- conflict.

Reuters. "Moody's Cuts Israel's Rating, Warns of Drop to 'Junk.'" September 27, 2024. https://www.reuters.com/world/middle-east/moodys-cuts-israels- rating-warns-drop-junk-2024-09-27.

———. "Netanyahu Rejects International Pressure for Palestinian State." February 16, 2024. https://www.reuters.com/world/middle-east/netanyahu- rejects-international-pressure-palestinian-state-2024-02-16.

Reynolds, John. "'Intent to Regularise': The Israeli Supreme Court and the Normalisation of Emergency." *Adalah Review* 104 (2013). https://www .adalah.org/en/content/view/8127.

Rezende Oliveira, Mariana. "Constitutional Courts in Transitions to Democracy: Limits, Critiques and Possibilities in Brazil and Argentina." *Latin*

American Law Review, no. 5 (August 2020): 27–44. https://doi.org/10 .29263/lar05.2020.02.

RFI. "UN Rapporteur Says Israel's War in Gaza Is 'Emptying the Land Completely.'" November 1, 2024. https://www.rfi.fr/en/podcasts/international-report/20241101-un-rapporteur-says-israel-s-war-in-gaza-is-emptying-the -land-completely.

Rimmer, Harris, and Susan Gail. "Reconceiving Refugees and Internally Displaced Persons as Transitional Justice Actors." *SSRN Electronic Journal* (2009). https://doi.org/10.2139/ssrn.1480974.

Rome Statute of the International Criminal Court. July 17, 1998. https://www .icc-cpi.int/resource-library/documents/rs-eng.pdf.

Ronen, Yaël. "Illegal Occupation and Its Consequences." *Israel Law Review* 41, no. 1–2 (2008): 201–45. https://doi.org/10.1017/S0021223700000224.

Rose, Emily. "Israeli Startups Act to Relocate over Judicial Shakeup, Survey Finds." Reuters, July 23, 2023. https://www.reuters.com/world/middle -east/israeli-startups-act-relocate-over-judicial-shakeup-survey -finds-2023-07-23.

Rosenberg, David E. "Will ICC Warrants Turn Israel into a Pariah State?" *Foreign Policy*, May 21, 2024. https://foreignpolicy.com/2024/05/21 /is-the-war-in-gaza-turning-israel-into-a-pariah-state/?utm_source= Sailthru&utm_medium=email&utm_campaign=Editors%27%20Picks%20 -%2005212024&utm_term=editors_picks.

Sarto, Raffaella A. Del, and Menachem Klein. "Oslo: Three Decades Later." *Israel Studies Review* 38, no. 2 (June 1, 2023): 1–11. https://doi.org /10.3167/isr.2023.380202.

Saunders, Christopher. "Analysing Namibia's Transition Towards Democracy: Historical Reflections." Workshop Paper, July 13, 1994. University of Witwatersrand, Johannesburg.

Savage, Kate. "Negotiating the Release of Political Prisoners in South Africa." Northern Ireland Programme at the Kennedy School of Government at Harvard. 2000. www.csvr.org.za/docs/correctional/negotiatingtherelease .pdf.

Scheindlin, Dahlia. *The Crooked Timber of Democracy in Israel: Promise Unfulfilled*. Democracy in Times of Upheaval 7. De Gruyter, 2023.

———. "Not Two States, Not One State: A New Way Out of Disaster for Israelis and Palestinians." *Haaretz*, November 30, 2023. https://www.haaretz.com /israel-news/2023-11-30/ty-article/.premium/not-two-states-not-one-state- a-new-way-out-of-disaster-for-israelis-and-palestinians/0000018c-1fc0 -d21c-abae-7ffc7f960000.

Schiff, Amira. "The Critical Role of Prenegotiations in Ethno-National Conflicts: Cyprus and the 'Annapolis Process.'" *Israel Studies Review* 26, no. 2 (January 1, 2011). https://doi.org/10.3167/isr.2011.260208.

Schneider, Tal. "For Years, Netanyahu Propped Up Hamas. Now It's Blown Up in Our Faces." *Times of Israel*, October 8, 2023. https://www.timesofisrael .com/for-years-netanyahu-propped-up-hamas-now-its-blown-up-in-our-faces.

Sewell, Abby. "Hamas Official Says Group Would Lay Down Its Arms If an Independent Palestinian State Is Established." AP News, April 25, 2024. https://apnews.com/article/hamas-khalil-alhayya-qatar-ceasefire-1967 -borders-4912532b11a9cec29464eab234045438.

Sfard, Michael. Blueprint interview. Video call, June 12, 2023.

———. "The Israeli Occupation of the West Bank and the Crime of Apartheid: Legal Opinion." Yesh Din, June 2020. https://www.yesh-din.org/en /the-occupation-of-the-west-bank-and-the-crime-of-apartheid-legal-opinion.

Shakir, Omar. *A Threshold Crossed: Israeli Authorities and the Crimes of Apartheid and Persecution.* Human Rights Watch, April 27, 2021. https:// www.hrw.org/report/2021/04/27/threshold-crossed/israeli-authorities-and-crimes-apartheid-and-persecution.

Sharp, Dustin N. "Addressing Dilemmas of the Global and the Local in Transitional Justice." *SSRN Electronic Journal* (2013). https://doi.org/10.2139 /ssrn.2288853.

Shehada, Yusif. "Does Foreign Aid Accelerate Corruption? The Case of the Palestinian National Authority." *Journal of Holy Land and Palestine Studies* 14, no. 2 (November 2015): 165–87. https://doi.org/10.3366/hlps.2015.0116.

Shezaf, Hagar, and Maya Horodniceanu. "Israel's Other Justice System Has Rules of Its Own." *Haaretz*, April 25, 2022. https://www.haaretz.com /israel-news/2022-04-25/ty-article-magazine/.highlight/israels-other-justice-system-has-rules-of-its-own/00000180-6566-d824-ad9e -e7664fa10000.

Shurafa, Wafaa, and Bassem Mroue. "Netanyahu Seeks Open-Ended Control over Security and Civilian Affairs in Gaza in New Postwar Plan." AP News, February 23, 2024. https://apnews.com/article/israel-hamas-war-news-02-23-2024-a5da6005cfa6734225af35ca460a75fb.

Smooha, Sammy. "The Israeli Palestinian-Arab Vision of Transforming Israel into a Binational Democracy." *Constellations* 16, no. 3 (September 2009): 509–22. https://doi.org/10.1111/j.1467-8675.2009.00555.x.

"South Africa: Human Rights Developments." In *Human Rights Watch World Report 1994*. https://www.hrw.org/reports/1994/WR94/Africa-07.htm.

South African Constituent Assembly. Constitution of the Republic of South Africa, 1996: As Adopted on 8 May 1996 and Amended on 11 October 1996 by the Constituent Assembly. Department of Justice and Constitutional Development, 2015.

South African Constitution of 1993 (Interim). August 17, 2023.

South African Government. "Intelligence White Paper." January 1, 1995. https://www.gov.za/documents/intelligence-white-paper.

———. "Safety and Security White Paper." September 1, 1998. https://www.gov .za/documents/white-papers/safety-and-security-white-paper-01-sep-1998.

South African Law Reform Commission. *Report on Activities of the South African Law Reform Commission 2022/2023.* 2023. https://www.justice .gov.za/salrc/anr/2022-2023-anr-salrc.pdf.

Stahn, Carsten. "The United Nations Transitional Administrations in Kosovo and East Timor: A First Analysis." *Max Planck Yearbook of United Nations Law Online* 5, no. 1 (February 9, 2001): 105–83. https://doi.org/10.1163 /187574101X00060.

State of Palestine, Ministry of Health. "Daily Report on the Effects of the Israeli Aggression in Palestine: From October 7th until May 21, 2024." May 21, 2024.

Stimec, Arnaud, Patrice Guillotreau, and Jean Poitras. "Ripeness and Grief in Conflict Analysis." *Group Decision and Negotiation* 20, no. 4 (July 2011): 489–507. https://doi.org/10.1007/s10726-009-9178-6.

Sultany, Nimer. "Activism and Legitimation in Israel's Jurisprudence of Occupation." *Social and Legal Studies* 23, no. 3 (September 2014): 315–39. https://doi.org/10.1177/0964663914521449.

Svetlova, Ksenia. "More Israelis, Palestinians Support the 'One-State' Solution." *Al-Monitor*, February 13, 2020. https://www.al-monitor.com/originals/2020 /02/israel-palestinians-west-bank-two-state-solution-one-state.html.

Taha, Hamdan, Ramzy Baroud, Ilan Pappé, Ibrahim G. Aoudé, Qassem Izzat Ali, Samaa Abu Sharar, Anuar Majluf Issa, et al. *Our Vision for Liberation: Engaged Palestinian Leaders and Intellectuals Speak Out.* Clarity Press, 2022.

Tang, Min, Narisong Huhe, and Qiang Zhou. "Contingent Democratization: When Do Economic Crises Matter?" *British Journal of Political Science* 47, no. 1 (January 2017): 71–90. https://doi.org/10.1017/S0007123415000095.

Teitel, Ruti G. *Transitional Justice.* Oxford University Press, 2002.

Thomas, Merlyn, Jake Horton, and Benedict Garman. "Israel Gaza: Checking Israel's Claim to Have Killed 10,000 Hamas Fighters." BBC, February 29, 2024. https://www.bbc.com/news/world-middle-east-68387864.

Thrall, Nathan. *The Only Language They Understand: Forcing Compromise in Israel and Palestine.* Metropolitan Books, Henry Holt and Company, 2017.

Times of Israel. "Netanyahu Says Palestinians Can Have a 'State Minus.'" January 22, 2017. http://www.timesofisrael.com/netanyahu-says-palestinians-can-have-a-state-minus.

———. "Police Unprepared to Deal with Multi-Front Outbreak of Violence, Chief Warns." June 6, 2023. https://www.timesofisrael.com/police-unprepared-to-deal-with-multi-front-outbreak-of-violence-chief-warns.

Tondo, Lorenzo, and Quique Kierszenbaum. "Israeli Soldiers and Police Tipping Off Groups That Attack Gaza Aid Trucks." *The Guardian*, May 21, 2024.

https://www.theguardian.com/world/article/2024/may/21/israeli-soldiers-and-police-tipping-off-groups-that-attack-gaza-aid-trucks.

Tondo, Lorenzo, Sufian Taha, and Jason Burke. "'Barbaric': Palestinian Lorry Drivers Recount Settlers' Attack on Gaza Aid Convoy." *The Guardian*, May 16, 2024. https://www.theguardian.com/world/article/2024/may/16/palestinian-lorry-drivers-israeli-settlers-attack-gaza-aid-convoy.

Turner, Mandy. "Creating 'Partners for Peace': The Palestinian Authority and the International Statebuilding Agenda." *Journal of Intervention and Statebuilding* 5, no. 1 (March 2011): 1–21. https://doi.org/10.1080/1750297 7.2011.541777.

UN Committee on the Exercise of the Inalienable Rights of the Palestinian People. "The Legal Status of the West Bank and Gaza." DPR Study, DPR Publication. https://www.un.org/unispal/document/auto-insert-203742.

UNESCO. "Request for the Admission of the State of Palestine to UNESCO as a Member State." UNESCO Digital Library. https://unesdoc.unesco.org/ark:/48223/pf0000082711_eng.

UN General Assembly. "The General Assembly of the United Nations Requests an Advisory Opinion from the Court in Its Resolution A/RES/77/247 on 'Israeli Practices Affecting the Human Rights of the Palestinian People in the Occupied Palestinian Territory, Including East Jerusalem.'" December 30, 2022.

———. International Convention on the Suppression and Punishment of the Crime of Apartheid. November 30, 1973. https://treaties.un.org/Pages/ViewDetails.aspx?src=IND&mtdsg_no=IV-7&chapter=4&clang=_en.

———. "Israeli Practices Affecting the Human Rights of the Palestinian People in the Occupied Palestinian Territory, Including East Jerusalem: Resolution /Adopted by the General Assembly." 77th sess., 2022–23, January 9, 2023. https://digitallibrary.un.org/record/4000001.

———. Report of the Special Rapporteur [Francesca Albanese] on the Situation of Human Rights in the Palestinian Territories Occupied Since 1967. A/77/356. September 20, 2022. https://undocs.org/A/77/356.

———. Resolution 181 (II), Future Government of Palestine, A/RES/181(II). November 29, 1947. https://undocs.org/A/RES/181(II).

———. Resolution 194 (III), "Palestine: Progress Report of the United Nations Mediator." A/RES/194, December 11, 1948.

UNHCR US. "Handbook on Procedures and Criteria for Determining Refugee Status Under the 1951 Convention and the 1967 Protocol Relating to the Status of Refugees." https://www.unhcr.org/us/media/handbook-procedures-and-criteria-determining-refugee-status-under-1951-convention-and-1967.

UN Human Rights Council. "Report of the Special Rapporteur on the Situation of Human Rights in the Palestinian Territories Occupied Since 1967." A/HRC/53/59, https://www.ohchr.org/en/documents/country-reports

/ahrc5359-report-special-rapporteur-situation-human-rights-palestinian.

——. "Report of the Working Group on Arbitrary Detention: United Nations Basic Principles and Guidelines on Remedies and Procedures on the Right of Anyone Deprived of Their Liberty to Bring Proceedings Before a Court." A/HRC/30/37, July 6, 2015. https://www.refworld.org/reference/themreport/unhrc/2015/en/106782.

United Nations. *2.10: The UN Approach to DDR*. February 2021. https://www.unddr.org/wp-content/uploads/2021/02/IDDRS-2.10-The-UN-Approach-To-DDR.pdf.

——. "Integrated DDR Standards." https://www.unddr.org/.

——. Report of the Special Rapporteur on the Situation of Human Rights in the Palestinian Territories Occupied Since 1967, UN Doc. A/72/43106, October 23, 2017. https://www.unwatch.org/wp-content/uploads/2009/12/Lynk-Report-Oct-2017-A_72_43106.pdf.

——. Report of the United Nations High Commissioner for Human Rights. Official Records (UN General Assembly). 2014. https://doi.org/10.18356/d9bf1c42-en.

——. "The UN Approach to DDR." Integrated Disarmament, Demobilization and Reintegration Standards. November 19, 2019. http://www.unddr.org.

——. *UNCITRAL Expedited Arbitration Rules 2021: UNCITRAL Rules on Transparency in Treaty-Based Investor-State Arbitration*. 2022. https://doi.org/10.18356/9789210021753.

——. Universal Declaration of Human Rights. December 10, 1948. https://www.un.org/en/about-us/universal-declaration-of-human-rights.

University Network for Human Rights. "Genocide in Gaza: Analysis of International Law and Its Application to Israel's Military Actions Since October 7, 2023." May 15, 2024. https://www.humanrightsnetwork.org/publications/genocide-in-gaza.

UN Peacebuilding Support Office. "DDR and Peacebuilding: Thematic Review of DDR Contributions to Peacebuilding and the Role of the Peacebuilding Fund." https://www.un.org/peacebuilding/sites/www.un.org.peacebuilding/files/documents/ddr_pbf_thematic_review.pdf.

UN Secretary-General. "The Rule of Law and Transitional Justice in Conflict and Post-Conflict Societies." UN Security Council, August 23, 2004. https://www.securitycouncilreport.org/un-documents/document/pcs-s-2004-616.php.

UN Security Council. Resolution 242, "The Situation in the Middle East." S/RES/242. November 22, 1967.

US Department of State. "Lustration and Vetting." May 2016. https://2009-2017.state.gov/j/gcj/transitional/257569.htm.

——. "Prosecuting Serious Crimes and Human Rights Violations." https://2009-2017.state.gov/j/gcj/transitional/257569.htm.

———. "Transitional Justice Overview." May 16, 2016. http://2009-2017.state
    .gov/j/gcj/transitional/257566.htm.

Van der Spuy, Elrena. "The National Peace Accord and Police Reform in South
    Africa: The Role of the Police Board as an Interim Policy Mechanism,
    1992–1994." *Journal of Contemporary History* 33, no. 1 (2008): 37–58.

"V. I. Gavrilov." *Acta Virologica* 19, no. 6 (November 1975): 510.

Wadi, Ramona. "The Palestinian Authority's Privilege and Freedom of
    Movement." *Middle East Monitor*, January 14, 2023. https://www
    .middleeastmonitor.com/20230114-the-palestinian-authoritys-privilege-
    and-freedom-of-movement.

Walsh, Dawn. "Constitutional Courts as Arbiters of Post-Conflict Territorial
    Self-Government: Bosnia and Macedonia." *Regional and Federal Studies* 29,
    no. 1 (January 2019): 67–90. https://doi.org/10.1080/13597566.2018.1511980.

———. "How a Human Needs Theory Understanding of Conflict Enhances the
    Use of Consociationalism as a Conflict Resolution Mechanism: The Good
    Friday Agreement in Northern Ireland." *Ethnopolitics* 15, no. 3 (May 26,
    2016): 285–302. https://doi.org/10.1080/17449057.2015.1024012.

Weinblum, Sharon. "Disqualifying Political Parties and 'Defending Democracy' in
    Israel." *Constellations* 22, no. 2 (June 2015): 314–25. https://doi.org/10.1111
    /1467-8675.12161.

Westhuizen, Christi van der. "South Africa's 1994 'Miracle': What's Left?" *The
    Conversation*, April 25, 2021. https://theconversation.com/south-africas-
    1994-miracle-whats-left-159495.

Wilde, Ralph. "Accountability and International Actors in Bosnia and Herze-
    govina, Kosovo and East Timor." *LSA Journal of International & Compara-
    tive Law* 7, no. 2 (2001). https://nsuworks.nova.edu/ilsajournal/vol7/iss2/18.

Williams, Dylan. Blueprint interview. Video call, June 23, 2023.

Wintour, Patrick. "Hamas Presents New Charter Accepting a Palestine Based on
    1967 Borders." *The Guardian*, May 1, 2017. https://www.theguardian.com
    /world/2017/may/01/hamas-new-charter-palestine-israel-1967-borders.

Yaron, Lee. "The October 7 Effect: The Israelis Leaving Israel, and the Diaspora
    Jews Replacing Them." *Haaretz*, September 6, 2024. https://www.haaretz
    .com/israel-news/2024-09-06/ty-article-magazine/.premium/the-october-7-
    effect-the-israelis-leaving-israel-and-the-diaspora-jews-replacing-them
    /00000191-b6b7-d13c-a39b-bebff9830000.

Yemen Justice. "The Yemen Declaration for Justice and Reconciliation." July
    2023. https://yemenjustice.org/files/The_Yemen_Declaration_for_Justice_
    and_Reconciliation_en.pdf.

Yesh Din, the Association for Civil Rights in Israel, Breaking the Silence, and
    Ofek. "Policy Paper: What Israel's 37th Government's Guiding Principles and
    Coalition Agreements Mean for the West Bank." January 2, 2023. https://
    www.yesh-din.org/en/policy-paper-what-israels-37th-governments-

guiding-principles-and-coalition-agreements-mean-for-the-west-bank
-january-2023/.

Yiftachel, Oren. "'Ethnocracy' and Its Discontents: Minorities, Protests, and the
Israeli Polity." *Critical Inquiry* 26, no. 4 (2000): 725–56.

Yimenu, Bizuneh. Review of *Federalism and Decentralization in the Contemporary Middle East and North Africa*, edited by Aslı Ü. Bâli and Omar M.
Dajani. *Publius* 54, no. 1 (2023): e5–e11. https://doi.org/10.1093/publius
/pjad033.

Yousef, Abdul. "The One State Solution: An Alternative Vision for Ending the
Israeli-Palestinian Conflict." PhD diss., CUNY, 2012.

Zalzberg, Ofer. "Beyond Liberal Peacemaking: Lessons from Israeli-Palestinian
Diplomatic Peacemaking." *Review of Middle East Studies* 53, no. 1 (June
2019): 46–53. https://doi.org/10.1017/rms.2019.9.

Zarpli, Omer. "When Do Imposed Sanctions Work? The Role of Target Regime
Type." *Journal of Conflict Resolution* 67, no. 7–8 (August 2023): 1482–1509.
https://doi.org/10.1177/00220027221139809.

Zartman, I. William. "Mediation: Ripeness and Its Challenges in the Middle
East." *International Negotiation* 20, no. 3 (October 26, 2015): 479–93.
https://doi.org/10.1163/15718069-12341317.

Ziv, Oren. "How Israeli Police Are Colluding with Settlers Against Palestinian
Citizens." *+972 Magazine*, May 13, 2021. https://www.972mag.com
/israel-police-settlers-lyd.

Index